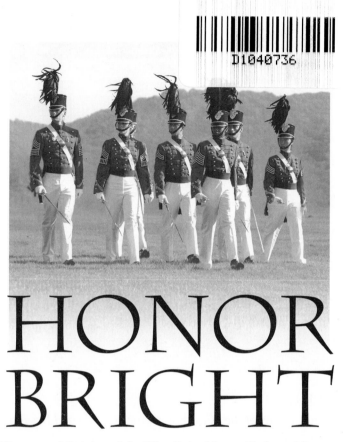

HONOR BRIGHT

History and Origins of the West Point Honor Code and System

Lewis Sorley

Learning Solutions

Boston   Burr Ridge, IL   Dubuque, IA   New York   San Francisco   St. Louis
Bangkok   Bogotá   Caracas   Lisbon   London   Madrid
Mexico City   Milan   New Delhi   Seoul   Singapore   Sydney   Taipei   Toronto

HONOR BRIGHT
History and Origins of the West Point Honor Code and System

4 5 6 7 8 9 0 DOC/DOC 16 15 14

ISBN-13: 978-0-07-353778-8
ISBN-10: 0-07-353778-0

Learning Solutions Manager: JD Ice
Learning Solutions Specialist: Michael Hemmer
Production Editor: Kathy Phelan
Cover Design: Fairfax Hutter
Printer/Binder: RR Donnelley

For the Corps,
and the Corps,
and the Corps

Guide us, thy sons, aright,
Teach us, by day, by night,
To keep thine honor bright,
For thee to fight.

The Alma Mater

Contents

Foreword

Our Army and Nation now find ourselves in an era of persistent conflict that is testing our resolve as well as our character. Despite the demands and hardships, our Army keeps getting better while continuing to accomplish its missions in service to our Nation because of its Values, its Warrior Ethos, and because of the strength of its People. As a result of their character and moral courage, Soldiers and leaders do what is right, no matter the situation, for mission accomplishment, for Soldiers, and for our Nation.

For nearly seven years our Nation's Army has been fighting for our own freedoms and to give others a chance at theirs with inspiring skill, courage, mission success, and yes, sacrifice against extremist fundamentalists who are opposed to our freedoms and way of life in regions of the world vital to our national security. During that time there has been an increasing velocity of change within the Army in order to adapt and stay out ahead of battlefield demands while simultaneously placing increasing operational mission demands on Army forces. Amidst such change and demands the Army aims to remain faithful to its enduring values that seal and sustain the continuing trust it has with the American people while accomplishing its complex battlefield missions for our Nation. The extended nature of this conflict has stretched the US Army, but its fundamental values remain firm. Our Army has not, and will not, compromise those values. As part of the US Army's continuing assessment of monitoring and strengthening this trust, and ensuring that value based fabric aids the Army in not only leading change but also in achieving mission demands, The Army Chief of Staff, General George Casey, chose the United States Military Academy at West Point, NY to serve as a Center of Excellence in this vital area of strategic importance to the advancement of our professional Army as a respected national institution—able to deliver mission accomplishment to the American people in this era of persistent conflict.

The United States Military Academy was born of necessity. In its earliest days our Nation found itself reliant on Armed Forces to first establish and then maintain itself in the face of external military challenges. Lacking experience and expertise in that realm, we were often obliged to look abroad for example and guidance. Fortunately, men of genius and dedication came forward such as Lafayette, von Steuben, and Kosciusko, yet clearly America needed her own school for professional officers. General George Washington had been advocating establishment of such an institution for many years, as had other senior officers of the Continental Army. Events in his presidency convinced Thomas Jefferson of the necessity, leading him on 16 March 1802 to sign a bill establishing the United States Military Academy at West Point, New York.

Developing and commissioning leaders of character for the United States Army has been West Point's mission ever since, with the inspiration and the challenge of its Cadet Honor Code setting a high standard for those who would choose to earn the right to lead America's Soldiers. That Code, and the system by which it is taught and administered, did not of course come to us fully developed. In this richly and thoroughly documented work of history, Lewis Sorley, himself a third generation graduate of West Point and a long serving public servant and inspiring writer of other works of America's military history, has laid out in detail the history and development of the Cadet Honor Code and its central role in making West Point, as General (Ret) Colin Powell stated in his Thayer Award acceptance speech in September 1998, *"the wellspring of my chosen profession— the place where the professional standards are set, the place that defines the military culture, the place that nurtures the values and virtues of Army service and passes them on from generation to generation"*.

To effectively accomplish its full range of missions, our Army needs agile and adaptive leaders who are culturally astute, creative and morally grounded. Today, a leader's character is more important than ever. In the complex, multi-dimensional security environment of the 21st Century, our Army is asking leaders at all levels—platoon to the highest headquarters—to exercise judgment and solve difficult and complex issues, many with strategic consequences. It's a challenge that our Army and Soldiers and leaders are meeting.

Today's graduates of West Point are meeting that challenge. No less than their predecessors in the Long Gray Line, while Cadets are still in their development, they embrace the Spirit of the Cadet Honor Code and see its value living among those who are of like beliefs at West Point. They also see the necessity to continue to perform their duties with Honor after they are commissioned as Officers. Thus, their concept of Honor includes not lying, cheating, or stealing, and not tolerating those who do, but also embraces the broader concept of honorable duty in treating all with dignity and respect as well as living up to the expectations of the Soldiers Creed, Warrior Ethos, and the ideals of West Point as included in Duty, Honor, Country. This generation's broader and more inclusive concept of honorable duty is both commendable and inspiring. They understand the expectations of Honor among the seven Army values: "Live up to all the Army Values."

Developed and refined over two centuries, the Cadet Honor Code is a foundation for a lifelong commitment to doing what's right. This text chronicles that journey through time, with impeccable research, and enlightening observations. There has long been a need for a definite history of the development of the Cadet Honor Code. Lewis Sorley delivers that definitive history in this book, but he also shows through the eyes of some of the most respected military leaders in our nation's history such as Dwight Eisenhower, Douglas MacArthur, Creighton Abrams, and Harold K. Johnson, and well-documented research, its central place in the development of leaders of character to serve our Nation. This comprehensive book stands as a definitive history of that development and indeed of the value and essential place of the Cadet Honor Code in the values of our Army and Nation.

I hope it will be widely read, as it will prove inspiring and educational to those who wish to reflect on the values of the military profession, and to better understand what West Point has meant to our Army and our Nation since its beginnings in 1802.

Frederick M. Franks, Jr.
General, US Army (Ret) Class of 1966 Chair
William Simon Center for the Professional
Military Ethic USMA, West Point

Prologue

What follows is an essay on the history of a concept and an ideal, one grounded in the ancient traditions of service, sacrifice, and honorable conduct by members of the military profession.

In their manifestation at West Point, and in the American Army in which West Point's graduates have served, the dictates of professionalism, of membership in a profession, have been particularly important, for from them have stemmed the imperatives of shared responsibility for setting, maintaining, and—when necessary—enforcing the profession's ethical standards and observance of its core values.

The elements of a profession are understood to include a sense of corporateness, a shared ethic, a discrete body of expertise based on both education and experience, a literature, and an acknowledged responsibility for self-governance in terms of both competence and values.[1]

In the Army there is also an acknowledged willingness—nearly unique, although shared with the other military services, with police, and with firefighters—to sacrifice for the greater good of others and of the nation, even if necessary at the risk of one's life. This willingness lends a particular gravitas to the profession, and to the act of making a long-term commitment to it. At the same time this unlimited liability, along with the shared hardships endured by soldiers and their families, produces bonds of fraternity unknown, and perhaps even unimaginable, to most who have not experienced military life.

This claim may require a little explanation. The Army, at least for those who embrace it wholeheartedly, is a way of life. It is in many respects a hard and supremely demanding one. But it has an attraction that for many is both vital and enduring. For those not seized with the sense of belonging, of contributing to a noble cause, of full use of whatever wit and talent one may possess, of shared purpose and shared service, of hardship and danger endured and survived, it is almost impossible to communicate the appeal of soldiering.

There are those who have not known the life, and indeed many who have had a taste of it without grasping—or without accepting—the professional outlook which characterizes the best soldiers at every level. These non-believers tend to focus on the hardships, the family separations, the frequent moves, the inevitable bureaucratic absurdities, the jealousies, the restrictions, the inequities. All of these, of course, are real.

Committed military professionals are seldom romantic idealists, unable to see the pain and suffering, the sacrifices of self and family, the unintended but inevitable and tragic impacts on the innocent and the unlucky incident to the use of armed might. These affect professionals in a profound way, shaping and deepening their essentially sober—some might say tragic—outlooks and their pervasive sense of the inevitable gaps between aspiration and achievement, between the precepts of professionalism and its practice.

For those who have made the commitment, though, the rewards are great and lasting and intensely satisfying. These include the company of soldiers, the privilege of living one's life among such men and women. Another fundamental is the opportunity to, as the Army's great recruiting slogan for so many years put it, "be all you can be." And it is not surprising that many who come to West Point are descendants of graduates of earlier days for, growing up as "Army Brats," they have gained a sense of what the life can mean and be.[2] "Soldiering is an affair of the heart," General Creighton Abrams often said, an affirmation that evokes the essential elements of service and sacrifice and deeply felt satisfaction, indeed all the touchstones of West Point's enduring motto "Duty, Honor, Country."

Charles de Gaulle has written splendidly on the sacrifices and satisfactions of the soldier's lot. "Men who adopt the profession of arms submit of their own free will to a law of perpetual constraint," he once stated. "Of their own accord they reject the right to live where they choose, to say what they think, to dress as they like. From the moment they become soldiers it needs but an order to settle them in this place, to move them to that, to separate them from their families and dislocate their normal lives. On the word of command they must rise, march, run, endure bad weather, go without sleep or food, be isolated in some distant post, work till they drop, [but] since the beginning of time armies have found in this life of drudgery, this vocation of sacrifice, their meaning and their joy."[3]

Membership in a profession, while thus gratifying in both personal and vocational terms, is characterized primarily by the responsibilities entailed. These include most conspicuously the obligations to achieve and sustain high levels of competence, to observe high standards of professional integrity, and—perhaps most important of all—to share corporate responsibility for ensuring that one's professional colleagues, in this case one's fellow soldiers, also live up to those obligations.

Accepting and acting according to such responsibility is an essential element of any profession, but none more so than military service. Indeed, as the Posvar Commission[4] (about which more later) noted in its report to the Army Chief of Staff, such values are not only desirable but literally essential, for, they had found, "contemporary sociological studies give empirical evidence of the need for and efficacy of a standard of truth and integrity in professional behavior."[5]

The profession of arms is an ancient and honorable calling. From out of the mists of antiquity has come our first appreciation of the code of honor, and of valor, followed and fiercely protected by the best of men at arms. Writing on "The Character Factor" in public service, columnist David Brooks recently recalled "an ancient sense of honor" which, he observed, "is different from fame and consists of the desire to be worthy of the esteem of posterity."[6] That is it exactly. When those who led the fight for independence of our country mutually pledged their lives, their fortunes, and their sacred honor, they were hazarding all that meant most to them—and doing so for a cause that mattered most of all.

Many inspiring discourses from antiquity illustrate the classic virtues, among the most appealing being that of Marcus Aurelius on emulating the

Roman emperor Antoninus Pius: "Keep yourself simple, good, pure, serious, and unassuming; the friend of justice and godliness; kindly, affectionate, and resolute in your devotion to duty. Strive your hardest to be always such a man as Philosophy would have you to be. Reverence the gods, succour your fellow-mortals. Life is short, and this early existence has but a single fruit to yield—holiness within, and selfless action without. Be in all things Antoninus's disciple."[7]

Those who are commissioned in the United States Army enjoy, as their commission states, the "special trust and confidence" of the Commander in Chief in their "patriotism, valor, fidelity, and abilities," essential attributes of principled leadership. This officership, as West Point's longtime Professor of Philosophy Brigadier General Anthony Hartle has written, is distinguished by "the quality and kind of expert knowledge required, in the depth of responsibility, and in the magnitude of the consequences of inaction or ineffectiveness." In one of their most important responsibilities, military leaders are also teachers and mentors, ensuring by precept, example, and inspiration that the professional ethic is transmitted to and perpetuated by successor generations of leaders. Thus is formed and sustained the Long Gray Line.

In older versions of *Bugle Notes*, the cadet handbook for plebes, there often appeared a short essay titled "The Army As a Career." It began by asking what advantages the Army as a career had to offer, then provided a response: "The answer is, paradoxically, practically none; [but,] in another sense, everything that is worthwhile in life. It depends entirely on your viewpoint . . . . If you measure success by things accomplished, by a niche well filled, by the gratification of duty well and faithfully done, if your joy in life finds fulfillment in playing the game for the game's own sake, of winning the love and respect of the men serving under you . . . , if you do not count the work, the trouble, the cost to yourself and do not stop to think of where the credit will go, but only of the success of the team, then in the Army you will find contentment."[8]

Pride in one's profession is essential, of course, and those in America's military service may draw on a rich heritage of selfless service not only to the nation, but to the cause of peace and justice throughout the world. In deterring or defeating aggression, in training and assisting others to maintain their independence and freedom of action, in helping to rebuild war-torn societies and economies, and in disaster relief the United States Army has throughout its long history earned the respect and gratitude of multitudes. Those who have led America's soldiers are sensible of the privilege of service, and of the compliment represented by their soldiers' trust. To become and remain worthy of such trust is a solemn obligation, one that is both inspiring and ennobling to those who accept it.

The Honor Code is West Point's defining feature. It has been, as it evolved over more than two centuries of the Military Academy's history, the essence of what has attracted fine men and women aspiring to become cadets and then officers, and to share in a life lived according to admirable standards of personal and corporate conduct.

The Honor Code is also, we believe, the central element in the process of self-selection that brings to West Point those who see it as an opportunity to, in the majestic words of the Cadet Prayer, "live above the common level of life," to be part of a community of shared values based on tenets of the Honor Code, along with commitment to service and to something greater than self.

For some this is a revelation that emerges only after joining the Corps of Cadets. Dawn Halfaker (USMA 2001) is a Californian who was recruited by Army to play basketball, something she did very well. Soon after arriving at West Point and getting to know some of her fellow cadets and the staff and faculty who were guiding them, she looked around and realized, with delight, "I had found my tribe!"[9]

Membership in such a tribe, with all its intangible rewards, also brings with it an obligation. It is simply a commitment to live by a shared code of values, thereby entering into a way of life which is infinitely rewarding in and for itself. The Cadet Honor Committee has proclaimed that commitment clearly and unequivocally to the Corps of Cadets: "You have chosen the profession of arms—an integral element of the profession is the acceptance of collective and individual responsibility for honesty and integrity as a way of life."[10]

Devotion to duty, honor, and country are not, of course, solely the purview of West Pointers. Soldiers of every origin, and of every rank, are expected to live up to the highest standards of professional conduct. Fortunately for our nation, we have in every crisis been blessed with large numbers who do. But as the oldest and most venerable national military academy, West Point bears a special responsibility for preserving and exemplifying the profession's finest values.

In this extended essay we shall trace the history and origins of the Honor Code at West Point, and of the Honor System by which its precepts are institutionalized and enforced. It is an inspiring story, but not without its challenges and crises. These have been met and overcome always by the actions of cadets and graduates deeply committed to West Point, to its ancient values and aspirations, and to the profession upon which they have embarked, one in which commitment to service, competence, and character are the immutable hallmarks.

Notes

1 In a paper on *Military Professionalism and Officership in America*, p. 2, Allan R. Millett suggests these as distinguishing characteristics of a profession: a full-time and stable job, serving continuing societal needs; regarded as a lifelong calling by the practitioners, who identify themselves personally with their job subculture; organized to control performance standards and recruitment; requiring formal, theoretical education; having a service orientation in which loyalty to standards of competence and loyalty to clients' needs are paramount; and granted a great deal of collective autonomy by the society it serves, presumably because the practitioners have proven their high ethical standards and trustworthiness.

2 There are many remarkable families. Rene DeRussy (Class of 1812), who later served as Superintendent, was followed by a son, two grandsons, two great-grandsons, three great-great-grandsons, and a great-great-great-grandson, six generations of them in succession, ten graduates in total. Israel Carle Woodruff (Class of 1836) spawned a total of eleven graduates. Although there were a couple of skipped

generations, his son, four grandsons, six great-great-great-grandsons, and one great-great-great-great-granddaughter, Katherine King Miller (Class of 1998), were all graduates, and Captain Miller is also the great-great-great-granddaughter of William Rice King (Class of 1863), who also had four grandsons and six great-great-grandsons join the Corps. Perhaps the all-time champion family are the descendants of Charles Walker Raymond (Class of 1865). Along with his two sons, four grandsons, six great-grandsons, and four great-great-grandsons they total seventeen graduates altogether. My personal favorites, while small in number, are the intellectually powerful family of Lieutenant General Ernest Graves Jr. (Class of 1944), who graduated second in his class. His grandfather, Rogers Birnie, graduated first in the Class of 1872; his father, Ernest Graves, graduated second in the Class of 1905; and his son, Ralph Henry Graves, graduated first in the Class of 1974. See "Genealogical Succession," *2000 Register of Graduates*, pp. 3-1ff.

3   Charles de Gaulle, *The Edge of the Sword* (1934), as quoted in Richard G. Trefry, "Ashes to Ashes?" *Parameters* (Summer 1995), pp. 58-59.

4   An outside group tasked to review honor matters was appointed by the Army Chief of Staff in 1989. Chaired by Dr. Wesley W. Posvar, it became known as the Posvar Commission. See *Final Report of the Special Commission of the Chief of Staff on the Honor Code and Honor System at the United States Military Academy*, 30 May 1989. More on this in later chapters.

5   *Final Report of the Special Commission of the Chief of Staff*, p. 6.

6   David Brooks, "The Character Factor," *The New York Times* (13 November 2007).

7   Marcus Aurelius, *Meditations*.

8   "The Army: The Army As a Career," *1924 Bugle Notes*, p. 109.

9   Captain Halfaker was grievously wounded while serving in Iraq as commanding officer of a military police unit. Subsequently medically retired, she is now CEO of a national security services firm which she founded. The company employs many who were wounded or injured in combat and operates under the inspiring motto "Continuing to Serve."

10 USCC Pamphlet 632-1, *The Honor Code and Honor System*, 1 June 1984, p. 1.

1 | Early Days

Recent classes from the Military Academy have often produced, after four years of arduous discipline and study, close to a thousand graduates. The first class, in 1802, consisted of two. They had, at the time they were graduated in October, been at West Point for just a little over a year, having received their appointments in the summer of 1801.[1]

Joseph Swift, who graduated first in that class, was Chief of Engineers during the War of 1812 and a brevet brigadier. For five years (1812–1817) he was also ex officio Superintendent of the Military Academy. Simon Levy, who graduated last in the class (but also second), served for only three years before resigning due to sickness.[2]

The Class of 1803 produced three graduates, the Class of 1804 two, and the Class of 1805 three again. There were no graduates in what would have been the Class of 1810. Colonel Jonathan Williams, writing in March 1808, observed that the Military Academy "was nothing more than a mathematical school for the few cadets that were then in the service. It was soon found that the government of young military men was incompatible with the ordinary system of schools, and, consequently, this Institution ran into disorder, and the Teacher into contempt."[3]

James Blackwell nevertheless credits Colonel Williams—Superintendent in 1802–1803 and then again during the period 1805–1812—with significant early measures designed to instill high standards of ethical conduct in cadets. In 1806, writes Blackwell, he "imposed regulations designed to shape the character of cadets as honorable men. He forbade drinking of alcoholic beverages and dueling. He also required attendance at chapel services every Sunday. He led discussions with cadets and officers about the demands for the highest standards of integrity on their word as officers."[4] Such actions would certainly have been right on the mark in schooling cadets in the path of honor and decency.

An early condensed history of the Military Academy describes practices under Captain Alden Partridge, Superintendent (1815–1817), which also would undeniably be contributory to imparting admirable ethical precepts to cadets. "There were prayers at reveille and at parade, at the latter of which formations the wings moved forward, and the battalion listened, bare-headed, to the kneeling chaplain. But even in those early days," reads a subsequent account, "that standard of truth and honor, which we now value as the highest attribute of the Military Academy, was already established."[5]

Austerity played an important role in the lives of these first cadets, and may have served a winnowing function. As described in a later *Howitzer*, since "the wooden barracks in which the cadets were quartered were almost uninhabitable in winter, a vacation was given from November to April." Also: "The cadets were at first obliged to manage for themselves the cooking of their rations; but a mess-hall, although a very poor one, was afterwards established, and they were allowed to board at private houses. They even had to forage on the post for the wood for their fires; a saw and sawbuck being considered necessary in every cadet's room. Their water was obtained from a spring on the hillside."[6] A certain grit and determination to persevere would seem essential to surviving those conditions, good qualities for future Army officers.

Nevertheless, during its entire first decade of existence West Point produced a grand total of just 71 graduates. At some point in 1812, says one source, "so slight was the interest in the Military Academy, that . . . there were neither cadets nor instructors at West Point."[7] Perhaps understandably, then, the following year's Class of 1813 consisted of but a single graduate. Things were off to a very slow start.

Establishment of a national military academy had been a long time in coming. Those charged with training and leading the Continental Army had early on become aware of the need for systematic development of officers and leaders of competence and character, and thus for an institution equipped for that task. General George Washington in particular had long advocated an academy and, in his very last days, was still doing so. "The establishment of an institution of this kind, upon a respectable and extensive basis," he wrote to Alexander Hamilton on 12 December 1799, only two days before his death, "has ever been considered by me as an object of primary importance to this country."[8]

General Friedrich von Steuben, who had done so much to help Washington train and discipline the Continental Army, laid out a recommended curriculum for a military academy. His suggestions surprisingly omitted any specific instruction in the ethical realm, perhaps because he assumed that the courses recommended would deal mostly with ethical improvement, as tended to be the case in those days. "Each cadet," he wrote, "shall be instructed in the following sciences and arts; Natural and experimental philosophy, eloquence and the <u>belles letters</u>, civil law and the law of nations, history and geography, mathematics, civil architecture, drawing, the French language, horsemanship, fencing, dancing, and music."[9] Few of these were in evidence during the early years, with the curriculum consisting solely of mathematics, French, and drawing. Looking back from the perspective of West Point's centennial, General Horace Porter judged that during the first decade of the Military Academy's existence "the instruction was then as meager as the rations."[10]

The curriculum was not the only element of early Military Academy life that was embryonic at best. There were, for example, no regulations as to eligibility for appointment. Joseph G. Totten (USMA 1805), admitted to West Point in November 1802, was then only fourteen years of age. That didn't seem to matter, though, as he subsequently rose to become Chief of Engineers. His unusual entry in the *Register of Graduates*, a publication that normally deals only in the unembellished details of assignments and promotions, depicts him memorably as an "eminent engineer" and "beloved gentleman."

There were other growing pains for early classes. In 1804 one officer wrote to Jonathan Williams, then between his two periods of assignment as Superintendent, to describe the current situation at West Point: "Everything is going to ruin.

Morals and knowledge thrive little and courts-martial and flogging prevail."[11] Nevertheless it may be discerned that, from the earliest days, there were influences at work and examples set that subsequently found their reflections in the central place occupied by devotion to honor at West Point and, by derivation, in the Honor Code as it evolved over time. A charming exposition of this early reality was set down by Morris Schaff (USMA 1862) in a memoir he entitled *The Spirit of Old West Point*. Schaff and his class had of course graduated in the midst of the Civil War, thereafter meeting on the fields of battle men they had known as

---

Lying

He who permits himself to tell a lie once, finds it much easier to do it a second and third time, till at length it becomes habitual; he tells lies without attending to it, and truths without the world's believing him. This falsehood of the tongue leads to that of the heart, and in time depraves all its good dispositions.

Thomas Jefferson
Letter to Peter Carr
19 August 1785

---

cadets, some even their own classmates. "West Point," Schaff remembered, "is a great character-builder, perhaps the greatest among our institutions of learning. The habit of truth-telling, the virtue of absolute honesty, the ready and loyal obedience to authority, the display of courage—that virtue called regal—to establish these elements of character she labors without ceasing. The primary agency in accomplishing her ends is, and has been, the tone of the corps of cadets."[12]

Schaff then related what he had experienced in his time as a cadet in the early 1860s to what took place during the earliest days. "This tone," he wrote, "the very life and breath of the Military Academy, tracks back to a fine source, to the character of Washington and the best society at the time of the Revolution." Since the day when Washington had had his headquarters at West Point, noted Schaff, it had been exclusively a military post, "completely isolated from the social ferment and adventitious standards of commerce and trade." In this environment "standards of private and official life, and those of the officers and the gentlemen of his day," were transmitted intact from one generation to the next. And it was at Washington's urging "that West Point as an institution of learning came into being; and its foundations were laid on the solid virtues of his example. And thus to him and to the high-minded men of his day, the tone of the corps of cadets for truth-telling, honesty, obedience to authority, and the considerate bearing of the gentleman, may fairly well be traced."[13]

Superintendent Alden Partridge

Captain Alden Partridge (USMA 1806), mentioned briefly above, served as Superintendent for just over two and a half years, beginning in January 1815 and continuing until July 1817. His tenure was, it seems fair to say, long on drama and short on discipline, to say nothing of vision. There was nevertheless evidence of an evolving code of honor during his superintendency. In 1816, for example, Captain Partridge dismissed a cadet "for lying in connection with a brawl in a local tavern."[14] And there was precedent for the desired standards of professional conduct. Thus, according to John Beasley, "the original Honor Code was actually an extension of the 'Code of Honor' then prevalent in the officer corps of the U.S. Army. This was a very broad code but, at least in the Academy's application, it meant that a cadet was to be fundamentally honest and accepted at his word."[15]

In commenting on the origins of the West Point Honor Code, an honor study of a much later day also made reference to the early officers' Code of Honor, which "stemmed from European values and customs, but [was] distilled through the experience of the American Revolution and Frontier."[16] Dr. Sidney Forman, longtime Military Academy Librarian, noted among antecedents of the Honor Code the standard promulgated in a military publication of 1793, which stated that "the Captain is to be true to his country, make service his business, true honor his object."[17] It is not hard to discern the precursors of "Duty, Honor, Country" in that formulation. Even so, Brigadier General Jack Capps, former Professor and Head of the Department of English, has common sense on his side when he observes that "the origin and history of the West Point Honor Code and System are steeped in faith, myth, and mystery."[18] The Code and System exert a no less powerful contemporary influence for that, however, and perhaps even gain in strength as a result of their knightly and even romantic origins.

The first USMA Chaplain, the Reverend Adam Empie, was appointed in 1813. He also served as Professor of Ethics, History, and Geography. Dr. Forman identified the chaplains as early sources of instruction in ethical conduct, along with "the course of religious and ethical training," the example of officers on the staff and faculty, and—as they evolved over time, presumably—traditions of the Corps of Cadets.[19]

Eventually Captain Partridge was court-martialed, found guilty of disobedience of orders and inciting mutiny, and sentenced to be cashiered. His case went all the way to the President of the United States, who approved the findings and sentence, but heeded a recommendation for clemency and remitted the punishment. Partridge then, in an uncharacteristically prudent act, resigned his commission.[20]

For our purposes in examining the history and origins of the Honor Code and System, the significance of this background is that it portrays an atmosphere in which it seems unlikely that much in the way of ethical development, much less anything systematic or institutionalized, could take place. That essential evolution awaited more settled times.

Thayer

All graduates of West Point know the significance of 16 March 1802, the date on which the United States Military Academy was founded. That occasion is celebrated by gatherings of graduates the world over, even in war zones, as the moment for camaraderie, reminiscence, and rededication to shared ideals and devotion to service.[21] West Point graduates should also know, and equally honor, 28 July 1817. That was the date on which Sylvanus Thayer, USMA 1808, become Superintendent of his alma mater. Thayer gave West Point its intellectual and ethical character, its pedagogical approach, its discipline, and its self-image. All these were critical elements of the young Academy's character and promise.

The late Colonel Thomas Griess, a highly regarded West Point professor and for many years head of its Department of History, has pointed out that Thayer had "been charged by the Chief of Engineers . . . to revitalize West Point, which had languished since the War of 1812 as a result of the mismanagement and unsuitable temperament of Alden Partridge."[22] That was putting it mildly indeed. The year before Thayer arrived, for example, what would have been the Class of 1816 produced no graduates whatsoever.

One scholar stated bluntly that West Point, "under the direction of Alden Partridge, was falling apart administratively."[23] There was that, and more—much more. The Chief of Engineers, General Joseph G. Swift, was clearly alert to the situation, as is revealed by his 17 July 1817 instructions to Major Sylvanus Thayer. "As soon as you can conveniently," he wrote, "I wish you to go to the Point and take charge of everything there." Swift warned Thayer that he would find those at West Point disposed to talk about their rights. "All the rights that any possess at West Point is the right of doing their duty," said Swift, adding reassuringly that in the exercise of his authority Thayer could depend upon his cordial support.[24]

A week later, with Thayer not yet having assumed command at West Point, Captain Partridge wrote to General Swift with an update on the situation there. "I have the honor to inform you," he stated, "that I have this day arrested Professors Mansfield and Ellicott, and also Mr. Snowden the military Storekeeper at this Place." That was not all. "I should have arrested Mr. Berard . . . but he is now absent. It is also my intention to prefer Charges against Capt. O'Connor." Partridge asked that General Swift make report of his proceedings to the Secretary of War and the President.[25] Three days later Thayer arrived to assume command. One of his first official acts, the very next day, was to advise General Swift that he had found the Professors of Natural and Experimental Philosophy, and of Mathematics, in arrest, and to express the hope that those gentleman could either be released from arrest or replaced by other instructors by the time the academic year began. Within a few days, gratifyingly, the Acting Secretary of War directed Thayer to "remove all restriction on the officers so arrested."[26] The tiny faculty was back in business.

When Thayer took over the Military Academy "nearly all the cadets were missing," noted Stacy Southworth in an assessment of Thayer's importance. "Evidently they had left for different parts of the country on furlough. Moreover, there was no registration enrollment which gave the cadets' place of residence." Faced with this surreal situation, a military academy with virtually no students in evidence and no information on their whereabouts, Thayer "actually had to resort to the newspapers to advertise for the return of the cadets."[27]

Thus Thayer's initial tasks involved recovering his student body, establishing discipline, learning in detail the record of each cadet, and dismissing disruptive recalcitrants.[28] In later nominating him for the Hall of Fame of Great Americans at New York University, the Military Academy's Association of Graduates noted that, when Thayer arrived to assume the duties of Superintendent, "he found . . . undisciplined personnel, a disgruntled faculty, a puerile curriculum. Within two years he had rebuilt and enlarged the curriculum, had subdued two mutinies, [and] had launched West Point on its glorious career."[29]

Thayer considered honor an essential element of cadet development, and George Fielding Eliot's biography of Colonel Thayer describes how he used honor to enhance discipline. As he "evolved it, the essence of his plan was that Honor would be the foundation required; Honor would draw all cadets together as a Corps; Honor, generated from within the Corps itself, would be the spirit, guiding the Corps for all time."[30] Going much farther in attribution of the Honor Code to Thayer, West Point Professor Colonel Herman Beukema stated his view that Thayer's greatest achievement lay "in the field of moral training. His experience prior to 1817," said Beukema, "had taught him that an army, to perform its mission, must have

---

Cadet Honor Code

A cadet will not lie, cheat, steal, or tolerate those who do.

---

at its core—the officer personnel—a rock-hard integrity in thought and word and action. And whatever the background of the entering cadet, he was still at an age permitting the inculcation of the principles of honor. Hence, the West Point honor code, established by Colonel Thayer. Wisely he understood the fact that honor recognizes no distinction of rank or position. The cadets themselves were made guardians of the inviolability of their code." Assessing the results, Colonel Beukema wrote in 1943: "How well Colonel Thayer builded is evident from the fact that the Corps honor code remains today in the minds of not only the Army officer but of the informed civilian as well, the distinctive feature of the 'West Point system.' "[31]

Before assignment to the Military Academy, Thayer had been sent to Europe, along with Colonel William McRee, on an extended mission to locate and acquire for the West Point Library the best contemporary works on military affairs, military maps and models, and related scientific instruments. What they collected over three years spent in France, England, Germany, and Holland, noted Sidney Forman, "formed the basic collection in the West Point Library," about a thousand volumes comprising "the principal military publications of Europe."[32]

The benefits derived from this scholarly collection extended well beyond the Military Academy. Under Colonel Thayer's guidance "the West Point Library became the largest and most important library in the United States in the field of military technology, and also in the related subject areas of the mathematical and physical sciences—a position of pre-eminence which it held until at least the end of the century," wrote Forman. "During Thayer's administration the library collection grew from 1,000 to 8,000 books and became one of the major vehicles through which European, particularly French, military technology, the physical sciences, and mathematics were introduced into American life."[33]

Not only scientific materials were introduced during Thayer's regime, however. In 1820 the first textbook in ethics was prescribed, William Paley's *Principles of Moral and Political Philosophy*.[34] The following year the standards of cadet conduct promulgated in regulations gave an indication of what Colonel Thayer set as the standard: "The cadets are not only required to abstain from all vicious, immoral, or irregular conduct, but they are also expected, on every occasion, to conduct themselves with the propriety and decorum of gentlemen: —any cadet who shall be guilty of conduct unbecoming an officer and a gentleman, shall be dismissed [from] the service."[35]

An early testimonial to Thayer's effectiveness came in the form of a report by the Chief Engineer dated 30 March 1822. In his view "the Military Academy may be considered as having been in its infancy until about the beginning of 1818," or in other words only a few months after Thayer assumed the Superintendency, "prior to which there was but little system or regularity. Cadets were admitted without examination, and without the least regard to their age or qualifications, [in violation of] the law of 1812. Hence the Institution was filled with Cadets who were more or less unfit for their situations. It is not surprising, therefore, that a large portion of them have been under the necessity of leaving the Academy without completing their education."[36]

What came to be known as the "Thayer System" included small classes (called sections) of only a dozen or so cadets, ranked in those sections according to their academic standing in a given subject, and resectioned periodically as their performance dictated based on daily graded recitations. There were obvious elements of character-building in the Thayer approach. Cadets had nowhere to hide, no opportunity to evade or avoid recitation and evaluation, no chance to let things slide and try to catch up later. Every man was obliged to be ready for inspection every day of his cadet life. In addition, Thayer established a standardized curriculum, regularized examination and promotion procedures, adopted a calendar of admissions, and prescribed a period of cadetship to qualify for graduation and commission. None of these standards and procedures had existed when he took charge; most were still in effect many decades after his departure. It is nearly impossible to overestimate Colonel Thayer's importance to West Point, and consequently to the Army of his times and for many years thereafter.[37]

Colonel R. Ernest Dupuy, an historian steeped in West Point lore, enumerated several of Colonel Thayer's innovations in the realm of military governance at West Point—organization of the Corps of Cadets into a battalion of two permanent companies, establishment of a forerunner of the Department of Tactics and appointment of an officer to function as Commandant of Cadets, creation of cadet officers with assigned responsibilities—and concluded that "the first steps in the inculcation of West Point's much discussed . . . honor system had been taken."[38]

Within a few months of taking command at West Point, Thayer also moved to introduce ethical considerations in determining the eligibility of dismissed cadets for service in the Army. This initiative served to penalize those dismissed from West Point for dishonorable conduct by barring them from such service, thus providing a further incentive for honorable behavior on the part of the Corps of Cadets. Specifically, his February 1818 *Proposition for the Re-organization of the Military Academy* included these proposals: "Persons who shall have been dismissed from the Academy to be ineligible to any office in the army for five years thereafter, and forever if dismissed for any action in itself dishonorable." Signed: Thayer.[39]

The necessity for some such provisions as defense against political preferment for the undeserving soon became clear. On 28 June 1818, nine Military Academy faculty members (acting with Thayer's approval), having just completed a laborious examination of cadets and being about to recommend certain of them for commissions, wrote to Secretary of War John Calhoun: "We beg leave to call the attention of the Secty of War to a subject in which the feelings of these young gentlemen and the welfare of the Academy are most deeply interested." These faculty members had just learned "with extreme regret" that two former cadets, "not long since discharged . . . under circumstances more or less disreputable, have been placed upon the Register of the Army as Commissioned officers of the same . . . ." This was intolerable. Not only had these two failed to learn and exhibit discipline as cadets, but "associated with the idea of subordination the undersigned are led also to appreciate certain moral principles which are considered as fundamental points in every system of Military Education."[40]

So long as those who conducted themselves in accordance with such principles prospered, and those who failed to do so did not prosper, all would be well. "But," and here was the heart of the matter, "should it appear in any instance that Idleness, Misconduct, habits of low and ungentlemanlike Behaviour or of disregard for the Rules of Discipline, are to be overlooked; that those who have been expelled from the society of Cadets on account of these vices, or rejected for gross and notorious incapacity, are nevertheless to be admitted to the confidance [sic] of the Government & clothed with Military rank: it is not to be wondered at, if the military ardour of the Cadets should be entirely subdued, and the spirit of obedience give way [to] that of disaffection and disgust."[41]

It is worth wading through such stilted and antique language to appreciate this statement as a powerful plea for maintenance of high standards of personal and professional conduct, not only at the Military Academy but in the officer corps at large. In closing their plea, these young officers nailed it down: "The honor of our country, and above all of the army which it is expected must receive its tone and character from the initial formation of its officers in this Institution, is deeply concerned in repelling all such attempts as would substitute dulness for genius, or idleness and vice for energy and a faithful discharge of duty."[42] This letter, endorsed by Colonel Thayer, offers some of the earliest and best evidence we have of efforts to establish and maintain high standards of honorable behavior at the Military Academy.

In his second year as superintendent Thayer introduced another important element of ethical instruction, compulsory chapel attendance for cadets.[43] Then known as "Divine Service," this practice continued for more than a century and a half. Only in 1972, under constitutional challenges based on the doctrine of separation of church and state, was compulsory chapel attendance brought to an end. With it went a potentially important contribution to the education of cadets in the realm of ethics and values. Even those who attended only grudgingly often in later years recalled appreciatively some aspects of the chapel experience, in particular the inspiring cadences of the "Cadet Prayer."

Cadet Prayer

O God, our Father, Thou Searcher of Human hearts, help us to draw near to Thee in sincerity and truth. May our religion be filled with gladness and may our worship of Thee be natural. Strengthen and increase our admiration for honest dealing and clean thinking, and suffer not our hatred of hypocrisy and pretence ever to diminish. Encourage us in our endeavor to live above the common level of life. Make us to choose the harder right instead of the easier wrong, and never to be content with a half truth when the whole can be won. Endow us with courage that is born of loyalty to all that is noble and worthy, that scorns to compromise with vice and injustice and knows no fear when truth and right are in jeopardy. Guard us against flippancy and irreverence in the sacred things of life. Grant us new ties of friendship and new opportunities of service. Kindle our hearts in fellowship with those of a cheerful countenance, and soften our hearts with sympathy for those who sorrow and suffer. Help us to maintain the honor of the Corps untarnished and unsullied and to show forth in our lives the ideals of West Point in doing our duty to Thee and our Country. All of which we ask in the name of the Great Friend and Master of all—AMEN.

Colonel Thayer, a bachelor, devoted his entire energies and attention to the education and discipline of his young cadets, even devising a stand-up desk in his basement office from which, while dealing with paperwork, he could observe drill through the head-high windows as it was being conducted on the parade field in front of his quarters. So pervasive was his influence, not only during his superintendency but for generations thereafter, that it is tempting to attribute to his stewardship virtually every element of the West Point experience. Thus a number of scholars have been led to credit Thayer with development of the Honor Code and Honor System, perhaps not in their fully evolved form, but at least in the initial concepts.

General Douglas MacArthur, who during his own superintendency faced difficult challenges and made important reforms, wrote of Thayer that "the high ethical standards and codes of conduct which, for more than a century, have been the predominant characteristic of West Point as an educational institution were established and nurtured by him." Going even further, MacArthur, while serving as Army Chief of Staff in 1935, wrote: "It is not too much to say that the reputation of the American officer corps for probity, integrity, and a high sense of honor and duty is traceable in large part to General Thayer's influence."[44]

Many later scholars and documents, including some official West Point publications, have attributed creation of the Honor Code in greater or lesser degree to Colonel Thayer. A pamphlet published by the Military Academy in 1976 and issued to cadets, for example, essentially endorsed this viewpoint. "The origin of the Honor Code has been attributed to Colonel Sylvanus Thayer, Superintendent of the Military Academy from 1817 to 1833," it began. "The lax and rebellious mood of the cadets at the time he assumed command in 1817 made abundantly clear the need for firm discipline, for the inculcation of a sense of duty, and for the establishment of a standard of honor which, resting in the hands of the cadets themselves, would provide the mold for future attitudes as officers."[45] Another official document published by the modern Military Academy states that "in the 1820's Sylvanus Thayer was the first Superintendent to expand the Code," a statement apparently postulating the existence of such a code at that early date, "to include [prohibition of] cheating."[46]

So respected a scholar as Colonel Ernest Dupuy wrote of "West Point's honor system, installed by Thayer." That system, he continued, "depended upon impetus from within the Corps itself to instill the unswerving truthfulness and sincerity which had become the hallmark of the Military Academy. Only by example, inculcation, and devotion, beginning in the long novitiate of the fourth-class year, would the individual realize what the bond of a cadet's word meant."[47]

In his history of West Point Stephen Ambrose credits Colonel Thayer with having "established the principle that a cadet's word is always accepted and consequently that a cadet is expected always to tell the truth. But neither Thayer nor his successors [until MacArthur, says Ambrose] ever spelled out the code or established any investigating and enforcing agency."[48] The latter portion of that statement requires some comment, since it has never been part of the officially sanctioned cadet responsibility to "enforce" penalties against honor violators.

That has been the exclusive purview of Academy authorities, usually carried out by means of courts-martial or dismissal. While the unofficial Vigilance Committees of another era (to be discussed later) did mete out rough justice, they did so with only the tacit consent, and perhaps not always that, of their superior officers.

Colonel Griess provides a balanced assessment of the likely state of affairs in Thayer's day and for some time thereafter. "Although superintendents, faculty members, and graduates habitually referred to the 'honor system' during the nineteenth century," he observed, "they meant the code of ethical behavior set forth as the ideal of the commissioned officer corps. Central to the ethical system was the idea that an officer's word was his bond. The penalty for failure to meet this standard was for the officer to be immediately cashiered and disgraced."[49]

Colonel Griess does acknowledge that during Thayer's time there was in operation "an embryonic honor system." He concludes that, in general, "this was a self-imposed code on the part of the Corps of Cadets. It was initially neither a formalized nor an officially recognized and sanctioned regulatory system. Indeed, the authorities at West Point generally sought to suppress the operative body, which usually consisted of a hastily formed committee of senior cadets."[50]

There occurred, late in Colonel Thayer's tenure, an interesting case in which a cadet successfully challenged the use in a disciplinary matter of a cadet's honor-bound obligation to tell the truth. Cadet Frederick A. Smith (USMA 1833) wrote to Secretary of War Lewis Cass: "Upon the 17th of October last, a report was recorded against me, for being 'Absent from quarters after taps.'" There was no validity to the charge, said Smith, "as I was not absent a moment." He then described a serenade having been given by three cadets to a lady then residing at West Point, indeed at the house of the reporting officer, and the subsequent reporting of six cadets for unauthorized absence from their quarters. Smith said that four of the six on report had had nothing to do with the incident, and suggested that they had only come under suspicion and been charged because of "a reputation for musical talent."[51]

Cadet Smith argued that the large number of cadets charged amounted to a fishing expedition on the part of the Commandant, Captain Ethan Hitchcock, who also happened to be the officer at whose quarters the serenading in question had taken place. Smith told the Secretary of War, in his very well written and logically argued letter, that "the question you are to determine is—whether the officers of this institution are to be allowed to charge all those whom they see fit—with offences, in order to discover the guilty."[52]

Secretary Cass saw the logic in Smith's argument, acknowledging that it was improper and unfair to charge cadets more or less at random, with no proximate basis for doing so. Cadet Smith could simply have denied the charges, and truthfully, but his objection rested on the more profound premise that it was an improper use of honor to almost randomly charge various cadets with an offense, relying on their obligatory truthfulness in responding to such reports to sort out those who were guilty. Secretary Cass therefore ordered the charges against Smith expunged from the record. "Reports, if mere conjectures are to be received, would be useless," said Cass. Otherwise they "would subject the M[ilitary] Academy to a species of inquisition, incompatible with the feelings of our Countrymen." And, he concluded, "it is better that many of these should go undiscovered or unpunished, than that such a practice should become established." Cadet Smith had made an important case persuasively, in the process bringing about limitations on the ways in which honor could be used to enforce regulations. He had also revealed himself as a man who understood proportionality, telling Secretary Cass that in his view "it was not considered an offence of a deep dye to Serenade a lady."[53]

Now back to Thayer. In the somewhat rococo language of his day, Stacy Southworth later put it this way in summing up for West Point's staff and faculty Colonel Thayer's importance to the Military Academy in terms of honor: "He set before you the standard of honor—it is nowhere higher; he laid deep the foundation of respect and reverence for law and liberty; he taught you by precept and example how a soldier and a citizen should live; he made his life the incarnation of the delicate honor of honesty."[54]

Soon after he became Superintendent in 1977, General Andrew Goodpaster provided what might well serve as the best capsule explanation of the Honor Code's origins and evolution. "The code, derived from the 'code of honor' of the officer corps of the late 1700's," he told a congressional committee, "after many changes in statement, application, and interpretation evolved into the present code."[55]

What now also seems clear, and fair to Thayer's legacy, is that in his example and the precepts he taught he gave West Point a simple and practical secular morality that was to become its essence, its central imperative, and its glory. We know it now as the Honor Code, here expressed in its current form: "A cadet will not lie, cheat, steal, or tolerate those who do."

Colonel Thayer resigned from the superintendency in July of 1833, frustrated and unhappy about continued interference by officials of the Jackson Administration and members of Congress, particularly with respect to reinstatement of cadets who had been discharged for academic or disciplinary reasons. Such issues were not, as we shall see, phenomena confined to Thayer's day, a reality perhaps not surprising at a national academy whose students are chosen primarily by members of Congress. Commenting on the years to follow, James Morrison accurately observed that "the history of the Military Academy is . . . among other things an exemplification of institutional development in a politically-charged environment."[56]

As for Thayer, though, his sixteen years as Superintendent had put an indelible stamp on the institution and those it would school for many years to come. Wrote Thomas Fleming with accuracy and appreciation, "Sylvanus Thayer's life remains a monument to the commitment to duty, honor, and country that is at the core of West Point's mission."[57]

Mid-Century

West Point from its earliest days was viewed, and properly so, as the most democratic of institutions. Its students were drawn from across the country, indeed from every Congressional district, without regard to economic or social status.

Only the desire to serve and demonstrated potential for doing the work determined who might be admitted.

This egalitarian admissions policy brought with it certain challenges, perhaps the most significant of which stemmed from varying cultural backgrounds with respect to values and standards of conduct. Captain Henry Brewerton (USMA 1819) addressed this matter with some eloquence when he was Superintendent (1845–1852). In a letter to the Chief of Engineers, a letter prompted by the necessity of convening a court-martial in the case of a cadet charged with lying, Captain Brewerton wrote: "It is, I think, to be expected, in an Institution like this, the members of which are youths brought from every section of our country and from the various grades of society in it, from the highest to the lowest, that the standard for truth should not be the same with all—that their moral perceptions in this respect should receive their color in a great degree from their different associations and the manner in which they have been reared at home. At the same time," he added, "it is evident we can have but one standard for truth and fair dealing at the Academy, and that [is] the highest—such as is acknowledged among gentlemen."[58]

Robert E. Lee

Captain Robert E. Lee (USMA 1829), soon to become one of West Point's most famous graduates as the nation descended into civil war, was Superintendent during the years 1852–1855. One honor-related incident is of particular interest and importance during his tenure.

It is widely believed that, until precipitating events in 1976 led to a dramatic change, there had invariably been imposed on convicted honor violators the single sanction of dismissal. Two cadets in the Class of 1857 were involved in an honor incident with a different outcome. Briefly the circumstances were these: the Cadet Officer of the Day, inspecting barracks, found Cadet Martin absent from his room. He asked Cadet Warner, who was orderly of the room across the hall, if he knew where the missing cadet was. Warner replied that he did not. Shortly thereafter, the Officer of the Day noticed Martin leaving the barracks. Upon the man's return, the Officer of the Day asked if he had been on an authorized absence, to which Martin replied untruthfully that he had. Subsequently, it came out that Martin had in fact been visiting (without authority) in the room of Warner, who had falsely denied knowledge of his whereabouts. This was all less complicated than it sounds. The simple fact was that both men had made false official statements, and one had also violated regulations by leaving his room without authority.[59]

Superintendent Lee considered the matter, then wrote of it to the Chief of Engineers (who in that day had supervisory responsibility for the Military Academy) addressing the actions of Martin, the cadet who had been absent from his room. "His full confession of his act & the clear perception he evinces of the errour of his conduct inclines me to believe he would not again repeat it, & the sincerity of his conviction is I think shewn by the offer of his resignation with the assent of his father."

Lee continued by broaching the possibility of a milder sanction than expulsion. "Should you therefore think that his punishment is not necessary to arrest conduct so derogatory to the character of the Corps of Cadets, & which he asserts has been practised by other members of his class; but I hope not to the extent he says; that the dishonour of such a course, can be otherwise clearly set forth to the Corps, I would respectfully recommend that as much leniency as possible be extended toward him, & that if his fault cannot be overlooked, that some milder punishment than that of dismissal be inflicted on him."[60]

Interestingly, the Secretary of War decided to accept the resignation of Martin, the cadet on whose behalf Colonel Lee had written, but left disposition of Warner's case to the Superintendent, cautioning only that "it is proper that the reasons which have determined [the Secretary] not to prosecute the matter further, should be understood."[61] Colonel Lee complied with those instructions by having his adjutant publish an order explaining his decision. "The conduct of Cadet Warner," it read, "is considered but little less culpable, than that of Cadet Martin. He should have replied with truth to the question of the Officer of the Day, or have remained silent. But in as much as the question of that officer was not called for in the strict line of duty; and as Cadet Warner upon reflection, saw his false step and corrected it, it is not considered necessary to be otherwise officially rebuked to prevent its repetition, than thus publicly condemned."[62]

Given a second chance in this early example of Superintendent's discretion, the cadet made good use of the opportunity. Graduating with the Class of 1857 and commissioned in the Artillery, he served on frontier duty in California and then, when war came, with the Army of the Potomac. He was breveted in the regular service to captain on 3 July 1863 for "meritorious services" at Gettysburg, to major on 13 March 1865 for "gallant and meritorious services during the siege of Petersburg," and to lieutenant colonel on the same date for "good conduct and meritorious services" during the war. In volunteer service he was breveted to colonel on 1 August 1864 for "gallant and distinguished services in the battle of Gettysburg and in the operations in front of Petersburg," and to brigadier for "meritorious services during the operations leading to the fall of Richmond and surrender of Confederate forces under General Lee."[63] There is no little irony in all this, particularly the last.

The Delafield Years

Major Richard Delafield (USMA 1818) was Superintendent in the five years leading up to the outbreak of the Civil War (1856–1861), years of increasing ferment and turbulence. This was the second time he had held the post, following up on a longer stint during the period 1838–1845. Delafield had strong views about cadets' accountability for their actions. Indeed, it has been maintained that he "frequently compelled cadets to give evidence against themselves in cases of misconduct, asserting that the oath each student took to uphold the regulations overrode the fifth amendment to the Constitution."[64]

"The highly legalistic, minutely regulated, cadet-administered honor code of today," wrote a scholar in a 1970 dissertation, "was unknown at ante-bellum West Point. The cadet of that era, like his officer counterpart, was expected not to lie or steal, and if apprehended in either of these offenses, he risked dismissal, although in a few cases mitigating circumstances reduced the penalty."[65] The latter observation is of particular interest, since a century and more later the issue of variable or proportionate sanctions for honor violations would become the centerpiece of heated controversy, remnants of which persist even to the present day.

Cadets of this era received elements of moral instruction from the chaplain, who chaired a Department of Ethics conducting classes in moral science or moral philosophy along with a mixed bag of other subjects, among them rhetoric, law, and grammar.[66] Such instruction by the chaplain may itself be considered an important element in the evolution of the Honor Code as the Military Academy developed and matured in these early days. There lay ahead, for West Point as for the nation, the divisiveness and trauma of a protracted civil war.

Notes

1   Theodore J. Crackel, *West Point*, p. 50.
2   *2000 Register of Graduates*, p. 4-2.
3   Report of 14 March 1808 as quoted in Edward C. Boynton, *History of West Point*, p. 193.
4   James A. Blackwell, *On Brave Old Army Team*, p. 96.
5   *1900 Howitzer*, p. 207.
6   Ibid.
7   *1946 Bugle Notes*, p. 22.
8   This statement is engraved in a prominent place in the West Point Room of the USMA Library. Washington departed this life on 14 December 1799, just two days after penning his final endorsement of a national military academy. At the Military Academy's Centennial in 1902, Lt. Gen. J. M. Schofield, President of the Association of Graduates, provided this background: "But in 1793 . . . Washington as President instituted measures looking to the establishment of a Military Academy. This resulted in the act of Congress of May 9, 1794, which provided for a Corps of Artillerists and Engineers of four companies, each company to have two Cadets, etc. Several subsequent acts authorized the appointment of Cadets in limited numbers and provided for their instruction; and finally the act of March 16, 1802, which authorized the organization of a separate Corps of Engineers, provided that the said corps, when so organized, should be stationed at West Point and should constitute a Military Academy." *The Centennial of the United States Military Academy*, I:58. Many years later Secretary of War Robert P. Patterson would observe that "West Point is the existing embodiment of the patriotism of its spiritual founder, the Army's first and foremost leader, General Washington." Quoted in 1947 *Bugle Notes*, p. [i]. Washington himself, in one of his most famous statements, expressed this aspiration: "I hope I shall possess firmness and virtue enough to maintain what I consider the most enviable of all titles, the character of an honest man." Letter to Alexander Hamilton, 28 August 1788.

9   Quoted in Edgar Denton III, "The Formative Years," p. 9. The curriculum of the early years was far more modest, featuring only mathematics and French at first, later to be supplemented with drawing. Subsequently many of the other recommended subjects were added, including dancing, the latter to the chagrin of many during the era of male-only cadets when one's instructional dancing partner was often a roommate.

10   *The Centennial of the United States Military Academy*, I:34.

11   Quoted in Denton, p. 43.

12   Morris Schaff, *The Spirit of Old West Point*, p. 77.

13   Ibid., pp. 77-78. In a foreword to his collection of West Point songs Frederick C. Mayer, long-time organist of the Cadet Chapel, cited "the treasured traditions, the versatile activities, and the resolute 'will-to-do' which inspire the imperishable standard of efficiency, character, and Service known to the world as 'The Spirit of old West Point.' " *West Point Songs*, p. ix. Many commentators share Schaff's view of the derivation of cadet concepts of duty and honor as stemming from the code of professional officers, but a dissenting view was set forth by Col. Harry A. Buckley, who concluded that the Honor Code and System had their roots in cadet perceptions of what standards of behavior for individuals would enhance the quality of their shared experience. Thus, according to Buckley: "Cadets determined over time that the quality of their lives was enhanced when they could be sure that their fellow cadets would honor their possessions and their word and would not take advantage of them in the highly competitive academic arena." And: "I think it is important to note that these honor norms were originally intended to enhance cadet life and were not established as rules for Army officer behavior." Memorandum, Col. Harry A. Buckley (Leadership) to Col. J. M. Pollin, Subject: Cadet Honor Code and System, 14 November 1977, USMA Archives. Such a view has a certain plausibility, especially given the youth and limited academic background of cadets in the early days, who might not be expected to have known much about historic codes of chivalric behavior and the like, but the two theories are not mutually exclusive.

14   Lesson Outline, History of the Cadet Honor Code, 1963, File: Honor Code—Historical (JUL 63–JUN 64), USMA Archives.

15   Major John H. Beasley, "The USMA Honor System," p. 3.

16   *Final Report of the Special Commission of the Chief of Staff*, May 1989, p. 5.

17   Sidney Forman, "Scandal Among Cadets," p. 485.

18   Letter to Sorley, 5 May 2007.

19   Forman, "Scandal Among Cadets," p. 486.

20   Denton, p. 174. Also, as per Denton: "Throughout his life he [Partridge] continued to attack the Military Academy at every opportunity, but with no lasting success. After his return to his native Vermont he . . . made numerous attempts to establish military schools, of which only one, which later became Norwich University, was successful." It is interesting to note that "Partridge's entire military career was spent at West Point." Like his successor Sylvanus Thayer, Partridge attended Dartmouth College, but left after three years to enter West Point. Subsequent to graduation in the Class of 1806, he was immediately appointed to the first of a succession of assignments at the Military Academy, culminating in the Superintendency. "Unfortunately," noted a later evaluation, "his administration tended to become more arbitrary and autocratic. In his final year, he intentionally disobeyed the orders of the President and the Secretary of War, convinced that he alone was qualified to determine what was best for the academy." *2006 Register of Graduates*, p. 1-25. Partridge did get on a postage stamp, however, an eleven-cent issue of 12 February 1985 in the Great Americans Series, being honored primarily as the founder of Norwich University. He looks very handsome and soldierly in his high-collared dress uniform coat.

21   The Military Academy was actually in operation well in advance of the formal date of its statutory establishment, with classes for the first cadets commencing in late

September 1801. As Theodore J. Crackel has pointed out, passage of the Military Peace Establishment Act of 1802, which included provisions for the Military Academy at West Point, constituted Congressional sanction of what President Thomas Jefferson had already accomplished administratively. See Crackel, *West Point: A Bicentennial History*, pp. 53-55. This is an early example of how, on the larger scale of the entire Academy, what we will observe repeatedly with respect to the Honor Code and Honor System was typical: practice became established, only later (sometimes much later) to be codified officially in written form.

22 Thomas E. Griess, "Dennis Hart Mahan: West Point Professor and Advocate of Military Professionalism, 1830–1871," Ph.D. dissertation, Duke University, 1968, p. 45.

23 James L. Morrison Jr., "The United States Military Academy, 1833–1866: Years of Progress and Turmoil," p. 36.

24 Letter, Gen. Joseph G. Swift to Maj. Thayer, Portland, 17 July 1817, *The West Point Thayer Papers*, Vol. II.

25 Letter, Capt. Alden Partridge to Gen. Joseph G. Swift, 24 July 1817, *Thayer Papers*, Vol. II.

26 Letter, S. Thayer to Gen. Joseph G. Swift, 28 July 1817, and response of 2 August 1817, *Thayer Papers*, Vol. II.

27 Stacy B. Southworth, "The Life and Character of BG Sylvanus Thayer," An Address Presented by the Headmaster of Thayer Academy in South Braintree, Massachusetts, to Officers of the USMA at West Point on 14 December 1922. Reprinted in the *2002 Register of Graduates*, p. 1-61.

28 Edgar Denton, "Formative Years," pp. 181ff.

29 Association of Graduates, USMA, "Nomination of Sylvanus Thayer, Educator, to the Hall of Fame," n.d. USMA Archives. Thayer was elected in 1965. Partridge, for his part, was court martialed and sentenced to be cashiered. President Monroe remitted the sentence, after which Partridge resigned his commission. He had not forgotten West Point, however, in 1830 publishing under a pseudonym a pamphlet entitled "The Military Academy at West Point unmasked, or corruption and Military Despotism Exposed by Americanus." *Thayer Papers*, Vol. XI.

30 George Fielding Eliot, *Sylvanus Thayer*, pp. 134f.

31 Colonel Herman Beukema, *The United States Military Academy*, pp. 25-26, as quoted in Lt. Col. John W. Burtchaell, Memorandum of Law, 27 November 1961, USMA Archives.

32 Sidney Forman, "Sylvanus Thayer and the United States Military Academy Library," *1959 Register of Graduates*, n.p. Reprint in Thayer Vertical File, USMA Archives.

33 Ibid. There is in the Thayer Papers a candid letter from Colonel McRee to General Swift describing what he and Thayer had encountered in looking for materials to purchase: "Among the military books there must inevitably be found a considerable portion of trash. We were indeed too little acquainted with them to determine from our own knowledge their individual worth. Their general character or that of the author was, in most cases, the only rule by which we could regulate our choice." Letter of 8 January 1817, *Thayer Papers*, Vol. I.

34 Sidney Forman, "Scandal Among Cadets," p. 486.

35 *Regulations*, USMA, 1821, Paragraph 102.

36 As quoted in Edward C. Boynton, *History of West Point*, p. 215.

37 Some academic authors have in recent years sought to debunk Thayer's sterling reputation, but to little avail. The fact is that he established the Military Academy on a level of excellence and efficiency far above what it had previously been able to achieve, and set it on a course of service and success that became its hallmark. His later election to the Hall of Fame for Great Americans was further evidence of the enduring value and importance of his accomplishments.

38 R. Ernest Dupuy, *Where They Have Trod*, p. 142.

39 *Thayer Papers*, Vol. III. It would be interesting to know what precipitated Thayer's letter a few months later in which he told General Swift that "the company of Bombardiers [Company of Bombardiers, Sappers & Miners] is undoubtedly the worst of the whole Army being principally composed of fugitives from justice & the refuse of society." Letter, 28 June 1818.

40 Letter, Nine USMA Faculty Members and Approved by Thayer, to Secretary of War John C. Calhoun, 28 June 1818, *Thayer Papers*, Vol. III.

41 Ibid.

42 Ibid. The dismissed cadets were Edward Polk and Wilson C. N. Armistead, former members of the Classes of 1818 and 1817 respectively. Armistead served until being honorably discharged as a first lieutenant in 1821. No further information about Polk is to be found in the *Register of Graduates and Former Cadets*.

43 Griess, p. 70, notes that "the first recorded instance of this compulsory attendance appears in an Academy order of 1818."

44 Letter, General Douglas MacArthur, 10 January 1935, USMA Archives.

45 *The Cadet Honor Code and System*, 1976, p. 3.

46 *USCC Pamphlet 632-1*, August 1992, p. 2.

47 R. Ernest Dupuy, *Where They Have Trod*, p. 357.

48 Stephen E. Ambrose, *Duty, Honor, Country*, p. 279.

49 Griess, p. 78.

50 Ibid. Some works flatly credit Colonel Thayer with establishment of the honor code and system. William Baumer (*West Point*, p. 7), for example, states that "the addition of a workable honor code . . . was accomplished by Brevet Major Sylvanus Thayer." Bennett Berman and Michael Monbeck (*West Point*, p. 48) maintain unequivocally that Thayer "started the honor system." My reading of the primary sources has not supported such claims, despite Colonel Thayer's undoubted superb example of principled leadership.

51 Letter, Cadet Frederick A. Smith to Secretary of War Lewis Cass, 9 December 1832, *Thayer Papers*, Vol. V.

52 Ibid.

53 Ibid. Cadet Smith went on to graduate first in his class, then later served as an assistant professor of engineering at the Military Academy and, on a later assignment, superintending engineer for the construction of Central Barracks.

54 Southworth, p. 1-63.

55 Statement, Lt. Gen. Andrew J. Goodpaster, Superintendent USMA, before the Subcommittee on Military Personnel of the Committee on Armed Services, House of Representatives, 5 October 1977.

56 James L. Morrison Jr., "Progress and Turmoil," p. 2.

57 Thomas Fleming, "A New Country Starts a School for Soldiers," in Robert Cowley and Thomas Guinzberg, ed., *West Point*, p. 44.

58 Letter, Henry Brewerton to Brig. Gen. Totten, Chief of Engineers, 1 May 1850, Superintendent's Letter Book, Vol. No. 2, USMA Archives.

59 Letter, R. S. Garnett, Commandant of Cadets, to Superintendent, 4 April 1854, USMA Archives.

60 Letter, Superintendent Col. Robert E. Lee to General [not otherwise specified, but in all probability the Chief of Engineers], 10 April 1854, Superintendent's Letter Book, Vol. No. 3, USMA Archives.

61 Special Order No. 57, USMA, West Point, New York, 19 April 1954, USMA Archives.

62 Ibid.

63 *2002 Register of Graduates*, pp. 4-42–4-43. Also *1908 Annual Reunion of the Association of Graduates*, p. 27.

64 Morrison, "Progress and Turmoil," p. 67.

65 Ibid., p. 134.

66 Ibid., p. 151.

2 | Vigilance

Civil War

As they were for the nation at large, the years leading up to and encompassing the Civil War were extremely traumatic for West Point. Cadets from southern states debated whether to leave the Military Academy and go home to join the Confederacy, weighing the agonizing questions of loyalties, friendships, and the dictates of duty as they interpreted it. Wrote Captain Edward Boynton (USMA 1846) in an early history of the Military Academy that reflected the Union outlook on these events, "The outbreak of the civil war was a signal for a number of the cadets who were appointed from the Southern States, influenced by family ties, tempting offers of position, and the examples in Congress, to tender their resignations and repair to their homes, in disregard of the sworn articles previously signed by them to serve faithfully the Government of the United States."[1]

Thus many southerners, but not all, returned to their home states and took up arms against the Union they had earlier sworn to support and defend. Their departures occasioned often tearful farewells to the classmates they left behind, both parties knowing all too well that their next meeting could take place on the field of battle. Many years later David Lipsky would write, with equal parts wit and accuracy, that "the Civil War was an armed West Point reunion, old friends catching up by firing at each other."[2]

Extreme turbulence characterized the administration at West Point during these years, with three different officers serving as Superintendent during the war's four years. This of course impacted heavily on all aspects of cadet training and education, to include the Honor Code and administration of the Honor System.[3]

In the very midst of this war Captain Boynton, serving a decade-long tour as Adjutant of the Military Academy, published his history of its development. Not surprisingly, he often emphasized the stringent demands of preparation for and leadership in battle. "It is admitted that the [West Point] system is rigid," he noted, "and it is all-important that is should be so; for the destiny of the cadet is not like that of a student in a private college. He is, and is to be, a soldier. Obedience is his first duty, it is the pivot on which his profession and the whole army can alone successfully move. Thoughtlessness, carelessness, and inattention are not tolerated; for the faithful performance of the most minute duties on the part of a soldier is indispensable to military efficiency."[4]

Boynton also celebrated West Point's democratic nature, observing that at West Point wealth and privilege had no influence, but that instead "native talent, with good conduct, is the true and real source of respectability."[5] He also understood the fundamental importance of ethical conduct to military leadership, quoting to good effect General J. G. Barnard, a pre-Civil War West Point Superintendent who went to war and wound up serving as Chief Engineer for Ulysses S. Grant. West Point's graduates, attested Barnard, "have maintained the highest reputation for integrity, zeal, efficiency, and high moral character—without which last attribute there can be no real integrity, zeal, or efficiency."[6]

Post-War Period

"The cadets of the antebellum Academy had been expected to adhere to the code of the commissioned officer," wrote Colonel Thomas Griess, "and this concept continued after the Civil War. Following the precedents set by Sylvanus Thayer, the statement of a cadet was accepted without question. If later events showed the cadet to have been untruthful, the institution moved against him in the form of a court-martial. Similarly, the antebellum Academy reacted against stealing among cadets with court-martial and dismissal. On the other hand, cheating was not considered to be a cadet violation of the officer's code, nor was it punishable by dismissal."[7]

> ### Grant As Exemplar
>
> Grant is as good a leader as we can find. He has honesty, simplicity of character, singleness of purpose, and no hope or claim to usurp civil power. His character, more than his genius, will reconcile armies and attach the people.
>
> General William Tecumseh Sherman
> Letter to his brother
> 5 April 1864

It was apparently in this period, also, that cadets first sought to establish and enforce standards of honorable behavior. Walter Dillard's dissertation research led him to conclude that "the reaction of the authorities at West Point and in Washington to the attempts of the cadets to establish an honor system to police and govern themselves reinforced the attitude of uncertainty that prevailed at West Point during the postwar years."[8] Colonel Griess, however, identified more continuity and purposeful change in the same period. "Concurrent with the incremental changes in the daily routine of cadets" in the post-war period, he wrote, "was the development of an early honor system, a forerunner of the system that was finally regularized and officially recognized after World War I."[9]

An instructive and well-documented incident took place in 1865, when Brigadier General George Cullum (USMA 1833) was Superintendent. Cullum described the matter in a letter (dated Christmas Day) to Brevet Major General Richard Delafield, Chief of Engineers and himself a former USMA Superintendent. While making his daily round of inspections on a recent afternoon, said Cullum, he had come across Cadet Orsemus Boyd "in citizens dress and on the road to the wharf." Cullum, thinking that Boyd was attempting to leave the post clandestinely, accosted him and inquired why he was off limits and out of uniform. "He said he had been forced to leave on an accusation of theft, of which he was not guilty." The Superintendent ordered Cadet Boyd to return to his quarters and get into uniform, but the young man "replied he dared not go back as the Cadets would tar and feather him (as had been the fate some years since of one similarly accused)."[10]

General Cullum thereupon ordered the Commandant of Cadets to "go to the Cadet Barracks, stop any disorder and investigate what had happened." Boyd he sent to his room. "I am happy to say that the energetic course taken by the Commandant, and the returning good sense of the Corps of Cadets, now conscious of their error, has prevented any further molestation of Cadet Boyd," Cullum told General Delafield.[11]

A Court of Inquiry was convened to establish the facts of the matter. Cullum felt some sympathy toward the upperclassmen who had taken matters into their own hands, though he condemned their actions. "The young gentlemen who have been the prominent actors in this highly unmilitary proceeding," he told General Delafield, "are most prominent for good character, intelligence, and elevated bearing as gentlemen and soldiers, and have acted upon a high sense of honor and from noble impulses, [so] that the fair reputation of the Corps of Cadets should not be sullied by the presence of one deemed guilty of so grossly disgracing his uniform, and so entirely unworthy of the association of gentlemen." On the other hand, Cullum viewed their actions as a "flagrant outrage" and "highly subversive of good order and military discipline." Thus he stated that, "while applauding their motives in ridding themselves of one deemed capable of the meanest crime, I cannot for a moment pass over this self redress of grievances."[12]

Boyd was apparently exonerated, graduating with the Class of 1867 (in which he stood third from the bottom among 63 graduates). Commissioned in the Cavalry, he served on frontier duty for more than a dozen years before dying in New Mexico at 46 years of age. His entry in the *Register of Graduates* is most unusual, noting that "Service as Cadet & officer marked him a heroic character."[13]

Boyd had been on firm ground in fearing he would be tarred and feathered, a fate that had threatened Cadet Charles Cockey only three years earlier. Colonel A. H. Bowman, then the Superintendent, had requested a Court of Inquiry to determine "the facts of the attempt, by certain Cadets, to tar & feather Cadet Cockey & for resisting & overpowering the Sentinel stationed at the public wharf, who attempted to prevent the contemplated outrage."[14]

Cockey had "been detected in stealing from his brother Cadets," wrote Colonel Bowman. "The proof was so overwhelming that he confessed his guilt and admitted that he had been engaged in it nearly the whole time since he entered the Academy." Bowman had the offender confined in prison, "as well for his protection from the just indignation of his classmates as to indicate the enormity of his offence." Cockey unwisely escaped from prison and made his way to the public wharf, where he was set upon by angry cadets intent on encasing him in feathers.[15] Clearly the tug-of-war between cadets, intent on administering their own justice as they saw fit in honor cases, and the authorities, desirous of adhering to prescribed disciplinary procedures, was to continue.

During this same period the Reverend J. W. French continued his very long tenure as Military Academy Chaplain and Professor of Ethics, in the process publishing successive versions of a text he titled *Practical Ethics*. In the closing year of the Civil War the then-current edition contained this observation, which was likely read with special interest by some of his former students: "In all these rules of prudence in temporal affairs, it should never be forgotten that success in life is not the great end of life. It is better to fail nobly than to succeed dishonorably."[16]

In January 1871 there occurred another well-documented case in which cadets banded together in taking action against other cadets thought to have violated the prevailing code of ethics. Three members of the plebe class were charged with giving false reports to sentinels by rendering an "all right" untruthfully. The "all right," in use for many years at West Point, was an affirmation at barracks inspections that those present in a room were authorized to be there and that any absent were authorized to be away.[17] In this case a cadet rendered a false "all right" to cover for his roommate, who was absent without authority. At about the same time another plebe, visiting another cadet's room without authority, had en route given a false "all right" to the sentinel.[18]

The following day the Commandant placed all three cadets in confinement and preferred court-martial charges against them. Determined to deal with the matter themselves, however, cadets of the First Class held a meeting at which they decided to force the three plebes to leave West Point. That was done the same night, and the following morning the three cadets who had been driven off were reported as "absent, breaking arrest, and deserting."[19]

Then things got messy. On learning the facts, the Commandant reinstated the three plebes, one of whom was soon thereafter dismissed for academic deficiency. The other two, confronted with the evidence against them, were told it would be best if they were to resign, which they did. But in the meantime elements in the Congress had learned of the matter and an investigating committee was appointed. Its report censured the authorities of the Academy for not investigating more thoroughly, for the mild nature of the punishment handed out to the senior class members for their actions, and for accepting the resignations of the two cadets who were underage without the consent of their parents as required by regulations.[20] Stephen Ambrose later concluded that both the Superintendent and the Commandant "believed the First Class had acted badly but from commendable motives."[21]

Colonel Emory Upton, the Commandant, "felt that the [Congressional] committee had been inspired in part by a desire to attack President Grant, whose son Fred had been involved."[22] He and the Superintendent, Colonel Thomas G. Pitcher, demanded a court of inquiry to clear their records. Nothing came of that, however, leaving two conclusions to be drawn. First, "this incident illustrated the determination of the cadets to enforce an honor code among themselves, and to take drastic action against those who did not meet their criteria of being honorable men." Alongside that was the demonstrated "unwillingness of the authorities to permit the cadets to handle violations of the code of ethics in their own fashion. This attitude," concluded Colonel Griess, "precluded the development of an honor system of the sort instituted after the turn of the century."[23]

That viewpoint is not universally accepted, however. In fact a Military Academy publication later distributed to the Corps of Cadets reflected an essentially opposite position, arguing that "sometime after 1871," some three decades before the turn of the century, "the Vigilance Committee, organized by the Corps, was entrusted with the handling of cadet honor violations." And "the Vigilance Committee was given official status as the authoritative voice of the Corps of Cadets in administering the Honor Code, and its rules and procedures were formalized. Although given official sanction and formal structure, the Honor Code and its means of implementation were deliberately left in the hands of the cadets."[24] An Army lawyer concluded in a later study that during the late 1800s, "although the Vigilance Committee had no official recognition by the Academy, its existence was tolerated and its decisions unofficially sanctioned."[25] This seems the more likely state of affairs at the time.

In any event the whole matter had precipitated a crisis of contending authorities and prerogatives in the realm of honor enforcement that dragged on for a number of months. According to the later recollections of a cadet of that day, in response to the actions taken against the offending plebes, the entire First Class was "confined to the limits of the [P]lain from the 10th of January until the 5th of June, during which time the whole matter was under the consideration of the Congress and the President."[26]

Sidney Forman, reflecting on the 1871 episode, noted that in taking the action it did "the First Class was influenced by the fact that during the previous years, a number of cadets who had been dismissed by courts martial, or who had been recommended for discharge by the Academic Board, were reinstated through the influence of members of Congress or by the intervention of the President or the Secretary of War." This, he suggests, led directly to establishment of a Vigilance Committee, a representative mechanism organized some years later and including class representatives from each cadet company.[27]

The cadet mechanism for dealing with suspected honor violators was, during these years, functioning in the broader context of cadet excess in general when they were handed the reins of authority. Wrote a reporter for the *New York Times* who had spent a day observing the reception and initial treatment of incoming plebes, "The Cadets are boys as yet, and like all boys they are overzealous in their task. When plebes or new-comers are placed in their hands for training they will fatigue themselves and nearly kill the former."[28] This accurate observation helps explain how the enforcement of a code of honor may at times have exceeded the bounds of justice and common sense when left solely in the hands of cadets and the Vigilance Committee.

Spanish-American War

Vigilance Committees were still functioning at the turn of the century, as shown by a 6 March 1899 memorandum to the Commandant of Cadets providing views of the Superintendent on a recent honor case. This had to do with the dismissal of two cadets from the Military Academy, said the memorandum (which the Commandant was directed to publish to the Battalion of Cadets). In this case it appeared that "in 1897, a so-called Cadet Court Martial investigated the alleged dishonorable conduct of one of the dismissed cadets, with the design of forcing his resignation, if guilty."[29] The memorandum serves, first of all, to document Vigilance Committee activity in these closing years of the nineteenth century.

Historical analyses often assert that the Vigilance Committees, while functioning without official status, did so with the tacit approval of the authorities. In this instance that was not the case. The memorandum, conveying the Superintendent's views, noted "the gravity of the above facts" as viewed by the authorities and drew cadets' attention to a pertinent provision of regulations. Thus, "while the Superintendent [Colonel Albert Mills at that time] believes that the motives animating the Cadets concerned therein arose from the praiseworthy desire to free the Academy of unworthy members, he cannot too strongly condemn such proceedings, for they not only are subversive of discipline, but they ignore the duties of constituted authority and if allowed would tend to destroy subordination and respect for law, the foundation of military efficiency." The memorandum then concluded with this caveat: "To preserve inviolate the high standards of truth and honesty always demanded at this Academy is the first duty of all Cadets, but departures therefrom are for the action of authority and must never be made the basis of unlawful judgment."[30]

Meanwhile a significant and longstanding influence in matters of honor and ethical behavior was terminated in 1896. Until that date a lecture course in moral ethics had been taught by the Academy Chaplain, emphasizing "the important role of truthfulness in the life of an officer, instilling in the cadet a deep-rooted desire to achieve and maintain standards of honor unequalled outside the Academy."[31] This development may have related to expansion over the preceding two decades of the course content in humanities. As advocated by the Rev. Dr. William Postlethwaite, history had been added to the curriculum in 1883 when he was appointed chaplain and, concurrently, professor of history, geography, and ethics. When Postlethwaite died in 1896, the teaching of history was transferred to a new Department of Law and History and "the chaplain's old department was dissolved."[32] The course in moral ethics seems to have been a casualty of these new organizational arrangements.

In dramatic fashion, early graduations were once again precipitated by war, this time with Spain. "On the afternoon of April 25 (the day war was declared in 1898)," wrote historian Edward Coffman, "at West Point, the fifty-nine first classmen were attending a law lecture when an orderly brought a message to the professor, who told the cadets that they were going to graduate at noon the next day."[33]

Superintendent Albert Mills (USMA 1879) had taken office in late August 1898, following gallant service in the late war. Perhaps influenced by that experience to instill strict discipline in the cadets, he soon ordered that cadet company commanders "certify on their honor in writing at the end of their daily detail in that position that they had reported all infractions of the regulations that had come to their notice." The cadets refused to make the required certifications, leading Lieutenant Mills to place sixteen recalcitrants in arrest and prefer court-martial charges against them. In the course of an investigation it developed that the cadets' refusal was due to their desire to shield fellow cadets involved in hazing plebes. Eventually the cadets recanted, whereupon the Superintendent in turn suspended the court-martial proceedings.[34]

Major Hugh Scott followed Mills as Superintendent at the end of August 1906. The Superintendency of Major Scott was an important period in the evolution of the Honor Code at West Point. Initially, as we have seen, that code dealt exclusively with the sanctity of a cadet's word and signature (his written word, as it were), reflecting the classic imperative that an officer's word was his bond. In the early days of the Military Academy other serious offenses, while not condoned, were also not considered to be covered by the Honor Code. One such offense was cheating.

Today, of course, we recognize that cheating is preeminently an attempt to take unfair advantage and therefore intolerable to honorable people. At West Point in particular, where so many important things depend on the competition for class standing—selection for cadet rank, academic recognition, and choice of branch and station upon graduation, among others—cheating harms not only the perpetrator but every classmate as well. An official document of fairly recent vintage, quoted earlier, attributes to Colonel Thayer an expansion of the honor code to include cheating. But, it goes on to add, "apparently it did not remain a fixture within the Code because the historical records suggest that the institutional response to cheating varied over the succeeding 100 years."[35]

Until the autumn of 1905, it appears, those found to be cheating were dealt with primarily within the military discipline system. Then there is an historical marker of a sort in the form of a response from the USMA Adjutant to a civilian college questionnaire. A cadet who was found to have cheated, he stated, would be severely punished, but not necessarily dismissed. "It is not a point of honor with cadets," he stated, to refrain from obtaining information in an unauthorized way. "By this, I mean that if a cadet is ever caught cheating his punishment while very severe does not necessarily include dismissal from the Military Academy. . . . The honor system which we have evolved is essentially this and only this: that the word of a cadet is never questioned."[36]

Soon, however, Superintendent Scott caused to be issued a document directing a radical change, significant enough in fact to be quoted at length. Signed by Captain J. S. Herron, the Adjutant, it directed the Commandant to provide a copy to each member of the Corps of Cadets "so that he may give it careful consideration." This was the guidance:

> The standards of truthfulness, honor, integrity and personal responsibility are believed to be as high among the student body at the Military Academy as at any other institution in the world. It is, therefore, the policy of the Military Academy to entrust to cadets in great measure the maintenance of honor and truthfulness, not only in matters of military discipline and official reports, but also throughout the entire daily routine of duties performed by them. With the object of furthering this policy the Superintendent directs that hereafter in the section-room, either at oral recitation or at written

recitation, all cadets shall be considered on honor to receive no information concerning their recitations or their lessons from any unauthorized source whatever. The preparation of a subject or recitation on the blackboard, or the submission of a written recitation or exercise whether signed or not, will be accepted without question as the individual work of the cadet preparing or submitting it, unaided by any improper or unauthorized assistance. As this matter is placed in the hands of cadets, it becomes their duty to safeguard in this respect also the honor and traditions of the Academy. A cadet unwilling to accept this trust, both in letter and spirit, had best sever his connections with the Military Academy.

The document concluded with the stipulation that, though cadets are honorbound not to cheat on recitations, they would continue to be monitored:

It is not the intention that the supervision of recitations by instructors should by this order be done away with. Instructors will supervise oral recitations, and written recitations as far as practicable, and perform their necessary duties at all recitations, as heretofore; and should any cadet be observed obtaining or endeavoring to obtain unauthorized information, an immediate report of the facts will be made to the Commandant of Cadets in writing.[37]

This was a highly significant departure, not only because it extended the coverage of the Honor Code to include cheating, but also because the initiative came from the administration. Up until this time, cadets had been the ones to develop through general practice what was later codified and accepted by Academy officials. In this very important instance, however, it worked the other way around.

Vigilance Committees continued to function during this period, although apparently in somewhat less draconian ways than earlier. The Posvar Commission reported, in fact, that during the early 20th century "some violators could be given a chance at rehabilitation."[38]

Centennial

As we have seen, except in the instance just discussed, written articulations of the Honor Code and other formal declarations of West Point values have followed, rather than determined, practice. This was demonstrated with particular clarity when, in anticipation of the Military Academy's 1902 centennial, a board drafted the now-famous motto, "Duty, Honor, Country." Sometime before 1898 such a board was appointed at West Point and tasked to design a coat of arms that could be used on diplomas and other documents, on the colors of the Corps of Cadets, on items of uniform, and on various structures. Part of this endeavor was creation of an appropriate motto for incorporation in the coat of arms.[39]

Colonels Edgar Bass (USMA 1868), Charles Larned (USMA 1870), and Samuel Tillman (USMA 1869), very senior professors at the Military Academy, constituted what became known as the Larned Board after its chairman, who was also Professor of Drawing. By the time of their deliberations, these officers had in the aggregate served a total of more than half a century at the Military Academy and were clearly steeped in its traditions, values, and lore. As one commentator noted, "When one reads the writings of early superintendents, professors, and graduates, he is struck by the constant recurrence of the three ideals set forth in the official motto." Of these, one is clearly preeminent, for "neither Duty nor Patriotism would be effective without the support and motivation of Honor." These values, acquired and practiced over a century and now institutionalized for the first time, were unveiled when the new coat of arms, bearing the also newly-developed motto, was first publicly displayed on the Battalion Colors of the Corps of Cadets at the time of the centennial. In its final report, the Larned Board stated its conviction that the words of the West Point motto expressed "the genius of this institution."[40] A subsequent official publication characterized the motto as "but a later generation's attempt to put Thayer's ideal into words."[41]

The 1902 Centennial was a time of celebration, reaffirmation, and rededication at West Point and for West Pointers everywhere. In June President Theodore Roosevelt attended ceremonies at the Military Academy, telling those assembled there of his unquestionable conviction that, "taken as a whole, the average graduate of West Point during this hundred years has given a greater sum of service to the country through his life than has the average graduate of any other institution in this broad land." This was particularly gratifying because, rather than singling out the most famous or prominent graduates, the President's remarks underscored the achievements and contributions of the rank and file.[42] The President closed his remarks by emphasizing West Point's essential values. "I do not have to ask you to remember what you can not forget," he said, "the lessons of loyalty, of courage, of steadfast adherence to the highest standards of honor and uprightness which all men draw in when they breathe the atmosphere of this great institution."[43]

Another distinguished speaker was Elihu Root, the brilliant Secretary of War whose reforms following the Spanish-American War had put the Army on a basis of professionalism previously unattained. "Happy augury of the future," he remarked, "that here where for a hundred years honor has ever ruled—honor made up of courage, truth, compassion, loyalty—is to be found the formative and controlling power of the American army of the future."[44]

The Centennial was also an important event in furthering reconciliation between graduates who had fought against one another during the Civil War, and the Association of Graduates played a major role in helping to reestablish ties of comradeship. Accordingly, a veteran of the Civil War was chosen as a principal speaker during festivities at West Point. The choice was a felicitous one, for Major General Thomas Ruger (USMA 1854) had left the Army only a year after graduation to become a lawyer, then had voluntarily returned to active duty when war came. He soon reached the rank of brigadier of U.S. Volunteers and, remaining in service after the war, eventually became Superintendent of the

Military Academy (1871–1876). He retired as a major general in 1897, forty-three years after graduating from West Point.[45]

General Ruger told the Centennial celebrants of the many graduates in civil life who voluntarily returned to active service when the Civil War broke out, naming among them Generals Grant, Sherman, McClellan, Rosecrans, Hooker, Burnside, "and many others of honorable fame and some also illustrious." He closed his remarks by saying how gratifying he found it to meet fellow graduates "at this place, where, as in the days of our youth, honesty and duty are still watchwords; where a man is estimated according to his qualities, and where favor can not be purchased. So may it always be."[46]

The emphasis on high standards of honorable conduct and on devotion to duty by virtually every speaker at the centennial fete served to underscore the fundamental importance those attributes had played in the professional example of West Point graduates over the first century of the Military Academy's existence and, gratifyingly, illustrated how thoroughly they were associated with the institution's reputation.

Not long after the centennial an important publication made its first appearance at West Point. Initially issued in 1907 under the title *The West Point Hand-Book*, and in its early versions prepared and issued by the West Point chapter of the Young Men's Christian Association, this small volume soon came to be known as *Bugle Notes*. Every plebe knows it well, indeed knows much of it by heart. From the beginning it emphasized the importance of honor at West Point. In a foreword to the very first edition, Charles Larned wrote that "West Point stands for Duty, Honor, Country. The principles of sentiment and of conduct embodied in these three words penetrate the whole life of the institution and have been exemplified in the lives and deaths of her sons for over a hundred years." Thus "it is . . . essentially a question of character that makes the West Pointer distinctive."[47]

Truthfulness

Truthfulness is part of the honor of a soldier. Stratagems to deceive an enemy are lawful and right. But apart from this, a true soldier knows not how to violate the truth. So delicate is the military profession in this respect, that offences against the truth which public sentiment might mark as trivial in other relations, are there regarded as a lasting stain on honor. Also the whole system of military discipline is deranged, and there cannot be perfect reliance on personal and official statements. Let no one enter on military life as his profession, who is not unfaltering in veracity.

The Reverend John William French
USMA Chaplain and Professor of Ethics
Practical Ethics, 1868

In another essay some pages later, titled "Corps Honor," Larned explained that "there are, of course, different degrees of culpability, and there are certain infractions regarding which the Corps is wholly intolerant, the commission of which declasses the offender at once, and for which no excuse or palliation is accepted. Theft, cowardice, and deliberate falsehood have been offences of this nature. The traditions of West Point have held that the Corps is no place for him who is capable of these things, and that the high standards of integrity for which the institution is famous cannot be maintained if toleration for such is shown. A thief, a liar, and a coward cannot be extenuated in the eyes of the Corps, and it is no part of the function of West Point to become a reformatory of morals."[48]

There has long been, or so it seems, a strong element of self-selection among those who enter the Military Academy. They have a view of themselves, of who they are, of what their values are. They likewise have a conception of West Point and its values, of what it stands for and the kind of people who go there. Finding these two compatible, perhaps congruent, they seek to join the company of people like themselves, or as they aspire to be—honorable, decent, committed to excellence and integrity, to loyalty and fidelity, and to lives of devoted service.

This phenomenon is illustrated in part by the consistently large percentage of entering classes who are Eagle Scouts. Over recent years this has averaged more than 12 percent of male cadets. Perhaps some of those young aspirants have noted, at least subliminally, the nearly exact correspondence between the West Point motto of Duty, Honor, Country and the Scout Oath. "On my honor I will do my best," begins that classic statement, "to do my duty to God and my country . . . ," specifying in the very first words the same values of duty, honor, and country set forth by West Point. In an early version of the Cadet Prayer, additional congruent language was used: "Help us in our work and in our play to keep ourselves physically strong, mentally awake, and morally straight."[49]

The Scouting movement was begun by Lord Baden-Powell, a distinguished British army officer, in 1908, just a decade after West Point's motto had been conceived and adopted. It seems quite possible that there was a connection between the two, the West Point motto and the Scout oath. In developing his concept for the Boy Scouts, we are told by the famous *Handbook for Boys*, Powell "studied many organizations, like those of Dan Beard and Ernest Thompson Seton in the United States."[50] In his later formulation of the Cadet Prayer, it appears that Chaplain Wheat may similarly have been influenced by the Scout Oath crafted by Baden-Powell.

Through this period in West Point's development, the first century of its existence and a bit more, there is apparent a strong commitment to high standards of honorable behavior on the part of cadets, who devised their own mechanisms for imparting those standards to successive classes and for enforcing their observance. A life lived according to such standards was appealing to many who thus sought admission to the Military Academy. But there lay ahead difficult days in all these respects, and they would not be long in coming.

Notes

1 Edward C. Boynton, *History of West Point*, p. 251.
2 David Lipsky, *Absolutely American*, p. 7.
3 In a dissertation on "The Uncertain Years," Walter Scott Dillard indicates that there were five different superintendents during the Civil War. He apparently included two

who served in the early part of 1861, before war was declared, in arriving at that number. The 2000 *Register of Graduates and Former Cadets* explains this interesting sequence of events: "Bvt. Maj. P. G. T. Beauregard, Corps of Engineers, by order of John B. Floyd, Secretary of War, relieved Col. [Richard] Delafield on 23 January 1861 from the superintendency of the Military Academy, but was himself displaced 5 days later, on 28 January 1861, by direction of the succeeding Secretary of War Joseph Holt, the command again devolving upon Col. Delafield." And, adds the *ROG* account, "recently discovered official documents indicate that Beauregard may never have actually relieved Delafield." This is of course the same P. G. T. Beauregard who, only months later, by then a Confederate general, on 12 April 1861 ordered Confederate forces to open fire on the Union garrison at Fort Sumter, South Carolina, thereby opening hostilities of the Civil War.

4 Capt. Edward C. Boynton, *History of West Point*, pp. 276-277.

5 Ibid., p. 277.

6 Ibid., p. 281. For Barnard's service, see *2000 Register of Graduates*, p. 4-17.

7 Thomas E. Griess Dissertation, "Dennis Hart Mahan," p. 79.

8 Walter Scott Dillard, "The United States Military Academy, 1865–1900, the Uncertain Years," p. xii.

9 Griess, p. 63.

10 Letter, Geo. W. Cullum, Brig. Genl., Superintendent USMA, to Br. Maj. Gen. R. Delafield, Chief of Engineers, Washington, D.C., 25 December 1865, Superintendent's Letter Book, Vol. No. 4, USMA Archives. Emphasis in the original.

11 Ibid.

12 Ibid.

13 *2000 Register of Graduates*, p. 4-45.

14 Letter, Col. A. H. Bowman to Gen. J. G. Totten, Chief Engineer, 29 October 1862 (second letter of this date), Superintendent's Letter Book, Vol. No. 4, USMA Archives.

15 Letter, Col. A. H. Bowman to Gen. J. G. Totten, Chief Engineer, 29 October 1862 (first letter of this date), Superintendent's Letter Book, Vol. No. 4, USMA Archives.

16 Rev. J. W. French, *Practical Ethics*, p. 84.

17 Griess, p. 84. Col. Griess states that the "all right" had been in use at West Point since at least 1835. The 1871 case is addressed by most studies of West Point during the period, in part because the records of the incident are intact and fairly detailed. Early records are, as might be expected, incomplete, especially for the years before 1838, when a major fire destroyed many documents.

18 Griess, p. 85. One of the most detailed descriptions of the use and implications of the "All Right" appears in the 1877 Blue Book's discussion of sentinels in barracks: "The sentinels will open the door of each room in their Divisions, will ask '*All right?*' and will be able to identify the Cadet who replies. The reply 'All Right' will signify that all the occupants of the room are present, or if one be absent, that he is absent by proper authority, or for a necessary purpose; also that there is no person in the room who does not belong there, unless by proper authority. The sentinels will demand a prompt reply, and in no case will they inspect a room out of its natural order or more than once. The answer, '*All right,*' from sentinels, will signify that they have inspected in the prescribed manner, and that no Cadets were visiting, unless by authority, during their inspection, and at no time while on post with their knowledge and assent, and that no Cadets have been in the hall of Barracks unnecessarily, or have left the Division except by proper authority, reporting their departure, purpose and return." The term "for a necessary purpose" appears to be a euphemism for a visit to the latrine, which in those days was situated in a separate facility apart from the barracks.

19 Ibid.

20 Ibid., p. 86.

21 Stephen E. Ambrose, *Duty, Honor, Country*, p. 279.

22 Ibid. Frederick Dent Grant (USMA 1871) was commissioned in Cavalry, served on frontier duty, and was aide-de-camp to General Sheridan for eight years before resigning his commission ten years after graduation. He was New York City's police commissioner, returned to military service as a colonel with the New York National Guard in 1898, and subsequently became a brigadier of United States Volunteers, then of the United States Army, retiring in 1906 as a major general. *2000 Register of Graduates*, p. 4-49.

23 Griess, p. 87.

24 *The Cadet Honor Code and System*, 1976, p. 3.

25 Maj. John H. Beasley, "The USMA Honor System," p. 5. A century or so later a West Point committee including both officers and cadets expressed a retrospective view that the Vigilance Committee's work was "doubtless more swift than sure."

26 William Bixby, *Record of the Class of 1873*, p. 16.

27 Sidney Forman, "Scandal Among Cadets," pp. 488-489.

28 Issue of 12 June 1882.

29 Memorandum, 2d Lt. Samuel C. Hazzard, Adjutant, to Commandant of Cadets, 6 March 1899, USMA Archives. The memorandum begins with the words "The Superintendent directs" and is bound with the 1899 version of *Regulations, USCC*.

30 Ibid.

31 Lesson Outline for Instruction of New Cadets in the History of the Cadet Honor Code and System, [1961], File: Honor Code—Historical (1961–JUN 1963), USMA Archives.

32 Theodore J. Crackel, *West Point*, p. 163.

33 Edward M. Coffman, *The Regulars*, p. 6.

34 Walter Scott Dillard, "The Uncertain Years," pp. 309-311. Lieutenant Mills had, upon assuming the Superintendency, only just returned from Cuba and the Spanish-American War, where his gallantry had earned him the Medal of Honor. Near Santiago, on 1 July 1898, he was cited for "distinguished gallantry in encouraging those near him by his bravery and coolness after being shot through the head and entirely without sight." *2000 Register of Graduates*, p. 5-30.

35 *USCC Pamphlet 632-1*, August 1992, p. 2.

36 As quoted in *Report of the Superintendent's Special Study Group on Honor at West Point*, p. A-3.

37 Memorandum, Capt. J. S. Herron, Adjutant, to Commandant of Cadets, 4 September 1907, USMA Archives.

38 *Final Report of the Special Commission of the Chief of Staff on the Honor Code and Honor System at the United States Military Academy*, 30 May 1989, p. 13.

39 "Origin of the Motto: Duty, Honor, Country," *Assembly* (December 1978), p. 32.

40 Ibid. The Larned Board Report, dated 14 January 1898, is quoted on p. 33.

41 *Official Register of the Officers and Cadets, United States Military Academy, For the Academic Year Ending 5 June 1956*, p. 4.

42 *The Centennial of the United States Military Academy*, I:20.

43 Ibid., I:26.

44 Ibid., I:53.

45 *2000 Register of Graduates*, p. 4-34.

46 *The Centennial of the United States Military Academy*, I:71-72, 76.

47 *The West Point Hand-Book*, Vol. I, p. 4. Colonel Larned (USMA 1870) served at West Point as Assistant Professor and then Professor of Drawing from 1874 until his death in 1911.

48 Ibid., pp. 28-29.

49 See, for example, the *1941 Bugle Notes*.

50 *Handbook for Boys*, 5th edition (New York: Boy Scouts of America, 1948), p. 8. Daniel Carter Beard had, in 1905, founded an organization for boys stressing outdoor activities which he called the Sons of Daniel Boone. He merged this outfit with the Boy Scouts of America when they were established in 1910. Ernest Thompson Seton, author and wildlife artist, had established a somewhat similar organization known as Woodcraft Indians. Both men were among the founders of the Boy Scouts of America, and Seton became the first Chief Scout. *Wikopedia*.

3 | Evolution

World War I

World War I almost ruined the Military Academy. Perhaps more accurately, World War I policies of the War Department almost ruined the Military Academy. "Nineteen-eighteen was not a good year at West Point; for cadets as well as faculty, academically and in other ways it was the worst," read a later assessment in *Assembly*. Early graduation had already reduced the Corps to three classes. Then, in October, the Secretary of War ordered the graduation of the two remaining upper classes on 1 November. That left only the plebes, who had entered just four months earlier, to constitute the Corps. When, two months later, a second plebe class was admitted, it had to be designated Fourth Class B to differentiate it from the existing plebe class (now to be known as Fourth Class A) that they were "following close order behind." To further confuse the matter, only a month or so after being graduated the former yearling class, now designated "officer cadets," was returned to West Point to complete another academic year.[1]

Earl Blaik, a member of what became the Class of 1920 and later to become West Point's longtime football coach, remembered that "for the cadets the winter and spring of 1918–1919, brought gloomy days mixed with hazing, a cadet suicide, personal grudge fights, and a War Department investigation. Certainly an air of melancholy prevailed."[2]

A later Superintendent summed up the period succinctly: "World War I almost destroyed the Military Academy," said Lieutenant General Sidney B. Berry. "Emphasis on quickly producing large numbers of officers for the War led to early graduation of five classes, disrupted the staff and faculty, and virtually turned West Point into simply another training camp for officers. The War ended with Fourth Classmen as the only members of the Corps of Cadets."[3] The latter such class (of two sets of plebes) had, reported Colonel Dupuy, been "admitted without entrance examinations."[4]

Colonel Ernest Dupuy wrote of this period that "never in its previous history had West Point seen such conditions as existed during that winter of 1918–1919." The "most dangerous symptom of all so far as the future of West Point was concerned," he added, "was the canker in the honor system. [Colonel Herman] Beukema points out, 'Shortly it became . . . evident that something very precious was vanishing, or perhaps had already disappeared.' "[5]

Tactical officers had, concluded Colonel Dupuy, played a key role in reestablishing knowledge of and commitment to the Honor Code and System. Lacking the background of the normal undergraduate years, he wrote, "the then First Class was in no position to pass on the honor system." But there was a remedy. "It was the elixir of Sylvanus Thayer, the procedure he had adopted in evolving the system. So, ninety-nine years after Sylvanus had placed 'Old Zeb' Kinsley and Henry Griswold, his first tactical officers, into barracks as mentors and guides to his Corps, back into barracks on [Superintendent Colonel Samuel] Tillman's orders went the desks of the tactical officers of 1919."[6]

Given what happened in the immediate post-war years, it seems very possible that the wartime chaos, traumatic as it was for the Military Academy in every respect, had one very positive effect in making possible abolishment of the Vigilance Committee and establishment of a more formal and sanctioned Honor Committee. "Without the disruption caused by war," noted Colonel Lance Betros, "there probably would have been no impetus for change. With the removal of the upper three classes, however, there was no continuity for the Vigilance Committee, and therefore it was possible to move to a different system of honor enforcement."[7]

At least some of the credit for reclaiming the situation goes to the cadets of what became the Class of 1920. At a meeting on 3 August 1919, that class "reexamined the entire body of cadet traditions[,] eliminating deleterious practices which had crept in mostly during the war years. Their recommendations were accepted by the Commandant and the Superintendent and the Long Grey Line had overcome one of its greatest crises since the days of Alden Partridge."[8]

Meanwhile, in the estimation of Secretary of War Newton Baker, those graduates who had gone off to war measured up. "West Point does many things for its men," said Baker, "but the highest quality it gives them is character, and in the emergency of the World War, our success rested on the character of our leaders. It therefore finally rested on West Point."[9]

Vigilance Committees continued to operate at least as late as 1917, and probably until they were converted into institutionally sanctioned and formally recognized Honor Committees beginning in 1922. Colonel Crampton Jones (USMA 1916) later stated that he was one of six members of the Vigilance Committee in his class. Jones also described the committee's method of operating: "Our VC (Vigilance Committee) would receive reports on a cadet; we would have other cadets watch; we would finally confront the guilty cadet and let him resign or else be silenced—he always resigned."[10]

Carleton Coulter III (USMA 1956) remembers that his father, Carleton Coulter Jr. (USMA APR 1917), spoke of being a member of the Vigilance Committee. "Their justice was quite stringent," said the younger Coulter, recalling his father's accounts. In those times cadet rooms were furnished with Windsor chairs, which had spindle backs. On one occasion his father and the father's roommate broke a chair to get out the spindles, used them to beat a fellow cadet they thought had lied, then trussed him up and tossed him in a boxcar. "It was rough justice," said the son.[11]

The Chairman of the Class of April 1917's Vigilance Committee, later to become one of the Army's most famous and most admired combat leaders, was Matthew Ridgway. That role was documented in his entry in the *Howitzer*, which read: "Matt was Chairman of the VC—he kept the rest of us in line."[12] Clearly, then, by this date the existence and role of the Vigilance Committee was openly acknowledged and accepted.

Gratifyingly, despite all the turbulence, the *1918 Bugle Notes* continued to showcase honor as the most important element of instruction for plebes. Its first words: "West Point stands for Duty, Honor, Country." Its starkest pronouncement: "There is no compromise with honesty and virtue—you either are, or you are not."[13] These were the bedrock values the Vigilance Committees were seeking to protect and defend, as would before long their more formally constituted and fully sanctioned successors.

Perhaps reflecting on the war so recently concluded, Secretary of War Newton Baker made a famous observation on the demands of the professional military code in a May 1920 letter to the Chairman of the House Committee on Military Affairs. "The purpose of West Point . . . is the inculcation of a set of virtues, admirable always, but indispensable in a soldier. Men may be inexact or even untruthful," he wrote, "in ordinary matters, and suffer as a consequence only the disesteem of their associates, or the inconveniences of unfavorable litigation, but the inexact and untruthful soldier trifles with the lives of his fellow men, and the honor of his government; and it is, therefore, no matter of idle pride but rather of stern disciplinary necessity that makes West Point require of her students a character of trustworthiness which knows no evasions. In the final analysis of the West Point product, character is the most precious component."[14]

The MacArthur Years

Soon entering upon the confused post-war scene at West Point, in the summer of 1919, was Douglas MacArthur, at age 39 the youngest Superintendent of the Military Academy in nearly half a century. He replaced Colonel Samuel Tillman, then 71, whose Class of 1869 had entered the Military Academy just two months after the end of the Civil War.[15] MacArthur's influence on many aspects of life and practice at West Point would be profound, perhaps most importantly in establishing a more formal Honor System.

There were at that time only two classes in residence at West Point, and both were composed of plebes. As noted earlier, this represented a very serious problem in terms of perpetuating and transmitting such key values as those represented by the Honor Code and System. "The Military Academy had always depended on its upperclassmen to carry on the Code and the traditions, and to instill these in the new cadets," noted General Jacob Devers, a member of the Class of 1909 who served at West Point as a tactical officer during the period 1919–1924. Since "there was no written code of procedure," the transmission of these traditions and customs was entirely dependent on tutelage of entering cadets by upper classes. But there were no upper classes.[16]

MacArthur's initiative in restoring stability and continuity was recalled by a cadet of the day, citing "the important organization of an Honor Committee and the formal recognition of this group as the supreme court of cadet judgment on matters involving personal honor. "Heretofore," wrote Earl Blaik, "there had been precipitous action on a less formalized basis. This involved either a quick departure of the offender from the post, or the alternative to remain and live as a silenced cadet. The Honor Committee, organized and nurtured by MacArthur, has proved through the years the strength of his design."[17]

The Academic Board also played a key role in the rebuilding process, as later described by Lieutenant General Garrison Davidson. "The Academic Board has been USMA's senate," he observed. "In 1919 when all semblance of the traditional academy had been lost because of the war, superintendent Douglas MacArthur looked to the Academic Board for a statement of the Academy's mission as he sat in daily conference with the Board through the summer to plan the reconstitution of the Academy."[18]

Measures of Merit

Where you came from and what you are makes not the slightest difference. You are judged by your character, loyalty and endurance.

General Creighton W. Abrams
USMA Class of 1936

Developments in the realm of honor during his tenure as Superintendent were recounted by General MacArthur in his June 1921 annual report to The Adjutant General. In it he recalled stating bluntly in the previous year's report, his first as Superintendent, that, if the Military Academy were to accomplish its mission, it "must construct a new West Point in the spirit of the old West Point."[19] The tasks then articulated, he recalled, were those necessitated by living up to the Academy's motto of "Duty, Honor, Country." These tasks were "to implant as of old the gospel of cleanliness, not only of body but of mind and spirit, to introduce a new atmosphere of liberalization—in doing away with provincialism, in substituting subjective for objective discipline, in progressively increasing cadet responsibility that tends to develop initiative and force of character . . . , to broaden the curriculum . . . and to bring West Point into a newer and closer relationship with the Army at large."[20]

Such a thoroughgoing program of revitalization and reform was not, MacArthur noted, susceptible of accomplishment in a single year. Hence he reported on progress to date, and on further initiatives planned or underway, emphasizing the central place of honor in the life of the Military Academy. The objectives he sought, MacArthur stressed, were not confined to the life of a cadet at West Point, but were instead preparation for the awesome responsibilities of the professional officer corps. "In many businesses and professions," said MacArthur, "the welfare of the individual is the chief object; in the military profession the safety and honor of the state are involved. In the emergencies of war, success or failure with all their effect upon the future of a country, may depend upon an officer's word and upon his undeviating adherence to a principle or an ideal."[21]

In 1920 a pamphlet on *Traditions and Customs of the Corps of Cadets* published at West Point pointed out that "there is no place in the Corps of Cadets or in the Service for a quibbler, an evader, or a twister of the truth." That pamphlet apparently resulted from deliberations of a committee MacArthur had convened, using selected cadets from the senior class still at the Academy, to articulate—perhaps even to resurrect—key elements of two fundamentally important aspects of West Point's culture, the Fourth Class System (how plebes were trained and indoctrinated) and the Honor System.

Not long after, in 1922, the first formal Honor Committee was established with officially defined duties and responsibilities. "West Point now had, for the first time," wrote Sidney Forman, "an explicit honor code based upon reasoned consent."[22] While many authorities credit General MacArthur with creation of this first Honor Committee, it should be noted that it was not until sometime in the autumn of 1922 that the Committee was actually formed, whereas MacArthur's tenure as Superintendent had ended in June of that year, when he was succeeded by Brigadier General Fred Sladen (USMA 1890).[23]

That initial Honor Committee consisted of twelve men, one representing each cadet company, and a chairman. Cadet Lynn Brady (USMA 1923) was the first Honor Committee Chairman. "Initially," reported a later study, "the domain of the Honor Committee included 'all matters concerning the welfare of the Corps,' but the scope was quickly reduced solely to matters of honor." The Honor Committee's duties were to "keep alive the principles of the honor code" and "to report violators of the honor code to the Commandant."[24]

The Honor Committee is pictured in the 1923 edition of *The Howitzer*, the cadet yearbook, and in practically every year thereafter.[25] The Class of 1923 said in that *Howitzer*, reflecting on developments during the MacArthur years, that "during our sojourn at the Academy, the Honor Committee has evolved from what was formerly known as the Vigilance Committee. Practically the only changes have been in the name, and in the fact that the present body is a recognized, official one, acting with the sanction of and in conjunction with the Tactical Department."[26] Thus MacArthur had put in place one of the most significant changes in the long evolution of the Honor System, formal recognition of the fundamental responsibility of cadets themselves for administration of that System, and the administration's acceptance and endorsement of that role for cadets.[27]

MacArthur's important part in regularizing honor matters became the subject of much later commentary. Historian Stephen Ambrose reached an interesting conclusion about MacArthur's underlying philosophy, namely "that cadets could be high-minded, clean-living men in an age that ridiculed such phrases, but only if they saw some meaning to those virtues and only if they saw some connection between what they were doing at the Academy and what they would be doing as army officers."[28] Colonel Harry Buckley, participating in a later honor review, also commented perceptively on the MacArthur contribution. "The Honor Code," he observed, "was originally an articulation of norms that had developed within the Corps of Cadets, norms that developed because of the nature of their lives in barracks and in the classroom. . . . These norms became so generally accepted and were so well enforced by the Corps that General MacArthur quite properly institutionalized the honor concept."[29]

Some details of the origin and functioning of the nascent Honor Committee were provided in the *1922 Bugle Notes*. A committee for dealing with honor matters had existed for a long time, acknowledged this account, "sometimes with, and sometimes without the sanction of authority, for the purpose of investigating all such cases [suspected honor violations]. At present, the guardianship of the Corps' honor is placed by the Superintendent directly in the hands of the first class, more especially in the hands of the President of that class, who is also Chairman of the Honor Committee, which is composed of thirteen first classmen." In all honor cases, explained this account, charges would first be preferred by the chairman of the committee to the Superintendent, after which a hearing was held "in which one member of the committee binds himself to act on behalf of the accused, so that after the investigation is completed he may certify that every possible opportunity was given the accused to clear himself of the charges." Finally the committee's findings, along with a detailed account of the hearing, were submitted to "the Authorities" for approval.[30]

The *1924 Howitzer* also commented on the recently established Honor Committee. "The Corps is really a huge honor committee that has delegated certain inherent powers of tradition to a small group of men," it stated. "The fundamental reason for the creation of this body was the desire to remove such a serious question as honor to a more tranquil stratum, where the facts for and against could be carefully balanced, and a decision reached that would be uninfluenced by the popular hue and cry."[31]

Even many years after General MacArthur's tenure as Superintendent, Cadet Honor Committee Chairmen were still quoting him on the stark necessity for integrity in the military profession: "In the emergencies of war, success or failure, with all their effects upon the future of a country, may depend upon an officer's word and upon his undeviating adherence to a principle or an ideal."[32]

Codification

As noted earlier, Major Hugh Scott had, during his tenure as Superintendent, directed that cheating be construed as a violation of the honor code. This prescription "was formalized by the Academic Board in 1926,"[33] providing yet another example of how every element of the honor code existed in practice for a long while, sometimes a very long while, before being formalized.

Even earlier the Superintendent had been asked by the Commandant of Cadets to approve a statement of the functions of the Honor Committee. In a 16 July 1924 memorandum the Commandant set forth these duties: "To assure among cadets an appreciative understanding of the principles and standards of honor observed in the Corps" (an education task), "to guard against the birth of practices inconsistent with those principles" (a monitoring task), "when, in its opinion, regulations relating to these principles require interpretation, to consult with the Commandant of Cadets" (a liaison task), "to inquire into all irregularities, personal or official, on the part of members of the Corps that may be in violation of those principles" (an investigative task), and "when, in its opinion, such irregularities warrant remedial action, to report the facts to the Commandant of Cadets" (an advocacy task).[34] Thus, by July 1924 at the latest, the full range of functions performed by the Honor Committee as we now know it had been articulated and approved.

Two years later, at the behest of Superintendent Brigadier General Merch Stewart (USMA 1896), the Academic Board's General Committee was asked "to acquaint itself with the honor system now in vogue in its relation to the Academic work of the Military Academy." The Committee found that "this code shows a just attitude towards the fundamental question involved" and gave it their unqualified commendation. What that fundamental question involved, the Committee explained, was "the breach of trust in section room work or examination work committed by giving or obtaining unauthorized assistance in the performance of this task." The application of the honor system to academic work was not a new departure. This was made clear by the Committee's reference to its understanding of "the honor system as it has applied traditionally in the conduct of academic work at the Military Academy, and as it should continue to be applied in the future." This application was, the Committee stated, embodied in a fundamental rule: "No cadet shall impart or receive any unauthorized assistance, either outside or inside the section room or examination room, which would tend to give any cadet an unfair advantage."[35]

Less than two months later the Superintendent inserted himself directly into the process in a seriously unsettling way. General Stewart was a veteran of long service at the Military Academy, including three years as a Tactical Officer and then later three years as Commandant of Cadets, a post from which he had had the unusual experience of being elevated directly to that of Superintendent. Now he sought to lay down as a rule that "cadets suspected of dishonest methods in their academic work must be given one warning before being brought to trial."[36]

This matter seems to have been the subject of controversy and perhaps some negotiation for a very extended time, since we know that voluminous back-and-forth correspondence which had begun in 1926 was still flowing as late as 1935. By that time General Stewart had long since retired for disability, and in fact his third successor was in office. Lieutenant Colonel Simon B. Buckner Jr., Commandant of Cadets, summarized some of the byplay over the intervening years. "It appears," he wrote, "that the then Superintendent on October 5, 1926, gave instructions to the General Committee apparently to the effect that it would not be considered dishonorable for a cadet to receive unauthorized assistance in a section room by copying problems or other matter from the board of another cadet until he had committed two offenses of this nature and had been warned after committing the first one. In other words, every cadet might have the privilege of deliberately copying from other boards until he had been caught the second time."[37]

Apparently some version or variation of such a policy had continued in effect, for Colonel Buckner wrote at this juncture that "this is so inconsistent with the views of both cadets and graduates and is so far from accomplishing the purpose outlined by the Academic Board, namely, to upbuild and uphold the honor code of the Corps of Cadets, that I believe the matter merits further study and consideration."[38]

Obviously Colonel Buckner had done some research, for he then noted that "it is the opinion of some officers who were here at the time that the Superintendent's instructions in October 1926 were based upon special considerations applicable at that time. It is not believed that any such conditions exist at present and that the application of the general policy of warning cadets when they have definitely been caught cheating will have a lowering effect upon the very standards which the Academic Board has sought to maintain." Colonel Buckner thus recommended that "the provision for warning after the first offense . . . be discontinued."[39] These views seem to have prevailed, for no such policy of warning cheaters was in evidence in later years.

A Written Honor Code

While it seems hard to believe in today's era of voluminous documentation of virtually every utterance, no matter how evanescent or trivial, it appears that the West Point Honor Code itself was not set down in formal written form until 1932. In the autumn of that year, Honor Committee members of the Class of 1933 undertook the task. Even then, however, the result did not take the concise form familiar to us today, but was more of a hybrid code and system.

Cadet Lawrence Lincoln was the principal drafter, and his handwritten version still survives in the USMA Archives. Lincoln (later a lieutenant general) subsequently recalled his belief that "prior to the fall of 1932 the so-called Honor Code had never been codified. It had," he said, "been passed on by word of mouth, with some help from an informal record of decisions and interpretations by the Cadet Honor Committees, which had been kept in a large book in diary form."[40]

The precipitating factor for producing a written version of the Code is of some relevance. In the summer of 1932, according to Lincoln, the Class of 1933 Honor Committee had become concerned that "the Tactical Department was easing its own problems by overloading the Honor Code." Thus "the Honor Committee decided to publish the code to the Corps without benefit of prior consultation with Academy authorities. But first it had to be written." The Corps was at that time in summer camp, living in tents. "We didn't want the Tac Department to know of our plan[,] so it was very carefully and almost surreptitiously done," Lincoln recalled. He did the typing under a dim light in his tent after taps, producing a rather dramatic document on orangish yellow paper in a large font.[41]

When the document was ready, the cadets had it printed by the same outfit that did various cadet publications (such as the *Pointer* or the *Howitzer*), then distributed the printed copies throughout the Corps. "The Commandant found it on his desk the same morning that the cadets got it," remembered Lincoln. "The Honor Committee Chairman and the First Captain had a few bad moments with the Commandant that day," but ultimately he decided to let it stand.[42]

Lincoln was modest but accurate in attributing his work to the ages. "The Code was not my product or even the product of the entire Honor Committee," he acknowledged. "It was the product of a hundred years of the Corps developing the Honor System and passing it on, in part by the Honor Book; but mainly by word of mouth and practice. It was really the product of those who preceded us in the Long Grey Line."[43]

Acknowledging this contribution, a later Superintendent, Major General Donald Bennett, wrote to Lincoln in 1967: "Too often we believe that such wonderful arrangements as the Cadet Honor Code have existed forever, and too seldom do we realize that it took the actions of a few dedicated individuals such as you and the other members of the Class of 1933 to provide a formal edition of the Honor Code, an action probably that was most necessary at that time. We find today that it would be impossible to ask the cadets to administer the Code or to subscribe to it whole-heartedly if all aspects of the Code were not formalized in writing."[44] That concluding observation of course was, as much as anything, a commentary on the times.

Even so, what Lincoln and his fellow cadets had produced was still not the succinct one-sentence statement of the Honor Code that we know today, but rather something of an interim description of such a Code embedded in details of a System. Nevertheless their work constituted, without any question, very significant incremental progress in the history of the Honor Code and System.

> ### Character
>
> Men may be inexact or even untruthful, in ordinary matters, and suffer as a consequence only the disesteem of their associates, or even the inconveniences of unfavorable litigation, but the inexact or untruthful soldier trifles with the lives of his fellowmen, and the honor of his government; and it is, therefore, no matter of idle pride but rather of stern disciplinary necessity that makes West Point require of her students a character of trustworthiness which knows no evasions. In the final analysis of the West Point product, character is the most precious component.
>
> Secretary of War Newton D. Baker
> Letter to the Chairman of the House
> Committee on Military Affairs
> 17 May 1920

Further Documentation

In a flurry of documentation promulgated near the close of World War II several documents, all describing the Honor System, were published in less than a year. The version of 6 December 1944, for example, cited non-toleration as an integral part of the Honor Code:

> The Honor System of the U.S. Corps of Cadets is the outgrowth of many years of development and trial. It belongs to the Corps of Cadets and has

been built up and perfected by the cadets themselves because they believe in it. Under the Honor System the word of a cadet is accepted as the truth, and is doubted only when an actual discrepancy appears which puts his honor in question. The indoctrination of the cadets in and the maintenance of the Honor System are in the hands of the cadets themselves, a fact which is predominantly responsible for its practical efficacy. In the eyes of the Corps, the Honor System is mightier than any individual, friend, or stranger. In keeping with this impartial outlook any cadet will report any other cadet, or even himself, for a violation of honor.[45]

A similar document published on 5 November 1945, soon after Major General Maxwell Taylor became Superintendent, responded to tasking by Major General Francis Wilby, the preceding Superintendent, in which he had asked the Standing Committee on the Cadet Honor System to "prepare a brief paper on the origin of the Cadet Honor System and the developments and changes in this system from its inception to the present day." The paper resulting began by citing the Military Academy's motto—Duty, Honor, Country—and then quoting President Theodore Roosevelt's remarks, previously noted, at West Point's 1902 Centennial Exercises: "I do not have to ask you to remember what you cannot forget—the lessons of loyalty, of courage, of steadfast adherence to the highest standards of honor and uprightness which all men draw in when they breathe the atmosphere of this institution."[46]

The Academic Board's Standing Committee also reported, however, that "exhaustive research among the early files relating to West Point has failed to reveal any precise date upon which the Honor System may be said to have been instituted." Looking back, they noted "uncontroverted evidence that the highest standard of Honor existed from and after the regime of Colonel Sylvanus Thayer and it is probable that the elevation of the system to its subsequent high level was among the many reforms instituted by him," citing as evidence of this the responses collected by General George Washington Cullum when he sent questionnaires to all living graduates in 1872.[47]

Considering the initial cadet-produced document and these others published by the authorities to be for the internal edification and guidance of subordinate elements at the Military Academy, USMA Historian Dr. Stephen Grove concluded that "the first time the Academy [publicly] articulated the cadet honor code was in a publication by Superintendent Maxwell Taylor titled 'The West Point Honor System' dated 23 July 1947." Dr. Grove suggested that "the stimulus for the action came partly from a famous January 1946 letter the Superintendent had received from Army Chief of Staff Eisenhower."[48] In that letter General Eisenhower stated his view that it was "important that individuals now at the Academy, both officers and Cadets, both clearly and definitely understand . . . that under no circumstances should [the Honor System] ever be used at the expense of the Cadets in the detection of violations of regulations."[49]

Eisenhower had thought deeply about the Military Academy and the preparation its graduates received for their responsibilities as officers. Technique and technical work at West Point, he thought, were "of far less importance than the larger questions" of honor and character development. He closed with this eloquent observation: "In your efforts to graduate succeeding classes in which each individual will have, as an officer, a very definite feeling of responsibility toward the country, a very lively and continuing concern for his personal honor and for the honor system at West Point, and who finally will approach all his problems with a very clear understanding of the human factors involved in developing, training, and leading an Army, then indeed West Point will continue to occupy its present place in the national consciousness and will be worth any sum that we must necessarily expend for its maintenance."[50]

Evidently as a means of providing input to General Taylor as he prepared to write his pamphlet, Commandant of Cadets Brigadier General George Honnen set forth some basics of the Honor System as it was operating in early 1946. "Although the Honor System at the United States Military Academy has never been set down on paper," he stated, "the fundamental principle is known to all concerned." (Apparently General Honnen was unaware of the version written and printed by the Honor Committee in the summer and autumn of 1932, discussed previously, or even of a five-page letter describing the Honor System issued by the Superintendent's office two years earlier, during General Honnen's own tenure.[51]) "This fundamental is that the word of any cadet at any time is always assumed to be the truth and the whole truth. A Cadet's word, personal and official, is accepted as the absolute truth unless there is positive evidence to indicate otherwise. From this broad statement the code has branched out until it reaches into every aspect of a cadet's life here at the Military Academy and after he leaves the Military Academy. It is the heart of the system of building character."[52]

In his short pamphlet General Taylor quite properly observed that "the Honor System at West Point is the outgrowth of many years of development and experience." Honor at West Point, he added, drawing on the language of the Cadet Prayer, "is not a complicated system of ethics, but merely 'honest dealing and clean thinking.'" Not until he was well into the essay did General Taylor state the essence (and, surprisingly, he alludes to the Honor System rather than the Honor Code in doing so): "the System has never outgrown its simple meaning—that a cadet will neither lie, cheat nor steal."[53]

Elements of the Honor Code, or statements closely related to it, have over many years appeared very prominently in *Bugle Notes*, the handbook for plebes prepared each year by the First Class. In a number of volumes the opening words are these: "West Point stands for Duty, Honor, Country." Many editions also feature "Advice from the First Captain." In 1936, for example, William Westmoreland wrote to the new plebes: "You have inherited a duty to the Corps. The preservation of the sacred traditions and customs of West Point has become an obligation of your class. The foremost of these traditions is honor." In that same edition, in a discussion of the guiding principles of honor, this statement is made: "Everyone is honor bound to report any breach of honor which comes to his attention." Taken sequentially, the annual editions of *Bugle Notes* further illustrate the way in which elements of the Honor Code have become practice, then reduced to writing, and only last entered into the official record. This process is not only of historical interest, but also demonstrates how literally the Honor Code has emanated from the cadets themselves. Not only have successive generations of cadets made it their own, but it sprang originally from the character and commitment to honorable behavior of their predecessors. In this realm is demonstrated, perhaps more concretely than in any other, the reality of the Long Gray Line.

That commitment to standards of honorable behavior, it seems almost certain, can trace its lineage to ancient traditional codes of behavior incorporating the martial virtues, thence to the code of chivalry, and eventually to our Articles of War and successor documents such as the Uniform Code of Military Justice. In a pamphlet explaining West Point's Honor Code and System to officers assigned to the Military Academy, the UCMJ's Article 133 (Conduct Unbecoming an Officer)—which applies to "any officer, cadet, or midshipman"—was quoted at length to illustrate the legal basis for the punitive aspects of the Honor Code and System:

> Conduct violative of this article is action or behavior in an official capacity which, in dishonoring or disgracing the individual as an officer, seriously compromises his character as a gentleman, or action or behavior in an unofficial or private capacity which, in dishonoring or disgracing the individual personally, seriously compromises his standing as an officer.
>
> There are certain moral attributes common to the ideal officer and the perfect gentleman, a lack of which is indicated by acts of dishonesty or unfair dealing, of indecency or indecorum, or of lawlessness, injustice, or cruelty. Not everyone is or can be expected to meet ideal moral standards, but there is a limit of tolerance below which the individual standards of an officer, cadet, or midshipman cannot fall without seriously compromising his standing as an officer, cadet, or midshipman or his character as a gentleman. This article contemplates conduct by an officer, cadet, or midshipman which, taking all the circumstances into consideration, is thus compromising.[54]

Surprisingly, or so it seems to me, an *Honor Guide for Officers* published at West Point as late as 1958, while maintaining that "the term Honor Code is now generally used to designate the ethical precepts which the Corps of Cadets has agreed to uphold," goes on to state that "there is no formal document setting these forth in clear cut fashion but they are contained in the statement, 'A cadet will not lie, cheat, or steal.'"[55] Reading that drove me back to the 1952 *Bugle Notes*, published for the guidance of my Class of 1956, where I was sure I would find the classic statement of the Honor Code so well known to us from our plebe days forward. To my dismay, it was not there. The Commandant of Cadets tabulated elements of the Code in that handbook when he advised us, in a note of welcome, to "cherish the honor system. By that I mean," he explained, "die a thousand deaths before you lie, steal, or cheat."

Elsewhere in this edition of *Bugle Notes* an eight-page essay on honor made numerous references to "the code," pointed out in reference to some elements of the Code as we know it that "lying, quibbling, evasive statements, or technicalities in order to shield guilt or defeat the spirit of justice will not be tolerated," that "anything to which a man signs his name means irrevocably what is said, both as to letter and spirit," and that "every man is honor bound to report any breach of honor which comes to his attention." But nowhere did it simply state the Code in its most highly distilled formulation, nor were stealing or cheating specifically addressed. Despite this lack of codification, however, cadets of that day knew with absolute certainty what the Code comprised and what adherence to it required, including non-toleration.

The unknown authors of the *Honor Guide for Officers* acknowledge a degree of mystery surrounding the origins of the Honor Code. "Interestingly enough," they begin, "there is no background material which states how the Honor Code and System operate in developing a strong sense of honor." The authors speculated that it was developed by empirical methods over a period of years, and that it was built around three complementary ideas: (1) "The voluntary and enthusiastic acceptance of an exacting Code of ethical standards based on the professional ethics of the Army officer." (2) "The acceptance of an Honor System which results in the cadet putting the Code into action many times each day for four years." And (3) "The policing of the Code and System by the cadets themselves with the strong backing of the authorities—separation from the Corps being the penalty for violations."[56] This analysis seems to be right on the mark.

Honor Book

Commencing in about 1928, Honor Committee chairmen began maintaining a remarkable journal, known informally as the Honor Book, in which they recorded—typically just before graduation—thoughts on their experiences in the position and, quite often, instructions and encouragement for their successor. Nearly all the entries are handwritten and rather succinct, two or three pages being typical. An early entry, dated July 1932, consists of hand-printed excerpts from an essay on honor by Robert Wood first published in *The Pointer*, the cadet magazine of an earlier day, including this: "Military men the world over value honor for its sterling worth, its vital force in any army, its power to make something or nothing of a man."[57]

Another early entry records duties of the Cadet Honor Committee as approved by the Superintendent in April 1928:

1. To keep alive in the Corps the principles of its honor code and transmit them from class to class.
2. To inquire into irregularities of conduct, personal or official, with a view to bringing them to the attention of higher authority, if the circumstances warrant such action.

3. To bring to the attention of higher authority regulations pertaining to matters of honor, when, in their opinion, they are not clearly understood.
4. To guard against the springing up of practices inconsistent with our honor code.

Drawing attention to an important change from days of the Vigilance Committees, the June 1928 entry notes that "it is no function of the Committee to interpret regulations" and that "the Honor Committee has no punitive power," then goes on to provide a little instructive history: "Contrary to common belief, the Honor Committee existing as a punitive body is not an old tradition of the Academy. At that particular time in the past when it first assumed for itself the right to punish officially and by legislative action another cadet, it exceeded its authority."[58]

The matter of the "silence" was also addressed in this early entry, but not as definitively or finally as its author may have anticipated. Referring to a 28 March 1928 meeting between the Superintendent, Major General William R. Smith (USMA 1892), and the Honor Committee, the Honor Book records Smith's having pointed out to the Committee the limits of its authority and responsibilities, then quotes him directly: "This, in a few words, means that you have no right to 'silence.' There is no longer such a thing as 'silence.' Forget about it." General Smith had at that point been on the job for about four weeks. One imagines that as his tenure grew longer he developed a keener appreciation of the strength of customs and tradition and of the limitations of leadership by fiat. We will, in any case, return to the subject of the silence in subsequent pages.

Over the years the Honor Book served as a kind of barometer of the state of honor at the Military Academy, or at least of the Honor Committee Chairman's view of its status, in the process illustrating that such a matter is not static but rather highly dynamic. In the 1930 entry, for example, the Honor Chairman wrote: "The Honor Committee feels that the Corps has upheld the Honor System very well this year and that there has been good cooperation between the Committee and the rest of the Corps." There follows an interesting endorsement from Lieutenant Colonel Robert Richardson Jr. (USMA 1904), Commandant of Cadets: "The Honor Committee of the Class of 1930 functioned admirably. The Honor of the Corps of Cadets has never been brighter nor the standard higher than at the present time."

Only a short time later, however, the 1937 Honor Committee Chairman wrote that, "proud as we are of our Honor Code, we cannot help but admit that the last two years have seen a decline in the interest of the Corps in the system. This is a calamity not to be left unnoticed, for the Honor Code is our most valuable heritage—not alone in the academy, but in the service in general." Cadet Eugene Stann then sought to explain the postulated decline: "The lack of interest—and what is worse, a growing lack of faith—in the system may be due to several things." He suggested first that it was the result of "the large classes that have been admitted as plebes these last two years. Regardless of how we may feel as to the personal integrity of every man in the Corps, it cannot be denied that there are men entering every year who do not belong." Thus: "It is your duty to weed them out. The best cure for this, if this is the cause, is more instruction, especially for the plebes."[59]

Cadet Stann thought another contributing cause in cadet loss of interest in the honor program might be that the Tactical Department had "placed too heavy a burden on the system by its insistence upon including more and more pure regulations in the system," a perennial complaint of cadets. The system, he maintained, "was not designed to require a cadet to report himself for every violation of regulation. The primary principle of the system," he asserted, "is that we give our word in return for certain privileges."

Honor Committees over the years have taken seriously their stated responsibility to "guard against the springing up of practices inconsistent with our honor code." One unusual case was recorded in the Honor Book in 1930: "About May 1, 1930, Cadet Christian Keener Cagle, our nationally known and immensely popular football captain was found to be married [cadets were not allowed to be married, and it constituted a violation of honor if a cadet had gotten married and did not acknowledge it upon signing in] and allowed to resign." There followed an entry dated 4 June 1931: "On May 13 the Honor Committee wrote Cagle and requested that he refrain from appearing at functions of the Corps to which the general public was not invited. He had attended two hops and had seemingly been welcomed as though violation of the honor code could be overlooked in his case." The 1931 issue of *Bugle Notes*, the handbook for instruction and indoctrination of plebes, included a relevant entry: "Offenders against the code of honor are never granted immunity."

The West Point practice of administering identical quizzes and examinations to cadets reciting at different times has long been problematical, as this entry in the 1930 Honor Book illustrates: "There should be no question in anyone's mind as far as section-room conduct is concerned. Men reciting the first hour should make no mention whatsoever to cadets reciting the second hour of what went on in the section-room. Even to say that the writ was hard or easy gives the second hour man an advantage which the first hour man did not have. The guiding principle should be that of fairness; the cadets reciting second hour should have no advantage not possessed by first hour men."

Some Honor Committee Chairmen have included in their Honor Book entries specific advice to their successor. One such entry of particular interest was penned in 1943 by Cadet Merle Carey: "Go to the Commandant: Col. Gallagher has a high sense of honor and will back you absolutely in any way. He will steer you along a straight road of good advice from experience. Have implicit faith in him. Also, your friends on the Academic Board are Colonels Beukema and Fenton, the tradition-wielders."

Over this long sweep of the Military Academy's history, from before the Civil War until World War II, the Honor Code evolved into a close approximation of its contemporary statement, was first rendered in written form, and became ever more firmly established as the defining essence of what West Point was all about. At the same time the Honor System, although in more or less continual flux, achieved official recognition and sanction. As the Honor Book makes clear, those who led the Honor Committee took their responsibilities seriously, understood the twin imperatives of education and enforcement, and were passionately committed to maintaining the honor of the Corps "untarnished and unsullied." Ahead, with war once again in the offing, their successors would face equally challenging responsibilities.

Notes

1 Theodore J. Crackel, *West Point*, pp. 185-186.
2 Earl Blaik, "A Cadet under MacArthur," *Assembly* (Spring 1964), p. 8.
3 Lt. Gen. Sidney B. Berry, Address, "The United States Military Academy," Newcomen Society, 17 November 1976, p. 19.
4 Col. R. Ernest Dupuy, *Where They Have Trod*, p. 356.
5 Ibid., p. 357.
6 Ibid., pp. 357, 358. When Colonel Tillman (USMA 1869) became Superintendent in June 1917 he had been in retirement for nearly six years after service spanning 46 years, 36 of them spent at West Point, the last 31 as Professor of Chemistry, Mineralogy and Geology. Ibid., p. 354.
7 Comments on draft manuscript. Colonel Betros (USMA 1977) is Professor and Head of the USMA Department of History.
8 *1946 Bugle Notes*, p. 33.
9 As quoted in Dupuy, p. 352.
10 *Notes of a Board of Officers*, 13 August 1951, p. 14. Colonel Jones was, at the time he made this statement, the USMA Inspector General.
11 Telecon, Dr. Carleton Coulter III with author, 6 June 2007.
12 As noted, and quoted, by Cadet Michael Starz in his essay on "The Non-Toleration Clause," p. 3.
13 *1918 Bugle Notes*, pp. 7 and 99.
14 Letter of 17 May 1920 as quoted in *The Cadet Honor Code and System*, 30 August 1976, p. 1. The statement is quoted in numerous other sources with relatively minor variations in punctuation and wording.
15 Theodore J. Crackel, *West Point: A Bicentennial History*, p. 330n77.
16 Jacob L. Devers, "The Mark of the Man on USMA," *Assembly* (Spring 1964), p. 17.
17 Blaik, p. 9.
18 Lt. Gen. Garrison H. Davidson, "West Point at the Crossroads—A Return to Basic Principles," unpublished paper, Dr. John A. Feagin Jr. Collection.
19 *1921 Annual Report of the Superintendent of the United States Military Academy*, p. 3.
20 Ibid., pp. 3-4.
21 Ibid., p. 9.
22 Sidney Forman, "Scandal Among Cadets," p. 490. As USMA Historian Dr. Stephen Grove has noted, Dr. Forman was probably referring to an "Honor System" rather than an "Honor Code," since a written Honor Code had not yet been formulated.
23 As noted in an excerpt from the *1923 Howitzer*, USMA Archives.
24 *Report of Superintendent's Special Study Group on Honor at West Point*, 23 May 1975, p. 10. Often referred to as the Buckley Study for Col. Harry A. Buckley Jr. of the Office of Military Leadership, who co-chaired the study with Cadet William J. Reid of the Class of 1975.
25 No Honor Committee photograph appeared in the 1970 *Howitzer*, a matter cited by the 1971 Superintendent's Honor Review Committee as evidence of a disturbing development: "The committee has noted with regret a subtle loss in prestige of the

Cadet Honor Committee and its activities in the eyes of the Corps of Cadets."
"Report of the Honor Review Committee—1971," 30 April 1971, USMA Archives.

26 Excerpt from *1923 Howitzer*, USMA Archives.

27 Alongside MacArthur's laudable actions in establishing the Honor Committee, however, were some countervailing factors which, emulated by others, would later give
rise to severe honor problems. MacArthur had, and manifested while Superintendent, an uncritical devotion to football and football players. That gave rise to severe
criticism from another (later very senior) officer, Omar Bradley. "On one matter I
was sorely disappointed by MacArthur," wrote General of the Army Bradley in his
memoir *A General's Life*, p. 52. "He backed the varsity sports squads to the hilt,
often appearing at practices, offering suggestions and exhorting the men to do their
utmost. Among the 1920 plebes there was a standout athlete, Walter E. French, who
starred in both football and baseball. French was a borderline student: it was doubt-
ful he would make it academically. MacArthur deemed French so vital to West Point
athletics that he passed the word to the academic department that French would be
'found' [meaning failed academically] over his—MacArthur's—dead body. This act
of favoritism was a blatant, even outrageous, corruption of West Point tradition and
honor, and it more than rankled the academic department. In our eyes, it was 'relax-
ing' the high standards at West Point a bit too far." In June 1922 MacArthur was
reassigned, replaced as Superintendent by Brig. Gen. Fred Sladen. "To his credit,"
continued Bradley, "General Sladen promptly dealt with the controversial case of
our star athlete, Walter E. French, whom MacArthur had been shielding academically. French was properly 'found' and forced to resign." That was not the end of
Mr. French's career, however. The *2000 Register of Graduates* indicates that he was
subsequently commissioned (from another source, apparently) and later retired,
after a long career, as an Air Force lieutenant colonel.

28 Stephen E. Ambrose, *Duty, Honor, Country*, p. 281.

29 Memorandum, Col. Harry A. Buckley (Leadership) to Col. J. M. Pollin, Subject:
Cadet Honor Code and System, 14 November 1977, USMA Archives.

30 *1922 Bugle Notes*, pp. 34-35.

31 *1924 Howitzer*, as quoted in *Report of Superintendent's Special Study Group on
Honor at West Point*, p. A-6.

32 Briefing on the Cadet Honor Code & System by the Chairman of the Cadet Honor
Committee, 1964–1965, File: Honor Code—Historical (JUL 64–JUN 65), USMA
Archives.

33 *USCC Pamphlet 632-1*, August 1992, p. 2.

34 Memorandum for the Superintendent from M. B. Stewart, Commandant of Cadets,
Subject: Functions, Honor Committee, 16 July 1924, USMA Adjutant General Files,
351.1 Honor System, 1924–1925, USMA Archives.

35 Memorandum to Superintendent, USMA, Subject: Application of Honor System in
Academic Work, Signed by Members of the General Committee, 11 May 1926,
USMA Adjutant General Files, 351.1 Honor System, USMA Archives.

36 As referred to in 3rd Indorsement, General Committee, 5 October 1926, to Superintendent USMA, to Memorandum from Maj. H. B. Lewis, Adjutant, HQ USMA, to
Commandant of Cadets, Subject: Honor System, Cadets, 28 June 1926, Adjutant
General Files, 351.1 Honor System, USMA Archives. According to his obituary in
the Association of Graduates' *Annual Report* of 11 June 1936, p. 200, Stewart was
"never brilliant in academic work and a 'clean sleeve' [no cadet rank] during his four
years as a cadet." During his assignment as a Tactical Officer Stewart, an Infantry-
man, campaigned so strenuously against the Army's policy of paying mounted officers more than dismounted ones that he antagonized the War Department and was,
as a consequence, summarily relieved from duty at West Point, issued a reprimand,
and posted to the Philippines. Ibid., p. 202.

37 Wrapper Indorsement dated 17 May 1935, Lt. Col. S. B. Buckner Jr., Commandant of Cadets, to Superintendent, Adjutant General Files, 351.1 Honor System, USMA Archives.

38 Ibid.

39 Ibid.

40 Letter, Lt. Gen. L. J. Lincoln to Maj. Gen. D. V. Bennett, Superintendent USMA, 22 November 1967, USMA Archives. The writer refers to the honor "code," but in fact seems to be addressing the honor "system."

41 Ibid.

42 Ibid. The First Captain was Kenneth E. Fields, who also stood first in his class academically and was a starting back on the football team. He was commissioned in the Corps of Engineers, won a Silver Star while commanding an Engineer Combat Group in Europe during World War II, and rose to the rank of brigadier general. The Commandant of that day was also an interesting officer, Lt. Col. Robert C. Richardson (USMA 1904). A Cavalry officer, he had been awarded a Silver Star and the Purple Heart for actions while fighting against the Moros in the Philippines, commanded at high levels in the Pacific during and after World War II, retired as a lieutenant general, and was posthumously promoted to full general.

43 Ibid.

44 Letter, Maj. Gen. D. V. Bennett, Superintendent, to Lt. Gen. L. J. Lincoln, 6 December 1967, USMA Archives.

45 Letter, "Honor System, U.S. Corps of Cadets," Headquarters USMA, 6 December 1944, USMA Archives. This version superseded one dated 5 October 1944, only a month earlier, and was in turn superseded by a version dated 5 November 1945, the 1945 version being published shortly after Maj. Gen. Maxwell D. Taylor had succeeded Maj. Gen. Francis B. Wilby as Superintendent.

46 Letter, unsigned, "The Honor System at West Point," 5 November 1945, Adjutant General File 351.1, Honor System, USMA Archives.

47 Ibid.

48 Memorandum, Dr. Stephen Grove, USMA Historian, "Origin of USMA Articulation of 'A cadet will not lie, cheat, nor steal' as the Cadet Honor Code," 3 February 1992, USMA Archives.

49 As quoted in "Honor Violations at West Point, 1951: A Case Study," USMA Archives. A research group directed by Col. Anthony E. Hartle, Professor of Philosophy, produced this case study, which was forwarded to the Superintendent on 10 September 1990.

50 Letter, Army Chief of Staff Gen. Dwight D. Eisenhower to Maj. Gen. Maxwell D. Taylor, Superintendent USMA, 2 January 1946, USMA Archives.

51 See Letter, "Honor System, U.S. Corps of Cadets," Headquarters USMA, 6 December 1944, USMA Archives.

52 Memorandum, Brig. Gen. George Honnen, Commandant of Cadets, for Superintendent, USMA, 8 January 1946, USMA Archives. The memorandum has the typed signature "G.H." At that time, shows the *Register of Graduates*, the Commandant was General Honnen.

53 Maj. Gen. Maxwell D. Taylor, *West Point Honor System*, pp. 3, 5. In another short Taylor dissertation, also published at West Point, he suggests that "all the great leaders of the past and the present have been conspicuous for the following three qualities. First, they have been devoted to the welfare of their troops. Next, they have been richly endowed with human understanding. And finally, they have stood out by their professional competence and ability." Noticeably missing from that short list is any reference to integrity or honor, although one might consider those qualities to be subsumed under the heading of professional competence. Maj. Gen. Maxwell D. Taylor, *Leading the American Soldier*, p. 4.

54 *Honor Guide for Officers*, pp. 2-3.

55 Ibid., p. 6.

56 Ibid., p. 7.

57 *Honor Book*, United States Corps of Cadets. This journal is maintained and safe-guarded by each Honor Committee Chairman in turn and upon graduation passed along to his successor. Robert J. Wood (USMA 1930), whose editorial "On Honor" was published in the 12 April 1929 issue of *The Pointer*, went on to a distinguished career in which he reached the rank of full general.

58 An admirably succinct and accurate definition was provided by Cadet Charles Lea in his 1957 Honor Book entry: "The function of the Honor Committee is to teach people to think and act honestly and to insure that they do."

59 Cadet Stann was right about the dramatic increase in class size. The Classes of 1936, 1937, and 1938 had graduated 275, 298 and 301 men respectively. The Classes of 1939 and 1940 graduated 456 and 449, representing an increase of approximately 50 percent in class size over the immediately preceding classes. *2000 Register of Graduates*, passim.

4 | Cohesion and Separation

World War II

As had been the case in World War I, certain classes at the Military Academy during World War II were graduated early, commissioned, and sent off to fight in the war. This time, however, early graduation measures were not carried to the extremes of the earlier day—when, as we have seen, at one point the Corps of Cadets was reduced to only two classes (and, for a few months, only one class), both composed of plebes.

The Class of 1942 completed a normal four-year course of instruction before graduating on 29 May. General George Marshall, the Army's great wartime Chief of Staff, presented their diplomas. Earlier that year, however, the Army had decided that subsequent classes would complete a three-year course, and that this policy would continue in effect for the duration of the war. The Superintendent, Brigadier General Robert Eichelberger, had stressed the need to "save West Point from its sad lot of World War I."[1] The wise decision to settle on a three-year curriculum headed off a repetition of the earlier chaos.

There were still significant problems, even from the perspective of the Corps. "There can be no doubt but that the present is a critical time in the history of the Military Academy," Cadet Scott, a regimental commander, wrote to the Commandant of Cadets in February 1943. "The magnitude of the present war, the radical changes resulting therefrom in the administrative departments of the Academy, and especially the calibre of the new class of the Academy demand immediate and sagacious action." Cadet Scott then added his views on the Honor System, which he characterized—along with the Plebe System—as one of the two great foundation stones of the Academy. "Surely there is no doubt but that the Honor System has maintained itself steadfastly through these many years because it belonged to the cadets themselves; the cadets alone have administered,

---

Conscience

The only guide to a man is his conscience; the only shield to his memory is the rectitude and sincerity of his actions. It is very imprudent to walk through life without this shield, because we are often mocked by the failure of our hopes and the upsetting of our calculations; but with this shield, however the fates may play, we march always in the ranks of honour.

Winston Churchill
Commons
12 November 1940

---

enforced, and carried out the principles of the Honor System [so that] today there is no question as to the workability—and permanence—of that system."[2] While that may not have been entirely accurate, in that the Honor System had for a number of years been managed through partnership with the Military Academy's administration, it did demonstrate an admirable and essential sense of cadet responsibility for maintaining high standards of honor.

Graduation for the original Class of 1943 was accelerated by a matter of months, to 19 January, at which time they were redesignated the Class of January 1943. Close behind, graduating on 1 June after three years as cadets, was the original Class of 1944, now to be known as the Class of June 1943. The Class of 1944, which had the distinction of graduating on 6 June of that year, D-Day for the Normandy invasion, had originally been the Class of 1945. Thus it, too, had completed three years at the Military Academy before being commissioned. Two more three-year classes followed, the Class of 1945 (entered 1942, graduated 5 June 1945) and the Class of 1946 (entered 1943, graduated 4 June 1946). The Class of 1947 was an anomaly. It had entered in 1944 as the three-year Class of 1947, but in 1946 was divided into approximately equal halves to form the three-year Class of 1947 and the Class of 1948, the first post-war four-year class.[3] The Class of 1949 was the first to enter after World War II (or nearly so, just a month before the surrender of Japan), with it returning to the traditional uninterrupted four-year experience.[4]

This history is pertinent to the health and perpetuation of the Honor Code and System, since it ensured that there would be upper classes on hand who had themselves received adequate instruction and experience with honor issues and procedures, and were therefore competent to provide such instruction to succeeding classes. Noted an entry in the *1944 Bugle Notes*: "West Point has been able to meet the present emergency and yet maintain the same high standards it did through the years of peace. There can be no doubt that it learned its lesson well from the catastrophic years of the First World War."[5]

Nevertheless certain problems arose. "In the past five months the Class of June '43 has had the reins, and an Honor Committee little prepared for the task has attempted to carry out a time-honored tradition—maintaining the high ideals and standards of honor in the Corps," wrote Cadet William Kilpatrick in the Honor Book. During that time, he noted, the Honor Committee had "asked for and received the honor resignations of three fourth classmen—an unprecedented number for such a short time—besides asking for, and not receiving, the resignation of a classmate." These developments, suggested Mr. Kilpatrick, were the result of "an enlarged plebe class and an ever diminishing amount of time available for the adequate instruction in principles of honor."

The Honor Committee Chairman of 1945, the last wartime graduating class, took a realistic view of the situation his successor would inherit: "I emphasize the importance of your responsibility because while our nation is at war it is only natural for everything that is not contributing directly to the war effort to get lax, including possibly the stiff requirements for entrance to West Point." And again the increased size of entering classes was identified as a source of potential problems: "This possibility, plus the enormous size of the 'war classes,' makes your job one worthy of constant, undivided, conscientious effort."

But there were optimistic notes. Brigadier General George Honnen had served as Commandant of Cadets during much of the wartime period (1943–1946). In a memorandum to the Superintendent, Major General Maxwell Taylor, soon after the latter took office, General Honnen described a World War II situation gratifyingly different than that which had characterized the World War I period. "I do not believe that the Honor System has fundamentally retrogressed to any extent during the period of the war," he said, "and [that it] is still as effective a force in the life of a cadet as it has been for the past decades."[6]

The noted military historian Martin Blumenson, writing retrospectively about senior military leaders in Europe during World War II, provided a warm testimonial to the successful inculcation of values during the preceding decades. "The military ethos was so ingrained and so strong among much of the officer corps," he observed, "that it required no definition. No one found it necessary to explain, for example, what the West Point motto—Duty, Honor, Country—meant. Everyone simply knew."[7]

Post-War Years

As noted earlier, in 1945 one of the most famous combat generals of World War II was assigned as Superintendent at West Point. Major General Maxwell Taylor (USMA 1922) had graduated third in his class and was commissioned in the Corps of Engineers, later transferring to Field Artillery. First as division artillery commander of the 82nd Airborne Division, then as commanding general of the 101st Airborne Division, he was a glamorous, popular, and highly successful troop leader during the war in Europe, earning among many other decorations a Distinguished Service Cross, two Silver Stars, and the Purple Heart.

His four-year tenure as Superintendent, coming just after four years of American involvement in war and the inevitable turbulence it introduced at the Military Academy, was marked by personal attention to honor and academics. Highly regarded as a soldier-scholar, Taylor was interested in every aspect of the Military Academy's functioning, to include a very keen and specific interest in the Honor Code and Honor System. That interest was reflected particularly by his personal authorship of a pamphlet entitled *West Point Honor System: Its Objectives and Procedures*. First emphasizing that the leaders developed by West Point "must have strength of character as well as intellectual and physical vigor," he then quoted Secretary of War Newton Baker's famous statement (cited earlier in this work) on the indispensable military virtues.[8] General Taylor got right to the essence in this short treatise, describing honor as "a virtue which implies loyalty and courage, truthfulness and self-respect, justice and generosity. Its underlying principal is truth."[9]

After some four months on the job, General Taylor wrote to General Dwight Eisenhower (USMA 1915), then Army Chief of Staff. "With regard to the Honor System," he said, "I believe that the Academy is on solid ground. There can be no question as to the danger to the System if it is allowed to become a device for the detection of the violation of regulations. The Commandant of Cadets and I shall exercise joint vigilance in preventing such abuses of the System as have arisen from time to time in the past." Taylor and Eisenhower were in strong accord on this issue. Three weeks later, summarizing what Eisenhower had told him in a recent face-to-face meeting, Taylor wrote: "He reiterated his strong opposition to any tendency to use the Honor System as a means of enforcing the Academy Regulations, and I assured him that this would never take place during my administration."[10]

Taylor also spoke of his efforts to ensure that the discipline of the Corps of Cadets rested with cadet officers and the First Class, not the Tactical Department. "I am sure that the four-year course," which was being reinstituted now that the war was over, "will bring forth a more mature First Class capable of assuming authority in the management of the Corps beyond that possible during the war-time course."[11]

The 1946 Honor Book entry reports an interesting change, one placing cadet officers of the day on their honor to report all violations of orders and regulations observed during their tours of duty. The timing of such an initiative is surprising, coming as it did during the first year of General Taylor's superintendency. The intent is equally surprising, as it appears clearly at variance with Eisenhower's guidance and Taylor's assurances to him. "The Corps was opposed to this step during most of the year," wrote Cadet Dwight Burnham, "but now it is generally agreed that it worked out rather well." That interesting conclusion is not further explained, but the provision continued in effect for a number of years.

Thus cadets of a certain era, roughly a decade later, will remember officers of the day jingling their large ring of keys to give other cadets warning of their approach, and some will remember in contrast an officer of the Tactical Department who gained the nickname "The Owl" for his zealous nighttime attempts to detect cadets engaged in wrongdoing. A minor triumph for cadets of that day occurred the night The Owl went out a second-floor stairwell window onto the roof of the stoops in the old Central Barracks, the better to snoop for illicit activity, only to be stranded there when an alert cadet locked the window behind him.[12]

In May 1950 a most interesting situation developed when, for reasons now unknown, one of the academic departments, "in a series of problems [academic quiz questions], inserted a trap in an effort to determine whether cadets were cheating or not." When this became known to the Commandant of Cadets, Colonel Paul Harkins, he was incensed. "I am chagrined and disappointed to learn that such an action has been taken as a means of absolving the innocent and finding out who are the guilty, if any," Colonel Harkins said in a memorandum routed through the Dean to the Superintendent. "It has been, and will always continue to be, my sincere belief that, as a whole, the Corps of Cadets possesses an honesty above question and it has been my belief, and will always continue to be my hope that the officer corps stationed at West Point also believes this to be true and will be so guided in their actions."[13]

Continuing in this vein, Colonel Harkins declared: "It seems incompatible in my belief in the Honor System that any department at West Point should present to the cadets an approved solution which to the cadets implies that it is correct to the best ability of the department but which contains intentional errors injected on purpose to test the honor of the Corps." Then, concluding: "For such practices as this to be condoned and to continue will strike at the very heart of the Honor System and will do nothing but engender distrust, disbelief, hatred, and bitterness. I am sure you understand that I have no sympathy for a cheat, thief or liar, and I will do everything in my power to prove that a cadet guilty of cheating, stealing, or lying should be separated from the Academy. If an individual cadet is suspected, I have no objection to anyone checking on him in an effort to determine whether he is guilty or not. However, to insert falsehoods to determine the truthfulness of the whole Corps is another matter and I am far from being in sympathy with such methods."[14]

Colonel Harkins was apparently quite effective in stating his outrage and opposition to this ploy, for only four days later the Dean informed the Superintendent, in an endorsement to the Harkins memorandum, that "action has been taken by the head of the department concerned to prevent the repetition of the specific procedure to which the Commandant refers," adding "I do not think that this procedure has been in customary use in any department."[15] What makes this correspondence so intriguing is the date, less than a year before the 1951 cheating scandal (involving primarily football players and their associates). It would be very interesting to know which department was involved and whether this action was motivated by early indications of the problem that soon surfaced in such a major way.

Crisis

In the late spring of 1951, the most serious challenge to the viability of the Honor Code occured. First disclosed publicly in a 3 August 1951 announcement from West Point's public information office, it was described as "a serious breach of the West Point Code of Honor involving approximately ninety members of the Corps of Cadets." These individuals had been "receiving improper outside assistance in academic work." Those found guilty were being discharged, and in that group were "cadets who have been prominent in various activities including varsity football."[16]

It is scary that almost no one saw this coming. In fact the Cadet Honor Chairman of 1950 had written in the Honor Book that "the Honor Code in the Corps today is at a very high standard. The principles and standards of honor are well understood by each man." About to burst into the open was a major and shocking exception to that understanding, or at least to acceptance of its implications, football players and others closely associated with them. Perhaps the Honor Chairman did have certain misgivings, though, for he had also written, in apparent contradiction of his overall assessment, that "the spirit of our code as adhered to by each cadet is the only tenet which is not at an optimum. This year we have tried to improve on this point."

Colonel Arthur Collins Jr. was then the 1st Regiment Tactical Officer. He was assigned to chair a board tasked to investigate alleged violations of the Honor Code. Colonel Collins admired the Commandant, Colonel Paul D. Harkins, for the way he handled the matter. "This was one of those events . . . which meant very much to Colonel Harkins at that time and could have hurt his career," recalled Collins. "There was so little to go on, he could very easily have said, 'Let's see if we can get something more concrete,' and just have passed the envelope along to the new Command, <u>but he didn't</u>. His directive to let the chips fall where they may, get to the bottom of it, and get it cleaned up before he left, was inspirational."[17]

The board chaired by Colonel Collins concluded that the cheating dated back several years, but that initially it was confined to only a few blue chip football players. "All of a sudden," however, "in 1949 and 1950, West Point admitted a large number of football players who lacked the educational qualifications to cope with the academic program at the Academy." Then this disfunction mushroomed and eventually, and inevitably, became so widely known that it could no longer be kept secret.[18]

Initially many cadets brought before the Collins Board denied involvement in any cheating, but subsequently many returned and renounced their false testimony. "After the football players recanted," remembered Colonel Collins, "they brought in long lists of names of people they were sure were involved, but they could not be specific. Some of them told us later they had been told to involve everyone they possibly could—make it look as though the whole Corps was involved." But, said Collins, "When we started to track down their allegations, most of them disappeared into thin air."[19]

The Bartlett Board, so known because it was chaired by a very senior professor, Colonel Boyd Bartlett, was convened later that same summer of 1951, tasked to look into the causes of the honor crisis, and reached confirmatory conclusions. "On the basis of interviews with members of the Athletic Board and the Director of Athletics," read its report, "we believe that a general policy was established about 1940 that West Point would have winning football teams."[20] Much else derived from that aspiration. The then-Superintendent, Major General Robert Eichelberger, hired Earl Blaik away from Dartmouth to coach the football team. Blaik, who had resigned his commission less than two years after graduation from West Point, was given the rank of colonel and assigned to West Point, an arrangement that kept him from overseas duty in World War II.

Beginning in about 1943, special "cram school" or "monster school" sessions were organized for tutoring football prospects so they could pass the USMA entrance examinations. Recruiting of football prospects was also stepped up. The Bartlett Board found that the majority of both officers and cadets at West Point were opposed to intensified football recruiting and to the special cram school for football players.[21] Also, found the Bartlett Board, this was not a new problem. "The ring or conspiracy appears to have been in existence for several years," the board reported, "but does not appear to have been widespread prior to the academic year 1950–1951."[22] Thus: "We conclude that a small, closely confined cheating ring may have existed among the members of the varsity football squad as a hard core for subsequent expansion at least as early as the Academic Year 1949–1950, and that such a ring may have existed as far back as the fall of 1944."[23] In the wake of these findings the new Commandant of Cadets, Colonel John Waters, told the Bartlett Board: "I think we have got to decide who is running West Point—the Superintendent or the Director of Athletics."[24]

At the beginning of August 1951 Secretary of the Army Frank Pace and Army Chief of Staff General J. Lawton Collins went to see President Truman. They described the situation, telling him that those who had confessed to violating the Honor Code were to be dismissed. Truman's comment was succinct: "Can't do anything else."[25]

The most encouraging aspect of this sorry mess was that, as Colonel Collins observed, "the Corps as a whole supported what we had done. They had a feeling and a sense of the honor system, and the importance of it to West Point. It was just unbelievable to the couple of thousand cadets not involved that anything like that could happen."[26]

Cadet David Ahearn (USMA 1952) confirmed that view in an article prepared for publication in *Assembly*, the West Point alumni magazine. "There is no sympathy for the guilty cadets to be found in the ranks of the men who lived, worked, slept, and ate with them," he affirmed. Having surveyed the Corps, he reported that "in no instance did any cadet indicate that he would in any way tolerate the pardon of the ninety or their reinstatement in the Corps. In short, the Honor Code violators can find absolutely no sympathy from the men who knew them best."[27]

The source of the problem was very clear. "I say without any reservation," Colonel Collins later stated, "that everyone who was involved became involved through a football player—living with him, coaching him in academics, or on the squad with him. The football team was the source of the infection."[28] Even many years later, after various other related problems had emerged at several points, the Posvar Commission could write that "the worst scandals and the most virulent threats to the Honor Code stemmed from deception connected with football."[29]

The Army Chief of Staff, General J. Lawton Collins (USMA April 1917), provided some advice on that aspect of the matter, transmitted to the Superintendent in a letter from Lieutenant General Maxwell Taylor (USMA 1922), himself a former Superintendent then serving in the Pentagon as Deputy Chief of Staff for Operations and Administration. "It is the impression of the Chief of Staff," wrote General Taylor, "that a contributing factor to the recent incident has been the separation of the athletic groups, particularly the football squad, from the environmental influences of the Corps of Cadets. He desires the

Superintendent to assure that in the future the athletes are not so insulated from the rest of the Corps as to be deprived of the sustaining ethical influences of normal cadet life."[30] General Collins felt so strongly about this matter that he later went personally to West Point, where he met with the Academic Board to discuss the honor system "and whether any isolation of the football squad was still in effect."[31]

Colonel Collins was forthright in stating his view of the coach's role in all this. "If Colonel Blaik, a graduate, had brought these youngsters up in the true tradition of West Point," he stated, "there would not have been an honor scandal."[32] An analysis of correspondence and press items received at West Point reflected the public's agreement. According to the analysis, "only one voice was raised in defense of the athletic coaches. The remainder attributed responsibility for the episode to these officials."[33]

Blaik's full role in the scandal remained unresolved, as it does even to this day, but his attitude is well documented, including in his own statements. In August 1951 he held a press conference in New York City. "He defended the character of the boys, [and] stated that they should be honorably discharged," said a subsequent account in *Life* magazine.[34] Much later, well after his reign as the Army football coach, Blaik wrote a book in which he called the dismissed cadets "scapegoats" and serially condemned those officials responsible for ordering the dismissals, beginning with the Secretary of the Army and the Army Chief of Staff. Singling out one dismissed former football player, Blaik maintained that "his sense of integrity and character meet every standard of men of honor."[35]

To the Superintendent, Major General Frederick Irving, such views were anathema. "I wish to emphasize," he wrote to the alumni in *Assembly*, "that the organization of the cheating ring was deliberate, well planned, and designed to wreck a heritage that has been passed down for nearly 150 years."[36]

After much of the debris had been swept away, the Secretary of the Army asked Judge Learned Hand, one of the most respected jurists in the nation, to head a board to review how the whole matter had been handled. The judge was joined on the board by Lieutenant General Troy Middleton, who had commanded VIII Corps in Europe during World War II and was now president of Louisiana State University, and Major General Robert Danford, a former president of West Point's Association of Graduates.

Three key elements were at the heart of the board's examination: whether the cadets involved had been adequately schooled in ethical matters, whether the procedures followed in adjudicating their cases had been fair and just, and whether the punishments handed down should be sustained. As to the first: "The Board finds from cadets themselves that they have been thoroughly briefed and indoctrinated with the principles of the Honor Code; that they regard it the very soul of West Point, and that they approve and expect the drastic penalty which the Code imposes upon those who violate it."[37] The procedures of West Point's internal boards were also validated by the Learned Hand inquiry, which "concluded that the investigation by the Collins Board had been proper and adequate."[38] And finally, with respect to the punishments handed down: "The Board believes that the action recommended by the Superintendent [dismissal of all cadets found guilty of cheating] is the only possible one he could recommend as strictly adhering to the long established and cherished Honor Code." And: "Indeed the opinion is strongly prevalent among officers and cadets that failure to invoke such penalty in this case will completely destroy the West Point Honor System." Thus: "The Board concludes that the Report of the Board of Officers and the recommendations of the Superintendent should be affirmed."[39]

When these matters had been resolved, the Bartlett Board was convened to take a retrospective look and to identify, if it could, the causes of the debacle. The board had little trouble arriving at definitive answers. "The fundamental cause of the incident was a misalignment of values in the implementation of the mission of the Military Academy," read its conclusions. "Specifically the misalignment of values took the form of an over-emphasis on football." Then the consequences of such overemphasis were spelled out: "As a result there was created among the members of the varsity football team strong group and personal loyalties which transcended their loyalties to the Corps of Cadets and to the traditions of the Military Academy." And finally: "In the atmosphere of overemphasis, preferential treatment of varsity football team members on many counts tended to build up the feeling among many of the football players that they were a group apart and of such importance that they were not subject to the ordinary rules of cadet life."[40] And, lest there be any doubt, the Bartlett Board also stated its conviction that "the violations were premeditated and repeated. Those participating knew it was wrong."[41]

It is surprising that the 1951 Honor Committee Chairman wrote nothing at all about such an infamous honor crisis on his watch in his Honor Book entry. His principal observation, addressed to the new chairman, had to do with the "constant need for honor education." The 1952 Chairman had a lot to say about the matter, however, beginning with the fact that, since the scandal broke just before June Week of 1951, "and in the confusion of turning over the duties of the committee & graduating, the committee of 1951 was unable to tell us anything about it. In addition, our committee, all inexperienced, was busy with three honor trials that came up that same June Week." Subsequently the authorities had made some of the record available for review by the new honor committee. "We feel that the two most important points are," wrote Cadet Thomas Collier, "first, the case was finally uncovered by cadets reporting their suspicions to their company honor representatives; and, second, the Corps was solidly— really solidly—behind the expulsion of the violators and the unchanged continuance of the Honor System."

A later Honor Committee Chairman, 1957's Charles Lea, wrote insightfully about the 1951 honor crisis in his Honor Book entry. When it took office, he related, the 1957 Honor Committee inherited a thirteen-page document reflecting previous committee stands on everything from athletic property to sub-division inspector responsibilities. "It was the practice of the Committee," he noted, "to sit down with their respective companies the first of September and read as dogma this pamphlet of answers to questions." Mr. Lea saw some serious problems with this approach. "On the surface this appears to be a good, businesslike way to run a factory," he observed, "but the unfortunate consequence of this action was to cause most of the Corps of Cadets to quit thinking for itself."

Lea noted that "these mimeographed, even handwritten, poopsheets on many obscure points did not exist as late as 1945." He identified the earliest one as dating from 1947. "To me," said Lea, "this indicates that, somewhere in this era, there was a desire by at least some portion of the Corps to know exactly how much they could get away with." As Lea saw it, this related directly to the 1951 honor scandal. "This attitude, I believe, unwittingly helped along by several Honor Committees who spelled things out—gave answers to problems—led to the rather disastrous events of August 1951. As you know, 90 people went [resigned or were dismissed]—this meant that at least 4% of the Corps didn't give a damn about Honor, and I think the reason is the attitude which demanded that this fine line be drawn."

In 1958 an Academy publication entitled *Honor Guide for Officers* commented on the aftermath of the 1951 cheating incident for the benefit of officers assigned to West Point's staff and faculty. "As might be expected," it said, "honor matters after the 1951 difficulty needed careful handling. It appears that the Honor Committees in subsequent years were conservative but positive in reestablishing the traditional standards. As of now, the system is back on a sound basis, and recent honor committees have been insisting on the maintenance of high standards. This has resulted in a small increase in honor losses to slightly under 2% per class for their four years."[42]

Later Sidney Forman, longtime USMA Librarian, wrote insightfully about the honor problems of 1951 and their causes. In the 19th century, he observed, "cadets, motivated by a sensitive awareness of the character of an honor code, *voluntarily* entered into a social compact which demanded compliance with and enforcement of the necessary ethical system." Meanwhile "the officer corps understood their professional responsibilities *in loco parentis* and guided the cadets by example and exhortation to a mature appreciation of the ethical standards necessary for the very existence of the military forces in a democratic society."[43]

But in the 20th century, thought Forman, "change has undermined the traditional . . . supports for the honor code. Attitude patterns which were best sustained by a peer group have now become colored by administrative coercion." The Military Academy's environment and controls had also "been drastically affected by increases in the size and heterogeneity of the student body."[44] Given these pressures on the traditional methods of socialization and transmission of values, it is perhaps most remarkable that nearly all cadets still embraced the core values of the profession.

Captain John Eisenhower (USMA 1944), son of General Dwight Eisenhower (USMA 1915), was teaching English at West Point at the time of these honor problems. An article he prepared for the Associated Press commented on the often sensational press coverage of the affair. "It is regrettable," he wrote, "in the recent scandal that so much attention was paid to the testimony of a few offenders and so little attention was paid to the remainder of the Corps who stood adamant against those who had broken their code. The honor system is vital to West Point. The ability to live by that system is a requisite for a man who is preparing to be an officer." Consequently he stressed that "if a man cannot understand and adhere to the code while he is a cadet, there seems to be a grave danger that he will not be able to adhere to it under the much greater stresses of his officer service."[45]

Rebuilding

Each year a Board of Visitors comprehensively examines all aspects of West Point's organization and operation, typically formulating recommendations on a number of issues. In the first such visit after the 1951 cheating scandal, the Board looked at the totality of the influences in West Point life conducive to development of high ethical standards in the Corps of Cadets. Subsequently, West Point's Curriculum Committee summarized those influences in a useful communication to the Academic Board. "The Military Academy," it began, "has evolved a way of life in many diverse aspects of which the cadet is influenced by ethical considerations." Among the most important were "religious instruction at required chapel services," "the Cadet Honor System," "moral teachings and the ideals of duty, loyalty, and patriotism which are repeatedly stressed in academic and military instruction," and "standards of behavior and conduct absorbed by precept and example from a specially selected group of officers with whom cadets come in contact in every phase of their life at the Military Academy."[46] The vast majority of cadets who had been given full exposure to that complex of positive influences had adopted and faithfully adhered to the Honor Code. A minority, increasingly isolated and insulated from such influences, had failed to live up to its dictates.

In September 1955 the Superintendent, Lieutenant General Blackshear Bryan, appointed a Faculty Advisory Committee for the Cadet Honor Code. Chaired by Colonel Charles Broshous, Professor of Military Topography and Graphics, it also included the Deputy Commandant, Colonel William McCaffrey, and Colonel Walter Renfroe Jr., Professor of Foreign Languages. In its report of 8 May 1956 this committee rendered one of the most positive assessments on record, a unanimous opinion that "there is no major discernible weakness in the

> Trust
>
> My family have been traders and merchants in the Indian Ocean for centuries, under every kind of government. There is a reason why we have lasted so long. We bargain hard, but we stick to our bargain. All our contracts are oral, but we deliver what we promise. It isn't because we are saints. It is because the whole thing breaks down otherwise.
>
> Salim in A Bend in the River
> V. S. Naipaul

present operation of the Honor Code," and also concluding that "the major premise of the Honor Code, 'a cadet will not lie, cheat, or steal,' is without question universally subscribed to by all."[47]

The Broshous Committee also addressed the perennially contentious topic of the use of honor to enforce regulations, taking a stand in decided opposition to the purists who held that no tinge of such use was allowable. "There is no question that the Honor Code is used to enforce both Academic and Tactical Department regulations," said the report. "The Committee believes this practice is necessary and is useful in the development of character if used wisely."[48]

Surprisingly, during the course of 1956 a considerable controversy played out within the Academic Board, arguably the Military Academy's most conservative, and often most influential, body. Even more surprisingly, the issue was honor as applied to academic work. The Dean, Brigadier General T. D. Stamps, described the matter. "The basic question," he wrote in an internal memorandum, "is really whether or not we are going to put cadets on their honor when doing academic work. If we are, the policy on homework approved by General Bryan [the Superintendent] and my recommendations on the Broshous Board report are as far as we should go. They provide for a simple and clear system. If we are not going to have an academic honor system, we should say so and proceed accordingly."[49]

General Stamps observed that, "outside of themes [essays] and similar papers, there are only two academic honor requirements left (assuming approval of my recommendations)." Those were that a cadet may not cheat in class and that, for a period of two academic days, a cadet may not discuss with another cadet (who has not yet recited) what took place in class. In that second case, he observed, "We have a prohibition that has been in effect from time immemorial and has never given any difficulty except where a cadet deliberately set out to cheat. We cannot build honor in young men unless we give them practice in being honorable. To remove absolutely all temptation would be the worst thing we could do."[50]

At issue was a proposal by another member of the Academic Board, a Professor of Mathematics, for always "scheduling a writ [in-class examination] for all members of a class simultaneously." The Dean felt that scheme "would be strongly opposed by every head of department who conducts normal recitations. What he is really proposing is that we place no trust in the cadets and have the honor system inoperative for academic purposes."[51] General Stamps was correct in his assessment of how other members of the Academic Board would view this matter, and the customary pattern of giving writs to half the class at early and later recitations on the first day, then identical writs in the same manner to the other half of the class on the following day, was continued, at least for the time being.

Over the years a number of internal review committees have been appointed to study and assess the Honor Code and System, or specific aspects of one or the other. One such faculty committee, convened in 1957, considered whether new plebes, "youngsters accustomed to certain practices and codes suddenly faced with an abrupt transition to different standards," might during a probationary period be subject to lesser penalties, short of outright dismissal, for honor violations. "The Cadet Honor Committee," reported the officer panel, "viewed such ideas with strong disfavor." Ultimately the officers went along. "Though we have deep sympathy with the youth who, through one misguided act, seriously impairs his entire future," said their report, "we see no solution that does not prejudice the very roots of the Honor System."[52] That position, as we shall see, would in later years be subject to substantial modification.

There have also been some reevaluations and changes of position over the years that are hard to understand. "Whether cheating included writing on an exam after the command 'cease work' was not decided until 1954," according to an official publication, "when the Cadet Honor Committee reversed their predecessors and declared it to be a violation."[53] That such an action obviously constituted taking "unfair advantage" would seemingly have been as obvious to classes prior to 1954 as those then and after.

The 1954 Honor Chairman got to the essence of the matter in his Honor Book entry about finding a balance with respect to honor matters. "There are two principal viewpoints with regard to the Honor System," wrote Cadet Thomas Young to his successor, "strict interpretation and liberal interpretation. Adhere to the strict sense alone and you will soon become lost in a maze of detail and subject to continual interpretation of regulations. The liberal point of view characterized by the question—What is the man's intent in the matter?— will most often be the simplest and most clear cut manner of answering the questions men will bring to you, but don't ever let this simplicity of interpretation develop into laxity of interpretation." That described a hard task, but also an essential one.

The following year the Honor Chairman reported that "our Committee placed primary emphasis on the spirit of the Honor Code, and found later that we failed to emphasize enough the individual responsibility of each cadet to be certain that he was adhering to this spirit and to the Code in all respects." Cadet Robert Wiegand cited as examples of such problems the resale and use of football tickets and cadet theft of Army Athletic Association uniforms and equipment.

Senior Academy leaders of this era were forthright in advising entering plebes what to expect. Wrote Superintendent Major General Frederick Irving in a foreword to the *1954 Bugle Notes*, "Remember that this is a test; a test to weed out the weak and strengthen the strong; a test so gauged that only the most determined succeed." His successor, Lieutenant General Blackshear Bryan, adopted a similar tone: "Life at West Point is not designed for weaklings."[54]

Meanwhile new cadets were entering with expectations every bit as high and commitments every bit as serious as had their predecessors. At the end of his first day as a cadet, remembered Norm Schwarzkopf, entering West Point in the summer of 1952 and one day destined as a four-star general to become the celebrated commander of Operation Desert Storm: "Suddenly, you raise your right hand and commit your life to serving your country. It's a profoundly moving moment."[55]

In this same season an exchange between two widely admired and accomplished senior leaders framed the dichotomy between attritional and developmental models of cadet development, a centrally important issue that would continue to be debated for a number of years to come.

In 1955 General Maxwell Taylor had become Army Chief of Staff. We have noted earlier how General Eisenhower had, when he was Chief of Staff, cautioned General Taylor about improper use of honor to enforce regulations. Now General Taylor similarly advised Major General Garrison Davidson, the current Superintendent. The purpose of the Honor System, he wrote, "is to inculcate in every cadet a code of conduct based upon unqualified honesty and truthfulness. The provisions of the system must be kept simple, scrupulously fair, and consistent with common sense. Above all things, it must not be used as a device to make easy the administration of the Corps of Cadets or the work of the Tactical Department."[56]

General Taylor—who had his own problems with the defense policies of President Dwight Eisenhower featuring reliance on nuclear retaliatory forces and in the process significantly diminishing the importance of the Army's role—nevertheless maintained an active interest in West Point throughout his tenure as Chief of Staff. In November 1957, for example, he wrote to General Davidson that "the overriding purpose of the Honor System is to eliminate cadets who by their conduct have created such doubt as to their integrity and honor that they are deemed unworthy of being members of the Corps of Cadets." But General Taylor also offered a perhaps surprisingly accommodating view of how to deal with less than egregious honor violations. "The Honor System should not, in my opinion, become a means for eliminating cadets guilty merely of thoughtless or perhaps inconsequential acts even in formal violation of the Honor Code which do not carry a strong inference of moral turpitude," Taylor wrote in this highly significant communication.[57]

Only weeks earlier, Taylor had raised a similar issue, one to which the Superintendent responded vigorously. "In the opinion of the [Honor] Committee," wrote General Davidson, "every individual able to qualify for the Military Academy and sufficiently interested in coming here is capable, even under the stresses of the first day, of understanding the broad, basic principles that a cadet does not lie, cheat, or steal." The Honor Committee also made the point that "we either have an Honor System or we do not. They recited innumerable difficulties that would arise were any 'gray' areas recognized and pointed out the gradual deterioration of the System that would result." Thus: "I am in accord with the views of the Cadet Honor Committee as illustrated above."[58]

Now Taylor explained his position in terms of preparing cadets for leadership in the Army at large. "As we both know," he told General Davidson, "right and wrong in life outside the Military Academy is not pure white and black. It is one of the requirements of military leadership to establish standards of justice and correct behavior among officers and men. It is a defective preparation for the exercise of this kind of leadership to allow our cadets to believe that justice can be administered by formula and without deep reflection upon circumstances and motivation. They should learn early in life to inject toleration, judgment of human factors, and appreciation of sincere repentance into their decisions affecting the careers of their fellow cadets."[59]

"I realize," Taylor continued, "that the kind of approach to honor questions which I am suggesting cannot be accomplished by fiat. I do feel, however, that by discussion with the senior cadets you and your officers can do much to orient their thinking along these lines. They should be convinced of the importance of judging every honor case on its own merits, developing a judicial approach of the kind which we hope they will use in the discharge of their official duties in later life."

General Taylor then suggested a mechanism by which he might be advised of whether such matters had been taken into consideration in the handling of honor cases. "I have in mind," he wrote, "requiring the Superintendent to state in his endorsement recommending discharge for a violation of honor that the Honor Committee finds and that he concurs that the breach of honor in question was of such a nature and occurred under such circumstances as to create serious doubt as to the moral attributes of the cadet in question and thus render his retention in the Corps of Cadets against the best interests of the Military Academy and the Military Service. I would hope that the requirement to make such a statement would induce the members of the Honor Committee to think deeply about the inherent merits of each case."[60]

General Taylor asked the Superintendent for his reaction to these thoughts, and of course General Davidson was quick to provide it. "As I understand your concern," he began, "it is that the approach of the Cadet Honor Committee is not a sympathetic and understanding one and that its procedures are not as deliberate and painstaking as might be desired, thus leading to elimination of men who by their very act of self-reporting have demonstrated they have absorbed our lessons of integrity." Then General Davidson sought to make sure that General Taylor appreciated the magnitude and significance of what he was proposing: "In view of this latter circumstance, you advocate a rather fundamental change in our Honor Code."[61]

General Davidson offered his view that the primary purpose of the Honor Committee was "keeping alive in the Corps the principles of the Honor Code, interpreting the requirements of the Honor System when necessary, and guarding against the birth of practices inconsistent with its tenets." Thus he viewed the eliminative process as secondary, "a distasteful task which is necessary in order to weed out those who demonstrate inability to meet the established standards." He suggested that the degree to which the Honor Committee handled such cases with appropriate consideration and understanding was demonstrated by "the relatively few cases in which a finding of guilty" was reached, citing the recent statistics: some 150 potential violations considered since the previous June, of which 21 were recommended for formal investigation. Only 13 wound up being heard by the Committee as a whole, with seven findings of guilty the result. Unintentional violators were not being punished as guilty, he said, and "we are even understanding in the case of the false statement that borders on inadvertence and is corrected immediately its full import has struck home."[62]

Now General Davidson gave the Chief of Staff what amounted to a tutorial, sort of a refresher course on the matter under consideration. In view of the fundamental nature of that matter, his remarks are worth quoting at length. "The Honor Committee gives these cases as mature and deliberate a treatment as their legal knowledge and judicial experience permits," he began. "Motivation is examined and plays an important part in the decision. . . . In all cases in which the individual has been found guilty, the motivation has been to avoid punishment or some similar unpleasantness." "But we don't punish for the circumstances that result in a lie but for the demonstrated instinct to deceive." "Certainly by the process we will lose a few good risks. True, some poorer risks, undiscovered, will graduate. It has been the Academy philosophy for a long time that it is necessary to hazard these few regret[t]able losses for the good of the many and of our country rather than dilute the Honor Code by accepting 'the little lie.' Since receiving your letter I have wracked my conscience to disturb this philosophy but, try as I may, I always return to acceptance of its wisdom—and overall justice."[63]

General Davidson advised the Chief of Staff that "the members of the Honor Committee are strongly opposed to having proven honor violators remain in the Corps." And, he added, "the members of the Committee are keenly aware that we are only six short years away from 1951." Then he closed with a heartfelt personal appeal: "So Max, I have searched my soul and my conscience with regard to the point of honor you have raised and have discussed it widely. I understand your point of view and have tried to bring myself around to it. I find I cannot do so voluntarily. I hope you will not insist that I try to convert the Corps to a philosophy on such an important matter in which I do not believe."[64]

Apparently the Chief of Staff was persuaded by General Davidson's impassioned response, for the advent of institutionalized discretion in honor cases remained still some distance in the future. Meanwhile an Honor Review Committee appointed by General Davidson concluded, in its May 1958 report, "that the Cadet Honor System is fundamentally sound; that those entrusted with its care and operation are alert to their responsibilities; that they are striving conscientiously to further the indoctrination of the Corps of Cadets in the basic tenets of the System and to clarify nebulous areas to eliminate misunderstandings."[65]

In the summer of 1960 Major General William Westmoreland (USMA 1936) was assigned to West Point as the new Superintendent. His three-year tenure would take the Military Academy into the Vietnam era, a period repeating the by-now familiar wartime turbulence, a reality that was to be intensified by a Westmoreland initiative. "One of my goals as superintendent," he later wrote, "was to increase the size of the Corps from approximately 2,400 cadets to 4,400, roughly the strength of the Brigade of Midshipmen at the Naval Academy."[66]

Historian Theodore Crackel, noting that expansion was an issue Westmoreland "had considered while he was on the Army staff before coming to West Point," concluded that "it became the central focus of his superintendency."[67] While Westmoreland was clearly the prime mover in bringing about this expansion, vigorously advocating and lobbying for it, authorization and implementation did not actually take place until after he had moved on. When the expansion began in 1964 it proved to be ill-timed, coinciding as it did with wartime stresses and greatly increasing—as had all such major increases in strength over short periods of time—the challenges of socializing incoming classes, particularly with respect to honor.[68]

Serious problems had already been flagged by Cadet George Schein in his 1962 Honor Book entry. "At this time the Corps does not feel it is a part of the honor system but instead feels that the system is something that is against them which they must in every way possible beat," he wrote. Schein suggested that the root of the problem lay in the perennial issue of use of honor to enforce regulations. His recommended solution was to "take as much as possible away from the honor system and place it under duty where in reality it belongs." That might, thought Schein, take ten years to accomplish.

In a dramatic illustration of how difficult it is to gauge the sometimes fluctuating state of honor commitment and observance within the Corps of Cadets, at virtually the same moment Cadet Schein was making his pessimistic assessment, a faculty honor review committee was reporting to the Superintendent its findings that "the whole atmosphere of Cadet Honor has improved since last year . . . and many of the shortcomings noted previously have been eliminated." And, complimenting Cadet Schein and his colleagues, the officer board stated its view that "the present First Class Honor Committee has done a tremendous job in handling the problems of the Cadet Honor Code."[69]

Non-Toleration

Those new to the subject of the Honor Code sometimes have difficulty accepting the non-toleration clause, the concluding portion of the Code which, following the familiar proscriptions against lying, cheating, and stealing, goes on to declare that cadets will not tolerate those who do. The reasons for the difficulty are obvious. First, and most important, is that adherence to non-toleration imposes a very heavy psychological burden and a very tough duty. Second, there is the necessity for moving beyond playground notions of proper ethical behavior, and for understanding and accepting the enforcement of standards that goes with becoming a member of a profession responsible for the public good and the nation's survival. Third, for young men and women who are new to a very challenging and in some respects threatening environment, one in which every day represents multiple challenges to be met and overcome academically, physically, and militarily, there is the felt need for friends and supporters. Thus, as USMA Historian Dr. Stephen Grove once delightfully described it to the Superintendent, "the concept of non-toleration exists like a delicate flower in rough combat terrain."[70]

Non-toleration, however, admits of no compromise, rough terrain or not. It is in fact at the very heart of the Honor Code. It is the imperative of professionalism. Every pursuit worthy of being considered a profession understands the necessity for its members to establish admirable standards of conduct in their work and then, of crucial importance, to uphold and defend those standards, both as individuals and corporately. With such aspirations come obligations, very demanding ones.

The military profession stands apart by virtue of the ultimate responsibilities of leaders in combat. Its mission of teaching impeccable standards of ethical behavior operates in parallel with the responsibility to weed out those who cannot or will not accept and adhere to those standards. In both aspects cadets themselves play the central role.

Exemplifying again the manner in which customs arose and were established first in practice, only later to be codified in written form, what we now know as the non-toleration clause was not incorporated into the written Honor Code until 1970. This comes as a surprise to many cadets of earlier years who seem to remember clearly that it was known and observed in their day. Certainly that was the fact in practice, if not in the written formulations of the Code. As early as the *1908 Bugle Notes* there is a statement definitively indicating cadet responsibility for non-toleration, in that "the high standards of integrity for which the institution is famous cannot be maintained if toleration for such is known. A thief, a liar, and a coward cannot be extenuated in the eyes of the Corps, and it is no part of the function of West Point to become a reformatory of morals."[71]

The *1921 Annual Report of the Superintendent,* who at that time was Brigadier General Douglas MacArthur, articulated both the responsibility for non-toleration and its origin within the Corps itself: In this century-old democracy of the cadet body, tradition has developed a group pride for the Honor of the Corps which is responsible for the maintenance of high standards of individual conduct. Under its inspiration each cadet not only models his own conduct along high standards, but is jealous of the actions of every other member insofar as those actions relate to the reputation or well-being of the whole. An unwritten code imposes an obligation on the part of each member of the corps to report voluntarily, even to the disregard of personal friendship, any deception or falsehood. The code, with its rigid high standards, has developed spontaneously from the experience of generations of cadets, so that the Corps painstakingly models its own life and conduct. It is not the result of a disciplinary system imposed from above, but of the better discipline emanating from within the student body itself.[72]

In 1922 the non-toleration obligation was specifically stated in regulations: "Any cadet in the Corps has the authority and is honor bound to report any cadet without regard to class or rank for a breach of honor."[73] Similarly we find in the 1925 *Bugle Notes*: "Everyone, offender or not, is honor bound to report any breach of honor which comes to his attention."[74] Much earlier than that, however, non-toleration was an established aspect of honor obligations. As noted by a later commission, "it was commonly and widely understood as far back as 1900 that non-toleration was implicit in the Code and that toleration was an honor offense. Over the years, some cadets were expelled for having tolerated cheating, without being convicted of cheating themselves." And, observed this report, "the toleration violation was a factor in the football-based cheating scandal of 1951."[75]

Later, still well before formal incorporation of non-toleration in the written Code, the existence and imperative of the practice was explained in a guide for officers stationed at the Military Academy: "One of the tenets of the Code which [cadets] have elected to support and cherish is that each cadet is responsible for ensuring compliance with the Honor Code and System. If he does not do so, he too is violating the Honor Code. The effective self-policing of the Honor System is one of the major features which sets it above other such systems."[76]

Once non-toleration had been formally added to the Honor Code—which then read, in its classic formulation, "A cadet will not lie, cheat, or steal, nor tolerate those who do"—the official USCC pamphlet issued by the Honor Committee often included an explanation of the "philosophy" of non-toleration such as this: "The Honor Code is not an all-inclusive prescription for moral behavior, but it does contain a set of irreducible standards common to all honorable persons—we will not lie, cheat, or steal. Additionally, the Honor Code includes the fundamental tenet of self-enforcement—the requirement that we will not tolerate actions of those who are unable to adhere to the fundamental standards of conduct embodied in the Honor Code."[77]

Nevertheless the later Posvar Commission's report and other periodic evaluations of the Honor Code were understanding of the stringent demands placed on cadets, especially those newly introduced to concepts of professionalism and corporate responsibility for the enforcement of standards, by the obligations of non-toleration. Posvar acknowledged "the agonizing dilemma posed for cadets by the non-toleration clause, which imposes an obligation that many cadets see as conflicting with personal loyalty and the bonds of comradeship."[78]

Compounding this challenge, at least in some cases, was that serious breakdowns in observance of the Honor Code and operation of the Honor System were observed to have "correlated with internal group loyalties contradictory to the spirit of the Corps of Cadets itself," held Posvar. Such groups were "prep-school friends, company enclaves, and, most seriously, intercollegiate athletic teams."[79]

The Corps more generally has seemed to understand, support, and implement non-toleration. A useful commentary on this topic was evoked by a *New York Times* editorial in February 1965. The anonymous writer had alleged there was an unwritten law at the Military Academy that a cadet would not "turn in" another cadet for an honor violation. The Honor Committee Chairman commented in a memorandum to the Commandant of Cadets. "This contention," he began, is "unfair and totally unfounded. Of the possible cases brought to the attention of the Cadet Honor Committee since June 1964, 39% were reported by other cadets and 48% were self-reported cases. Of those cases reported by other cadets, 50% were reported by a cadet of the same class as the individual accused. These cadets who reported violations by classmates have continued normal relations with their classmates and other cadets." Thus: "These facts indicate a healthy attitude towards the toleration aspect of the Cadet Honor Code."[80]

The many commissions and study groups that have, over the years, been asked to examine honor at West Point have been unanimous in their conclusion that non-toleration is an indispensable element. But a major cheating episode in 1976, to be discussed more fully later, introduced some new issues into the discussion. Thus, beginning with the Borman Commission in 1976, there developed growing sentiment that, in order to encourage cadets to support and act in accordance with the duty of non-toleration, some provision should be made for sanctions other than dismissal of cadets found guilty of an honor violation. Borman stated such a view flatly and explicitly: "Sanctions other than dismissal should be authorized for violations of the Honor Code."[81]

Probably the Borman Commission has, of all the major study groups, been the most permissive in terms of its recommendations in this realm. Said Borman: "The nontoleration clause should be retained. However, a cadet should have options in addition to *reporting* an honor violation. A cadet who perceived a violation must counsel, warn, or report the violator. Some action is required, as distinguished from tacit acquiescence."[82]

The 1978 Honor Chairman, Cadet Robert Lamb, provided a powerful statement of the opposing view in his Honor Book entry. "The non-toleration clause of the Code has been and remains the most ambiguous and the most difficult to teach to men and women who enter the Military Academy," he acknowledged. "I believe this clause is essential if the Code is to continue to be a dynamic and moving force for moral and ethical development of cadets."[83]

In the wake of the Borman report the Superintendent convened a Special Committee on Nontoleration tasked to "examine the total issue and philosophy involved and to recommend ways that nontoleration can be strengthened and improved." Colonel Hal Rhyne, Special Assistant to the Commandant for Honor Matters, and Cadet Michael Ivy, the 1977 Honor Committee Chairman, co-chaired the committee, which concluded that "without the nontoleration clause, the Honor Code would be vitiated, and that a major facet of the strict adherence to a code of ethical conduct as a device to shape character—a major tenet of the Military Academy—would be obscured." "Ultimately," therefore, "the committee came to the conclusion that nontoleration was a vital and necessary aspect of the Honor Code."[84]

The committee understood full well, however, that there were problems with non-toleration and that these needed to be addressed. As members put it, "There were no illusions regarding the effectiveness of the nontoleration clause in recent years and specifically in light of the EE 304 experience." (The reference was to honor problems in a course known as Electrical Engineering 304, about which more later.) Citing the record of the previous seven years, they noted that only two cases of toleration had been reported, and that "during the past summer, not a single case of toleration in the EE 304 matter was reported to the Honor Committee." Thus: "Clearly, the sense of the committee that nontoleration was a vital aspect of the Honor Code was not being shared by the entire Corps at large."[85]

Two remedies suggested themselves. "It is in education that the Code and the spirit of the Code will be sustained," the committee maintained. In addition, "the Committee concluded that a modification to the single sanction would assist in overcoming the apparent reluctance of some cadets to report observed violations." Discussion of that finding led to "the recommendation for a dual sanction which would allow, under certain compelling circumstances, an opportunity for a cadet found guilty of an honor violation to resume his place in the Corps."[86]

In 1977, when the Military Academy was struggling to recover from the very serious honor crisis of the previous year, the Superintendent, Lieutenant General Sidney Berry, cited "one of the most fragile aspects of the Honor Code—the non-toleration clause." Fragile it might be, but—as we observed at the very beginning of this work in discussing the elements of a profession—it was equally indispensable. General Berry described non-toleration as "essential to the Honor Code, for it requires that each cadet be an active participant in the Honor System and it inculcates in cadets the higher loyalties and keen sense of duty required by the profession of arms."[87]

General Andrew Goodpaster, who followed General Berry as Superintendent in the summer of 1977, was equally clear on the essentiality of the non-toleration clause, as well as on the demands it placed on each individual to serve as a guardian of professional standards and hence, as we have noted, as a true member of a profession. General Goodpaster said the following in testifying before a congressional committee: "It is recognized that the non-toleration clause is definitely more demanding on the individual because it requires each cadet to become a moral guardian of the code, ensuring that suspected violations witnessed or known are reported and investigated. In doing so, the cadet acts in response to a firm commitment to integrity, a higher loyalty that must be pre-eminent over individual desires, friendships, or considerations of personal advantage."[88]

Addressing the same topic, the Posvar Commission subsequently reported that "discussions within the Commission and with outside ethicists emphasize that 'non-toleration,' meaning expulsion or severe punishment of any professional who passively accepts a breach of a system of professional integrity, is a keystone of that system."[89] It also affirmed that "non-toleration—prohibition by a professional group against violations of its norms—is integral to the spirit of the Code and essential to its viability."[90]

Writing in 1989, the Posvar Commission also noted "a connection between the perceived single sanction of expulsion, or its high likelihood, and a reluctance of some cadets to vote for a guilty verdict when there are ameliorating circumstances." And, added this assessment, "The statistical evidence of this is strong."[91] A year later, when Dr. Posvar met with Army Chief of Staff General Carl Vuono to review the status of the Army's actions on the Commission's twenty-five recommendations, twenty-three had been fully implemented and one partially implemented. The one recommendation not implemented, noted a contemporary account, "was a proposal to change the wording of the Honor Code's non-toleration tenet. Based on a survey of the Corps of Cadets, two-thirds of cadets opposed the change, so the superintendent decided not to implement it."[92]

The Posvar report also noted that, "over the long history of the Code and System, and particularly in the last 70 years [since the end of World War I, then], enforcement of the non-toleration clause has been a recurring and thorny issue. There have been recent occasions when, on the testimony of cadets themselves, acceptance of the non-toleration clause was in serious doubt."[93] This is an absolutely crucial matter, for if those joining a profession fail in their responsibility to monitor and police its standards, the profession itself will lose credibility and effectiveness. What cadets, and officers later on, are asked to do is put loyalty to the mission and to the larger organization ahead of personal ties to others, especially when those others have forfeited their right to the brotherhood of honorable soldiers by failing to live up to its standards. One Commandant of Cadets put it this way: The obligation of non-toleration requires the cadet "to value integrity more than friendship or close association. It requires him to act in response to a higher loyalty, a loyalty which must be pre-eminent over individual desires, friendships, or considerations of personal advantage."[94]

In earlier days cadets learned about the professional obligation underlying non-toleration by reading "Worth's Battalion Orders," which appeared in many annual editions of *Bugle Notes*. Thus stated Brevet Major William Jenkins Worth:

> But an officer on duty knows no one—to be partial is to dishonor both himself and the object of his ill-advised favor. What will be thought of him who exacts of his friends that which disgraces him? Look at him who winks at and overlooks offenses in one, which he causes to be punished in another, and contrast him with the inflexible soldier who does his duty faithfully, notwithstanding it occasionally wars with his private feelings. The conduct of one will be venerated and emulated, the other detested as a satire upon soldiership and honor.[95]

Major Worth, longtime (1820–1828) Commandant of Cadets, issued this straightforward view early in his tenure. Surely it deserves to be considered among the antecedents of the Honor Code, and especially of its non-toleration clause.

In a much later era, Deputy Commandant Colonel Clayton Moran, addressing the incoming Honor Committee during June Week of 1972, likewise laid it on the line: "A friendship changes if the friend concerned violates the Code."[96]

He might have done well to also quote the Roman philosopher Marcus Tullius Cicero, himself a soldier, who wrote: "Let this be ordained as the first law of friendship: Ask of friends only what is honorable; do for friends only what is honorable."[97]

Notes

1 Theodore J. Crackel, *West Point*, p. 207.
2 Memorandum to Commandant of Cadets, from Cadet Captain Ralph M. Scott, Commander, 2nd Regiment, USCC, Subject: Plan for Organization of the Plebe System, 19 February 1943, Adjutant General Files, 351.1 Honor System, USMA Archives. The Superintendent, Maj. Gen. F. B. Wilby, commented favorably on Mr. Scott's memorandum in his own 24 February 1943 memorandum to the Commandant.
3 USMA Historian Dr. Stephen Grove has provided this useful language from the *1946 Annual Report of the Superintendent*: "The split of the old Class of 1947 was accomplished on the basis of individual preference and maturity. The more mature cadets were assigned to the new Class of 1947 and the less mature cadets assigned to the Class of 1948."
4 *2006 Register of Graduates*, p. 3-163 and passim.
5 *1944 Bugle Notes*, p. 37.
6 Memorandum, Brig. Gen. George Honnen, Commandant of Cadets, for Superintendent, USMA, 8 January 1946, USMA Archives.
7 Martin Blumenson, "America's World War II Leaders in Europe: Some Thoughts," p. 11.
8 Maj. Gen. Maxwell D. Taylor, *West Point Honor System*, p. 2.
9 Ibid., pp. 2, 3.
10 Summary of Interview with the Chief of Staff, 24 January 1946, Maj. Gen. Maxwell D. Taylor, Superintendent, dated 28 January 1946, Adjutant General Files, 351.1 Honor System, 1946–1948, USMA Archives.
11 Letter, Maj. Gen. Maxwell D. Taylor, Superintendent USMA, to Gen. Dwight D. Eisenhower, Army Chief of Staff, 8 January1946, Adjutant General Files, 351.1 Honor System, 1946–1948, USMA Archives.
12 Author recollection.
13 Memorandum, Col. Paul D. Harkins, Commandant of Cadets, to Superintendent, USMA, Subject: The Honor System and Academic Procedures, 11 May 1950, USMA Archives.
14 Ibid.
15 Ibid. The archival record, at least insofar as I have been able to discover, does not provide additional information on this matter. Approximately forty letters sent by the author to surviving members of the faculty from that time brought a number of interesting replies but did not serve to locate anyone who had knowledge of the event, much less what may have precipitated it.
16 Public Information Office USMA Release, "Breach of West Point Honor Code Announced," 3 August 1951.
17 Lt. Gen. Arthur S. Collins Jr., Senior Officer Oral History Interview, U.S. Army Military History Institute.
18 Ibid.
19 Ibid.
20 *Proceedings of a Board of Officers*, p. 13.
21 Ibid.
22 Ibid., p. 7.

23 Ibid., p. 20.

24 *Notes of a Board of Officers*, p. 26.

25 Memo for the Record, Col. James B. Leer (PIO), Subject: Dismissal of 90 Cadets, 2 August 1951, Adjutant General Files, 351.1 Honor Violations (90) (PIO File), 1951–1952, USMA Archives.

26 Ibid.

27 Cadet David C. Ahearn (USMA 1952), "The Honor Code at West Point: A Statement from the Corps of Cadets," *Assembly* (January 1952), p. 6. An editor's note indicated that Cadet Ahearn had shown his article to First Captain Cadet Gordon D. Carpenter and the Honor Committee Chairman, Cadet Thomas W. Collier, and that both "feel that Cadet Ahearn's article accurately reflects the consensus of the feeling of the Corps."

28 Ibid.

29 *Final Report of the Special Commission of the Chief of Staff*, p. 12.

30 Letter, Lt. Gen. Maxwell D. Taylor to Superintendent, USMA, 3 August 1951, Proceedings of the Academic Board, Volume 63, 1951, USMA Archives.

31 Academic Board Meeting, 21 January 1952, Proceedings of the Academic Board, Volume 64, 1952, USMA Archives.

32 Ibid.

33 "Analysis of Correspondence and Press Items, 1 September 1951," File: Honor Code, USMA Archives.

34 *Life* (20 August 1951), p. 26.

35 Earl Blaik, *The Red Blaik Story* (New Rochelle: Arlington House, 1974), pp. 444-445.

36 Maj. Gen. Frederick A. Irving, "The Recent Violations of the Honor Code at West Point," *Assembly* (October 1951), p. 7.

37 Memorandum, Report of Board, Honorable Learned Hand to Secretary of the Army, 25 July 1951, USMA Archives.

38 "Honor Violations at West Point, 1951: A Case Study," p. 27, USMA Archives. Later some apologists for the cheaters sought to impugn Colonel Collins' motives and integrity, but without success. Wrote Thomas E. Courant, who had detailed knowledge of many of the people involved in the scandal as cadet in charge of the legitimate academic coaches for athletes: "I can assure you that (then) Lt. Col. Arthur 'Ace' Collins was a decent, honest, fair, conscientious soldier whose report contains the very best telling of the truth." Letter to Frank DeFord, 25 January 2002, copy provided the author by Col. Courant.

39 Ibid.

40 Excerpt, Conclusions of Bartlett Board, 31 August 1951, USMA Archives.

41 *Proceedings of a Board of Officers*, 13 August 1951, Adjutant General Files, 351.1 Honor Violations, 1951–1952, USMA Archives.

42 *Honor Guide for Officers*, p. 14.

43 Sidney Forman, "Scandal Among Cadets," p. 490.

44 Ibid.. pp. 490-491.

45 Capt. John S. D. Eisenhower, "West Point's Honor System Is as Broad as a Man's Life," article written for the Associated Press, File: Honor Code, USMA Archives.

46 Memorandum, Curriculum Committee, USMA, Subject: Recommendations of the 1952 Board of Visitors Concerning the U.S.M.A. Curriculum, 1 November 1952, Proceedings of the Academic Board, Volume 64, 1952, USMA Archives.

47 Memorandum, Col. Charles R. Broshous (Chairman, Faculty Advisory Committee for the Cadet Honor Code) to Superintendent, USMA, Subject: Review of Honor System, USCC, 8 May 1956, Adjutant General Files, 351.1 Honor System, USMA Archives.

48 Ibid.

49 Memorandum, Brig. Gen. T. D. Stamps (Dean of the Academic Board) to C/S [Chief of Staff], USMA, 8 August 1956, Adjutant General Files, 351.1 Honor System, USMA Archives.

50 Ibid.

51 Ibid.

52 Memorandum, Subject: Report of Committee Appointed to Review Cadet Honor Code, 13 May 1957, USMA Archives.

53 *USCC Pamphlet 632-1*, August 1992, p. 2.

54 A current senior faculty officer who reviewed this manuscript noted that these comments demonstrated how West Point at that time openly used an "attritional" model of development, as opposed to what he described as the "developmental" model currently in place. This, he observed, "helps to explain why USMA leaders and cadets [of the earlier day] could be so uncompromising when it came to the Honor Code."

55 Gen. H. Norman Schwarzkopf, "Introduction" to Robert Cowley and Thomas Guinzburg, ed., *West Point*, p. 14.

56 Letter, Gen. Maxwell D. Taylor, Army Chief of Staff, to Maj. Gen. Garrison H. Davidson, USMA Superintendent, 14 July 1956, Adjutant General Files, 351.1 Honor System, USMA Archives.

57 Letter, Gen. Maxwell D. Taylor (Army Chief of Staff) to Lt. Gen. Garrison H. Davidson (Superintendent USMA), 1 November 1957, Adjutant General Files, 351.1 Honor System, USMA Archives.

58 Letter, Lt. Gen. Garrison H. Davidson (Superintendent, USMA) to Gen. Maxwell D. Taylor (Army Chief of Staff), 18 October 1957, Adjutant General Files, 351.1 Honor System, USMA Archives.

59 Letter, Gen. Maxwell D. Taylor (Army Chief of Staff) to Lt. Gen. Garrison H. Davidson (Superintendent USMA), 1 November 1957, Adjutant General Files, 351.1 Honor System, USMA Archives.

60 Ibid.

61 Letter, Lt. Gen. Garrison H. Davidson (Superintendent USMA) to Gen. Maxwell D. Taylor (Army Chief of Staff), 4 December 1957, Adjutant General Files, 351.1 Honor System, USMA Archives.

62 Ibid.

63 Ibid.

64 Ibid. On 31 July 1958 General Davidson informed General Taylor that "as occurred with the Class of 1957, the trend in honor discharges continued to increase slightly with the Class of 1958; however, it now appears to be leveling out at a loss rate of between 1.5% and 2%." DA Form 1613-2, Superintendent USMA to Chief of Staff DA, Adjutant General Files, 351.1 Honor System (1958), USMA Archives.

65 Memorandum, 1958 Honor Review Committee to Superintendent USMA, Subject: Report of the 1958 Honor Review Committee, 21 May 1958, Adjutant General Files, 351.1 Honor System (1958), USMA Archives. Members of the Committee were Col. Vincent J. Esposito (Chairman), Col. Julian J. Ewell, and Lt. Col. Amos A. Jordan Jr.

66 Gen. William C. Westmoreland, *A Soldier Reports*, p. 36.

67 Theodore J. Crackel, *The Illustrated History of West Point*, p. 263.

68 The Class of 1967 (admitted in 1963) graduated 583 men. The next three classes graduated 706, 800, and 749 respectively, representing an average increase of about 28 percent over a very short period. *2000 Register of Graduates*, passim.

69 Memorandum, Honor Review Committee to Superintendent, Subject: Report, 2 April 1962, USMA Archives. The committee's members were Col. Elvin R. Heiberg (Chairman), Col. Frederick C. Lough, and Col. Paul V. Tuttle.

70 USMA Historian, DF [Disposition Form] to Superintendent, Subject: Environmental Factors Which Led to the Honor Scandals of 1951 and 1976, 21 October 1988, Palmer Files.

71 As cited by Maj. John H. Beasley in "The USMA Honor System," p. 6.

72 *1921 Annual Report of the Superintendent, United States Military Academy*, p. 8.

73 Orders, USCC, 1922, as quoted in Compilation, Lt. Col. Roger H. Nye, Department of Social Sciences, 1 February [1968?], File: Honor Code—Historical (JUL 67–JUN 70), USMA Archives.

74 *1925 Bugle Notes*, p. 57. In reviewing this manuscript Colonel Lance Betros, Head of the USMA Department of History, pointed out that the non-toleration clause had appeared in USMA regulations prior to official articulation of the Honor Code.

75 *Final Report of the Special Commission of the Chief of Staff on the Honor Code and Honor System at the United States Military Academy*, 30 May 1989, pp. 10-11.

76 *Honor Guide for Officers*, p. 5.

77 *USCC Pamphlet 632-1*, June 1977, p. 3.

78 *Final Report of the Special Commission of the Chief of Staff on the Honor Code and Honor System at the United States Military Academy*, 30 May 1989, p. 12.

79 Ibid.

80 Memorandum, Stanley G. Genega, Chairman, Cadet Honor Committee, to Commandant of Cadets, Subject: Editorial Comment, *New York Times*, 6 February 1965, dated 11 February 1965, File: Honor Code—Historical (JUL 64–JUN 65), USMA Archives.

81 *Report to the Secretary of the Army by the Special Commission on the United States Military Academy*, 15 December 1976, p. 19. The Borman Commission, which rendered this report, was appointed in the wake of a 1976 cheating scandal involving cadets enrolled in a course known as Electrical Engineering 304 (EE 304), about which more will be said in a later chapter.

82 Ibid. Emphasis supplied.

83 Cadet Lamb recalled his meetings with the Naval Academy's Honor Chairman and conversations with midshipmen familiar with the Naval Academy code and system. Each time, he said, he had become "more convinced that our non-toleration clause is necessary. In lieu of the non-toleration clause, the Naval Academy code and system substitute flexibility at the individual midshipman level in handling of apparent violations, yet the problems and inconsistencies which attend the flexibility are of such seriousness that, in my judgment, the value of the flexibility is negated."

84 Memorandum, Superintendent's Special Committee on Nontoleration, to Superintendent, Subject: Report of Superintendent's Special Committee on Nontoleration, 27 May 1977, Adjutant General Files, 1011-01 Curriculum Approval Files: Honor Code (1977), USMA Archives.

85 Ibid.

86 Ibid.

87 Letter, Lt. Gen. Sidney B. Berry, Superintendent, to West Point Graduates, 18 February 1977, USMA Archives. In 1974, when the Johns Hopkins University very reluctantly discontinued an undergraduate honor system that had been in use for decades, President Steven Muller described as the "greatest flaw" causing the system to fail "the unwillingness of students to turn each other in when offenses against academic integrity were observed." He cited as some of the causes of this reluctance "strong peer group orientation among young people, the growing tendency in our whole society to look the other way from trouble, and the regrettable fact that academic dishonesty is now more evident in pre-college experience." These views were reproduced and distributed to the West Point faculty in a 20 July 1976 Memorandum from the Dean, Brig. Gen. Frederick A. Smith Jr., USMA Archives.

88 Statement, Lt. Gen. Andrew J. Goodpaster, Superintendent USMA, before the Subcommittee on Military Personnel of the Committee on Armed Services, House of Representatives, West Point Honor Code, 5 October 1977.

89 *Final Report of the Special Commission of the Chief of Staff on the Honor Code and Honor System at the United States Military Academy*, 30 May 1989, p. 13.

90 Ibid., p. 15.

91 Ibid., p. 13.

92 Col. Larry R. Donnithorne, "An Update on Honor at USMA," *Assembly* (September 1990), p. 4.

93 Ibid. It seems clear that the expectations and outlooks of entering cadets are an important factor shaping their willingness to accept responsibility for non-toleration. The Posvar Commission stressed the importance of shaping accurate expectations and of character as a selection criterion: "The Commission is concerned that other sectors of the whole recruiting system, beyond the Academy, may give too little attention to the ethical qualities of candidates and to the ethical commitment expected of them." And: "Everyone involved in recruiting should be advised that personal character is a fundamental criterion for admission to the USMA. Those to be informed are applicants, guidance counselors, USMA representatives, coaches, and Congressmen," p. 16.

94 Memorandum for the Record, Maj. Gen. Philip R. Feir, Commandant of Cadets, Subject: After Action Report, 12 April 1975, USMA Archives. This massive document includes a 98-page memorandum and an additional seventeen attachments.

95 To be found, for example, in the *1964 Bugle Notes*, p. 115. Major Worth's Battalion Orders were dated 22 December 1820.

96 Deputy Commandant Col. Clayton L. Moran, Talk to 1973 Honor Committee, June Week 1972, File: Honor Code—Historical (JUL 70–JUN 72), USMA Archives.

97 In *On Friendship*, or *Laelius*. There are many variations in translation, another being: "We may then lay down this rule of friendship: neither ask nor consent to do what is wrong." Cicero also maintains that "true friendship is possible only between good men." See Ancient History Sourcebook at www.fordham.edu/Halsall/ancient/cicero-friendship.html.

Colonel Sylvanus Thayer, West Point's Superintendent 1817–1833, established the ethical climate and military and academic regimes that earned him the title "Father of the Military Academy."   Author Photograph

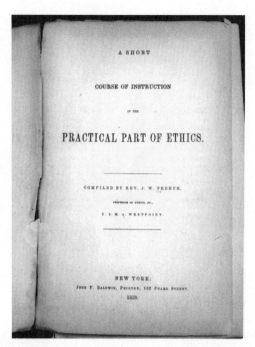

A SHORT

COURSE OF INSTRUCTION

IN THE

PRACTICAL PART OF ETHICS.

COMPILED BY REV. J. W. FRENCH,

PROFESSOR OF ETHICS, &C.,

U. S. M. A. WESTPOINT.

NEW YORK:
JOHN F. BALDWIN, PRINTER, 102 PEARL STREET.
1858.

The Rev. J. W. French, long-time USMA Chaplain and Professor of Ethics, published successive editions of this influential work on ethics.   USMA Library

Colonel Paul S. Reinecke, Class of 1911, composed the stirring words of the Alma Mater while still a cadet.   Reinecke Family Collection

The Class of 1923 Honor Committee was the first officially constituted, replacing the Vigilance Committees of earlier years.   1923 Howitzer

KLEITZ   MUNDELL   SILLS   BONNER   LINCOLN, T. J.   O'MALLEY   LARSON
HINE   FIELDS, K. E.   DOWNING, E. B.   PARK, R.   FULLER, W. H. G.

HONOR COMMITTEE

The Class of 1933 Honor Committee produced, then issued to the Corps on its own authority, the first written articulation of elements of the Honor Code and System.   1933 Howitzer

Cadet Lawrence J. Lincoln drafted the first written document on the Honor
Code and System, typing it late at night in his tent during summer camp.
1933 Howitzer

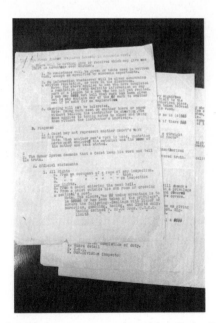

This excerpt of the original document produced by Cadet Lincoln, preserved in
the USMA Archives, includes the fundamental imperative that "the Honor System demands that a Cadet keep his word and tell the truth."   USMA Archives

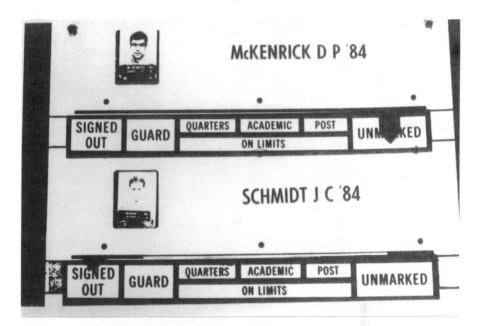

The Absence Card, shown here in one of its several versions, was for many years a feature of cadet life until finally being phased out in about 1990. USMA Archives

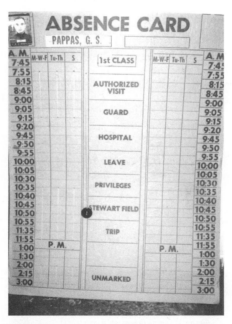

Another version of the Absence Card, which in its classic use placed cadets on their honor to observe regulations relating to the "five points" of gambling, hazing, limits, liquor and narcotics while absent with their card marked. Nininger Hall Display

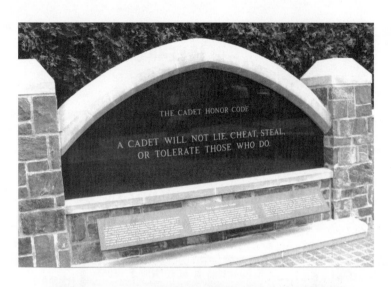

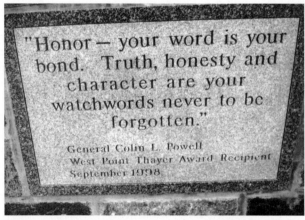

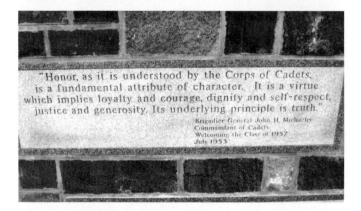

The Honor Plaza, located where most cadets pass it on the way to and from class every day, features the Honor Code in its current formulation and relevant quotations dealing with honor and fidelity.   Class of 1957 Project File

5 | Turbulence

The Vietnam Era

During the long years of the Vietnam War, as always, West Point neither existed nor functioned in a vacuum. Rather it was influenced by the currents of change and challenge in the larger society, not least because each year a new cohort of cadets reflected and brought with them as they entered West Point the attitudes and outlooks of that society. Meanwhile the Military Academy sent its own Superintendent off to war. General William Westmoreland, who had headed West Point during the period 1960-1963, then briefly commanded the XVIII Airborne Corps, was selected as Deputy Commander, U.S. Military Assistance Command, Vietnam, where he soon moved up to the top spot.

En route to Vietnam General Westmoreland visited West Point, where he made an address to the Corps of Cadets. During this brief stopover General Westmoreland also arranged to drive down to New York City and call on one of his famous predecessors as Superintendent, General of the Army Douglas MacArthur, who in his later years resided in the Waldorf Towers in Manhattan. MacArthur, Westmoreland later confided, gave him some advice on how to treat South Vietnamese officers: "Like cadets."[1]

General MacArthur had himself visited West Point not long before, a memorable occasion on which he was awarded the Sylvanus Thayer Medal and gave the Corps what came to be a very famous address. MacArthur was a wonderful speaker—dramatic, a master of timing, good resonant voice—and he made the most of all those qualities during what he told the cadets was his "final roll call with you." His theme, of course, was the Academy's motto. "Duty—Honor—Country. Those three hallowed words," he told his rapt audience of cadets and faculty, "reverently dictate what you ought to be, what you can be, what you will be. They are your rallying points: to build courage when courage seems to fail; to regain faith when there seems to be little cause for faith; to create hope when hope becomes forlorn."[2]

The words of the motto, MacArthur continued, "build your basic character, they mold you for your future roles as the custodians of the nation's defense, they make you strong enough to know when you are weak, and brave enough to face yourself when you are afraid. They teach you to be proud and unbending in honest failure, but humble and gentle in success; not to substitute words for actions, nor to seek the path of comfort, but to face the stress and spur of difficulty and challenge; to learn to stand up in the storm but to have compassion on those who fall; to master yourself before you seek to master others; to have a heart that is clean, a goal that is high; to learn to laugh yet never forget how to weep; to reach into the future yet never neglect the past; to be serious yet never to take yourself too seriously; to be modest so that you will remember the implicate of true greatness, the open mind of true wisdom, the meekness of true strength. They give you a temper of will, a quality of the imagination, a vigor of the emotions, a freshness of the deep springs of life, a temperamental predominance of courage over timidity, an appetite for adventure over love of ease. They create in your heart the sense of wonder, the unfailing hope of what next, and the joy and inspiration of life. They teach you in this way to be an officer and a gentleman."[3]

A more insightful, or more inspiring, gloss on the full meaning and implications of the motto would be hard to imagine. It was a timely message, too, for West Point, like the rest of America, was already being buffeted by powerful cross-currents of outlook on such fundamental issues as the proper balance between rights and responsibilities, between duties and entitlements, and on the proper course in the war then building in Vietnam and other parts of Southeast Asia.

The years of the Vietnam War (1960–1975) were particularly difficult and turbulent ones in America, pitting those who opposed the war against those who fought it, those in leadership roles against those who challenged authority of any kind, and often those of the younger generation against their elders. Fortunately for the Army, it was led during the years of the buildup in Vietnam by General Harold K. Johnson (USMA 1933). Said another senior officer admiringly, "He had a moral center to him. His moral compass was headed north. It wasn't headed north-northeast or north-northwest. He had a hard core ethical approach to problems."[4]

One of General Johnson's last duties before retirement was to deliver the commencement address to West Point's Class of 1968. He began by recalling that, at the graduation of his own class in 1933, the speaker had been General Douglas MacArthur, who stressed that "any nation that would keep its self-respect must keep alive its martial ardor and be prepared to defend itself." That warning had remained with him, Johnson said. "I pondered a long time about what I, who stand in the dimming twilight of my active service, could say to you who are the most recent marchers to join the Long Gray Line." Very conscious of the continuing war in Vietnam, which had dominated his four years as Chief of Staff, Johnson said, "It is sobering to recall how much has happened and yet how little has changed since that day when I listened to General MacArthur at Trophy Point. Men cried for peace then; men cry for peace now."[5]

In such circumstances General Johnson delivered a message emphasizing practicality and realism. "Above all," he said, "we must distinguish between the world of our dreams and aspirations and the tough, cruel demanding world of reality where advantage, gain, and privilege are accompanied by work, sweat, tears, and accountability for our actions." Those were the words of a man who had survived forty-one months of captivity in Japanese prison camps during World War II, won a Distinguished Service Cross as an infantry battalion commander in the first desperate days of the Korean War, and led the Army through the years of force buildup in Vietnam. "Against that backdrop of reality," he said, "you are about to become a part of an institution on which the very life of the Nation depends." In a closing insight we might now view as having great contemporary relevance, he laid out the fundamental aims of our national military philosophy: "We seek, first of all, to deter war and then, when deterrence fails, to win any kind of war that may be forced upon us without destroying the institutions of our civilization in the process."[6]

The war that the Class of 1968 would soon be joining was having a hugely divisive impact on the nation. At West Point, noted a later Superintendent, "resignations increased to a peak of 32 percent in 1970, surpassing peaks for previous wartime periods." There were undoubtedly multiple reasons for that, but he noted in particular that "cadets suffered often from the stinging criticisms of the military which became common and from the dichotomy of values and standards between the civilian and military communities."[7]

Even so, noted Lieutenant General Sidney Berry in a retrospective assessment, "The influence of Vietnam . . . affected the West Point staff and faculty more directly than the Corps of Cadets." Repetitive assignments to Vietnam induced abnormal turbulence within the faculty, and as a consequence "teaching and supervisory effectiveness suffered." Moreover, "each group of returnees from Vietnam introduced into the West Point community different experiences, attitudes, and levels of personal satisfaction or frustration, depending upon the nature of their most recent service in Vietnam." A pervasive feeling of sadness gradually permeated the community, induced in large part by the heavy cost in friends and colleagues exacted by the war. There were 264 West Point graduates killed in Vietnam, 114 of whom were buried at West Point. In only two years, 1968 and 1969, 49 war-related funerals were held at West Point. These had a "strong emotional impact" on the community, in particular on "members of the tenured faculty and their families . . . as month after month they attended funerals of many young officers who, as cadets, had become their friends."[8]

Cadet attitudes were, of course, also affected by the course of the war and the controversy it engendered. They were, recalled General Berry, "besieged by news media and peers alike with arguments against violence, against warfare, against the military, against involvement in Vietnam, against West Point, and against the national economic priority given defense over domestic programs." Also "cadets were confronted constantly with the values of their civilian peers which, to a greater extent than ever before, were at variance with the values and expectations of West Point." These forces inevitably had a negative effect on cadet outlooks, disconcertingly revealed when only 47 percent of the Class of 1971 answered "yes" when polled, shortly before their graduation, as to whether, if they could reconsider their decision, they would still come to the Military Academy.[9]

Overlaid almost exactly on the Vietnam War period was another disruptive development at the Academy—a massive increase in the size of the Corps of Cadets and parallel increases in staff and faculty. Under legislation signed into law in March 1964, the authorized strength of the Corps of Cadets went from

2529 to 4417—a jump of roughly 75 percent—to be achieved over a relatively short time. Just how short a time is illustrated by the growing size of entering classes over the twelve-year period beginning in 1964: 991, 1138, 1019, 1054, 1244, 1439, 1377, 1339, 1378, 1376, 1435, and 1435. That constituted a 15 percent increase from the first to the second year, and 45 percent from beginning to end of the period.[10]

At the same time, the staff and faculty grew from 412 in 1962 to 649 in 1975, an increase of about 57 percent, during a time when, as noted, turbulence of assignments was high. These developments, acknowledged General Berry, "affected the cohesiveness, attitudes, outlook, and environment" of West Point's people and the institution itself. There was, he added, "reason to believe that West Point's expansion occurred at a faster rate than its assimilative processes and that it became more impersonal and less cohesive."[11] Noting how the expansion of the faculty lagged so far behind that of the Corps of Cadets itself, a current department head suggested that may have been another factor in the weakening of the Honor System in the 1970s.[12] These developments, one almost surely must conclude, would be reflected in honor problems soon to come to light.

In July 1971 Colonel Robert G. Gard Jr. published an insightful analysis entitled "The Military and American Society" in *Foreign Affairs*. Gard described how the demands of combat operations called for "a set of values which to some extent are contrary to those held by liberal civilian society,"[13] but also postulated the military profession's need "to adapt traditional concepts and practices of military professionalism to changing requirements and radically new demands."[14]

Colonel Gard's conclusion was that "traditional values are not outdated; those vital to success in battle still must be inculcated in servicemen who may be required to engage in or support combat, both to ensure operational success and to prevent unnecessary loss of life."[15] At West Point, the challenge was to make that case in a persuasive way to each class of entering cadets, while in the Army at large it was both to attract the necessary talent to man what would soon be an all-volunteer force and to shape it into a cohesive, disciplined, and committed whole.[16]

In 1971 there appears a particularly poignant entry in the Honor Book, written by Cadet Patrick Finnegan, later brigadier general and Dean of the Military Academy: "The Honor Code is the most important thing that the Corps has and it sometimes seems that it is slipping away." Two years later Honor Committee Chairman Thomas Lubozynski had a more encouraging report. "My committee finally made some progress in destroying some beliefs of the selectivity of the Honor Committee," he said. "We found [meaning convicted] any cadet who we felt was guilty of an honor violation without regard to their class, color, or participation in sports or activities. I hope your committee," he told his successor, "can continue to foster the attitude of impartiality."

Soon after becoming Superintendent in July 1974, Major General Sidney Berry looked back at Vietnam's impact on West Point. "The last decade has, indeed," he concluded, "been one of turmoil, transition, and change."[17] During the latter years of the Vietnam War the top American post in Vietnam, and then that of Army Chief of Staff, was held by General Creighton Abrams (USMA 1936), who followed in each of those key billets his classmate William Westmoreland. General Abrams had sent his staff a handwritten note articulating his view of essential leader qualities: "What we want in our officer corps: character, integrity, respect for and devotion to the fundamental precepts of our government and our evolving way of life, intelligence, professional competence in a highly technical age, and a fundamental belief and confidence in human beings." Abrams had often come to West Point to address cadets during an earlier tour as Vice Chief of Staff, talking to them about soldiers, about the responsibilities of leadership, and about integrity as the indispensable quality.

Reputation

Officers, of course, hankered for advancement, but it was not the value by which they measured themselves. A general might be admired, or he might not. Admiration derived from something other than his badges of superior rank. It came from the reputation he held as a man among other men and that reputation had been built over many years under the eyes of his regimental tribe. That tribe was not only of fellow officers but of sergeants and ordinary soldiers as well. "Not good with soldiers" was an ultimate condemnation. An officer might be clever, competent, hardworking. If his fellow soldiers reserved doubt about him, none of those qualities countervailed. He was not one of the tribe.

John Keegan
A History of Warfare

"Nobody can take your integrity away from you," he observed. If you're going to lose it, "you have to give it up yourself." That was a wise observation on several counts, not least in its emphasis on how surely the individual holds in his own hands the priceless possessions of personal integrity and professional reputation.

In the autumn of 1974 General Abrams died unexpectedly, the only Chief of Staff ever to succumb while in office. In a eulogy delivered in the Chapel of the Most Holy Trinity at West Point, General Berry recalled a two and a half hour conversation he had had with General Abrams the preceding spring when Abrams had told Berry he was assigning him as the Military Academy's next Superintendent. "He spoke of the central importance of the ideals of West Point," recalled Berry. "He spoke of the need for officers who care for their men and who are willing to get down in the mud with their soldiers. He spoke of qualities he despises in others, particularly in officers: selfishness, careerism, arrogance, insensitivity to other human beings. Selfishness and insensitivity headed his list. He said that West Point must always develop a special kind of American leader—that leader who makes the difference between winning and losing. He said that the Army needs leaders who <u>like</u> people, who <u>believe</u> in others, who <u>want to serve</u> others. He described command of American soldiers as a rare privilege and opportunity which one accepts with humility."[18]

In 1975, the same year in which America withdrew its support of the South Vietnamese and essentially squandered a decade of sacrifice, Honor Committee Chairman William Reid reported a distressing situation at West Point. "This past year has been very difficult," he admitted. "The honor system is in transition, and has come very close to failing altogether. Although we may perhaps have arrested the demise of the system, there is still a great deal more to be done to restore a healthy one."

Simplification

Early in Academic Year 1970–1971, Honor Committee Chairman Patrick Finnegan sent a memorandum to all cadets on the subject of Cadet Honor Committee procedures. "This year there will be a new concept in the Honor System," he wrote, "in an attempt to simplify the procedures for unintentional violations. The new concept will be called an 'Unintentional Violation of the Absence Card.' Whenever the card is marked, whether or not it is inspected by a subdiver [cadet slang for a subdivision inspector], it is making an official statement."[19] This meant, explained Cadet Finnegan, that "whenever you mark your card, and then unintentionally go to an unauthorized place, you have made a false official statement, and you are honor bound to report yourself for an unintentional violation of the absence card."[20]

Absence cards were for many years a fixture of each cadet room, where the occupants posted their nametags on a card opposite a sliding marker which was used to indicate their whereabouts. Certain assurances—ethically equivalent to a verbal declaration—as to the authorized nature of such absences, and conduct during them, were inherent in the marking of cards. More about this mechanism shortly.

That the matter raised by Cadet Finnegan required clarification had become clear a few years earlier when a Superintendent's Honor Review Committee explored the issue of whether the absence card made a statement on the cadet's behalf when he marked it, or, alternatively, whether the marked card made such a statement only when it was inspected by someone acting in an official capacity. Noted the committee, "Interviewed cadets were far from unanimous in their understanding of when the absence card spoke. This difference was highlighted when the current chairman and vice-chairman [of the Honor Committee] expressed positions in direct opposition to each other."[21]

Finnegan further explained the new concept as "the first step toward a simplification of the Honor System. Our Honor Committee hopes to focus more attention on the Code and the Spirit of the Code, and the way we intend to do this is to simplify the many rules of the Honor System. If you take every action with the Code and its basic tenets in mind," he assured his fellow cadets, "you will not go wrong."[22]

In its original manifestation, marking the absence card constituted giving one's word that not only was the absence authorized, but that during the absence the cadet would obey the regulations governing gambling, hazing, limits, liquor, and narcotics, or what were commonly known as the five points. In 1963, which may in retrospect be seen as a way station en route to the demise of the absence card, its coverage was reduced to limits alone, eliminating the remainder of the five points.

In the following year, 1964, a faculty review committee commented favorably on this and other revisions of the system. "The Committee was reassured to find the high regard with which the Cadet Honor Code and Honor System are held by members of the Corps of Cadets," the committee's report told the Superintendent. "It noted the overwhelmingly favorable reaction to the present Honor System revised last June. The modified version, in the minds of cadets, has eliminated many 'gray areas,' has simplified procedures, and has facilitated the important task of indoctrinating the new class." Given later developments, however, it is apparent that this committee was too sanguine in concluding that "the revisions have practically eliminated the growing complaint that Honor was being used to enforce regulations."[23] Cadets' fondness for such a claim, regardless of the era, has remained one constant in an otherwise continually shifting landscape of outlooks and attitudes on honor.

Perhaps reacting to a perceived decline in cadet support for use of the absence card, the 1976 version of USCC Regulations added some rationalization for use of the card. "Moreover," read the relevant section, "the card is a great convenience to cadets. With respect to this convenience, the intent of the absence card is to preclude constant use of the company departure book or accountability formations."[24]

Even so, the absence card continued to be a matter of concern to authorities and cadets alike. In March 1977 General Berry sent a note to the Commandant: "Is this the time to review seriously and questioningly the entire question of the ABSENCE CARD? Philosophy, practice, benefits, abuses, attitudes, alternatives to accountability? We need to examine this issue searchingly no later than Sep-Dec 1977."[25] Such matters would continue to occupy both cadets and the administration until finally, in Academic Year 1989–1990, use of the absence card was abolished altogether. We will return to those residual issues.

Legal Challenges

Major General Philip R. Feir (USMA 1949), the Commandant of Cadets who was wrapping up his tour of duty in the spring of 1975, commented on the increasing tendency of cadets who had been found guilty of an honor violation by the Honor Committee to seek a hearing by a Board of Officers. He suggested several reasons for this, including "the emphasis on and requirement for due process that concerns so much of what we do. But young people are more legalistic too," he added, "perhaps legally sophisticated is the term to use, than has been the case in the relatively recent past."[26]

Problems and frustrations for both cadets and officers resulted from the fact that in a number of cases officer boards acquitted those the Honor Committee had found guilty. The Commandant described how the administration was trying to help cadets understand that "what may have been good enough for Honor Committees ten years ago simply will not suffice these days." This he attributed to "the nation-wide emphasis on due process," to the fact that "lawyers are playing a far more significant role in cases of this kind than formerly," and to the reality that boards of officers and their proceedings "are governed by different rules than the rules under which the Honor Committee operates."[27]

A 1957 internal committee that was convened to review the Honor Code looked back to identify some sources of procedural problems. "Since the affair of 1951 emphasis has been placed on removing temptation from the path of cadets in the field of academics," it noted, citing most recently a published policy on homework. "Having adopted a program of trying to codify the morally obvious in the academic field," the report commented with some asperity, "we have introduced the element of strictly legal interpretation. Current policy is interpreted as meaning that that which is not proscribed is permissible."[28]

This report precipitated an intense discussion of the honor issues involved. "Honor is not developed by avoiding situations where a cadet is on his honor; the reverse is true," wrote the Dean, Brigadier General T. D. Stamps, who added that "the cheating that culminated in the 1951 incident was not the result of any misunderstanding of what was right and what was wrong. The evidence clearly showed that the cheating was deliberate and that those who participated knew that they were cheating."[29]

General Stamps followed with an inspiring tribute to the cadets he had known and taught over his long career. "Anyone who has dealt with cadets in academic situations cannot help from being impressed with their high sense of honor. The exposing of a minute fraction who are not honest, and cannot resist temptation, prevents our sending such men out into the Service. Cadets are proud to be trusted; being honest in academic situations is no strain on them if our regulations are clear and simple."[30]

But increasing legalism in the larger society inevitably continued to have an impact on the Honor System at West Point. A young officer serving on the faculty in the early 1980s (who would later become the Army's Chief of Military History) commented on changes since his class had graduated a decade earlier: "The honor system is much more elaborate, much more detailed, has much more legal machinery, is much more complicated in its use," observed then-Major John Brown. "I think the Honor Code remains as intrinsic, valid, and valuable as it ever was. I think the Honor System is a little top heavy, but I frankly don't know what one could do to return to an earlier, simpler era. I mean, there are factors outside of the Academy's experience that have pushed us in that direction."[31]

He was right on the mark. As the society at large became increasingly litigious, West Point was not immune to such influences. In fact General William Knowlton, Superintendent during the period 1970–1974, often described himself as "the most sued Supe in history." A number of the lawsuits during his tenure and at other times, while quite provocative, eventually proved reassuring in that, in every instance, the elements of the Honor Code and System, and West Point's entitlement to prescribe and enforce their provisions, were upheld in courts at several levels.

In 1973, for example, a former cadet found guilty of lying brought a federal lawsuit charging that West Point's Honor Code enforcement procedures were unconstitutional. This matter reached the Second U.S. Circuit Court of Appeals, which held: "We recognize the constitutional permissibility of the military to set and enforce uncommonly high standards of conduct and ethics." The U.S. Supreme Court declined to review the case, leaving standing the Second Circuit's ruling.[32]

In a 1973 suit captioned White v. Knowlton, which raised the issue of whether separation was too severe a sanction for honor violations, Judge Knapp rendered this opinion: "The fact that a cadet will be separated from the Academy upon a finding that he had violated the Honor Code is known to all cadets even prior to the beginning of their careers there." "While separation is admittedly a drastic and tragic consequence of a cadet's transgression, it is not an unconstitutionally arbitrary one, but rather a reasonable albeit severe method of preventing men who have suffered ethical lapses from becoming career officers. That a policy of admonitions or lesser penalties for single violations might be more compassionate—or even more effective in achieving the intended result—is quite immaterial to the question of whether the harsher penalty violates due process."[33]

The 1976 Electrical Engineering 304 cheating scandal also spawned lawsuits, one contesting the constitutionality of the Honor Code and the Honor System and heard in the United States District Court in the Southern District of New York. In this case the cadet plaintiff had been charged with violation of the non-toleration clause of the Honor Code for having "asserted, at a meeting with the Undersecretary of the Army and various other cadets, that numerous cadets not then charged with Honor Code violations had engaged in acts comparable to the ones committed by those who had been charged. After he refused to answer questions about this statement put to him by the Chairman of the Honor Committee or appear before the Committee, he was found guilty of toleration by the Committee."[34]

The plaintiff, reported the court, "does not deny that he has violated the prohibition against toleration. Rather, he attacks its legal and moral basis, and

Principle

One must be true to the things by which one lives. The counsels of discretion and cowardice are appealing. The safe course is to avoid situations which are disagreeable and dangerous. Such a course might get one by the issue of the moment, but it has bitter and evil consequences. In the long days and years which stretch beyond that moment of decision, one must live with one's self; and the consequences of living with a decision which one knows has sprung from timidity and cowardice go to the roots of one's life. It is not merely a question of peace of mind, although that is vital; it is a matter of integrity of character.

Dean Acheson
Present at the Creation

that of the entire system of which it is a part." In rendering his opinion Judge Owen observed that "attacks upon the Honor Committee's functioning tend to indulge in the dubious assumption that it is intended to perform a judicial function." Recalling an earlier case and ruling, the judge noted that "the Constitution does not . . . prescribe any particular disciplinary code for use at West Point. It is a matter that has traditionally been left to the discretion of the military. As this Circuit has cautioned: 'the Academy's rigorous and exacting standards of discipline, behavior and personal decorum for cadets . . . should not be interfered with by the judiciary.' " The government had entered a motion for summary judgment, which would resolve the case in its favor. Said Judge Owen: "It is so ordered."[35]

A July 1976 opinion rendered by U.S. District Court Judge Vincent J. Biunno was subsequently quoted at length in the USCC Pamphlet on the Honor Code and System as follows:

> The Academy at West Point is the training place of military leaders. Such leaders bear an extremely heavy responsibility. They are called upon during their careers to make individual decisions that will affect not only those under their command but the many others whose protection it is their duty to provide. Such leaders are often called upon, especially in the heat of battle, to make decisions promptly as well as soundly, and often they have no one to consult but themselves. This concept requires that from the start of their training throughout their careers such leaders learn to rely on themselves so that others may rely on them. A habit of complete self-regulation as embodied in the Honor Code is essential to the development of such self-reliance.[36]

Even given the increased litigiousness of the larger society, there were a few actions brought against the Military Academy or its senior officials that appeared to be frivolous. One such, previously mentioned, White v. Knowlton, was described in these terms by the Commandant of Cadets: "Cadet White and several others were found to have violated the honor code and were separated. White chose to appeal to the courts essentially, it seemed to me, on the grounds that the Military Academy had denied his fundamental constitutional right to cheat." The courts found in favor of West Point, with Brigadier General Philip Feir noting that "the language used was persuasive."[37]

There was one aspect of cadet life with profound ethical implications in which a legal challenge successfully reversed longstanding Academy policy. That was the termination of mandatory chapel attendance. The Commandant of Cadets at the time, General Feir, had some interesting observations on the change, which he acknowledged constituted a major departure from existing procedures. "In the past," he wrote, "the USMA position has been that compulsory chapel was necessary because it was the basic means by which the Academy fulfilled its responsibilities for the religious, moral, and ethical training of cadets. This has always been a weak reed." If the Military Academy really does have an obligation to provide such training to cadets, said General Feir, *"now is the time to change course and make some meaningful moves to fulfill this obligation."*[38]

End of the Silence

Up to this point, we have seen occasional brief mentions of the old cadet discipli-nary device called the "silence." It is time now to examine this practice in greater depth. For generations the Corps of Cadets had available to it, and from time to time made use of, a technique known as the silence. This involved total Corps ostracism of a man believed to be guilty of an honor violation, but who refused to resign and was not dismissed by the authorities. In an effort to force the dis-graced person out, no other members of the Corps would have anything to do with him beyond the bare minimum required by official actions. No one would speak to the subject except in the line of duty, no one would room with him, no one would sit with him at meals or in social settings. This isolation was almost invariably enough to persuade the honor violator to resign.[39]

"The formalization of the [Honor] System in 1926," noted a later Academy publication, "provided a two-tiered process of adjudication. The first tier was review by the Cadet Honor Committee." Cadets found guilty in such reviews could then "go to the second tier, an officer review board in which protection of due process rights was more substantial." Should the officer board find the cadet not guilty and return him to duty, the Corps had the option of imposing the silence. "Few cadets could withstand the pain of silencing, and so few cadets went through the formality of an officer board."[40] Instead, they routinely accepted the findings of the Honor Committee and submitted resignations.

An internal officer research project determined that the silence "had been used prior to 1920 when the honor committee had no official recognition." Thereafter, however, at least according to this source, it was not until Academic Year 1940–1941 that use of the silence was reintroduced. "In this year," it is maintained, "the honor committee assumed an even greater amount of finality, by 'silencing' a man who was found guilty by it, but was acquitted by a court-martial."[41]

According to a 1975 study the silence had been invoked "about 15 times in the last half-century." It was, observed the Commandant of Cadets, "not some-thing which cadets ever have done hastily or without what they considered suffi-cient reason."[42]

Early episodes in which imposition of the silence was less than fully success-ful began to erode support for the technique, so much so that in 1962 a faculty committee tasked to review honor matters told the Superintendent in its report that "perhaps this method of punishment may now be archaic or at least impracticable with the growth of the Corps to its present size."[43]

The Class of 1973 was the last to see the silence officially sanctioned by the Honor Committee. Several mutually reinforcing influences led to its abandonment. One was that the greatly increased size of the Corps of Cadets (4400, as compared to 2496 only a few years earlier) had made it increasingly difficult for cadets to recognize the offender and behave accordingly. General Feir expressed his view as Commandant that the silence was not very "effective in a Corps of 4,000, many of whom did not even know one another."[44] When it became necessary to post photographs of such persons on cadet company bulletin boards so others would know whom to silence, the practice began to fall of its own weight.

The case of a cadet who had been found guilty of cheating, but whose conviction by the Cadet Honor Committee was not upheld by a board of officers, further undermined use of the silence. This individual, unlike most before him, persisted throughout the remaining two years of his cadetship and graduated.[45] Failure of the technique in this case to achieve the desired effect further eroded support for it.

Eventually, in September 1973, the Honor Committee issued this statement to the Corps: "Monday night the Cadet Honor Committee voted to discontinue the formal sanctioning of the tradition of social ostracism known as the Silence. This is NOT a change to the Honor Code which states simply: 'A cadet will not lie, cheat or steal nor tolerate any cadet who does.' All other procedures of the Cadet Honor System will remain the same."[46]

Later, the Commandant of Cadets observed that many people assumed that publicity over the silenced cadet who stayed to graduate "forced the Academy to abandon the silence. Nothing could be further from the truth," he said. "Long before this publicity occurred the efficacy and appropriateness of the silence had been discussed at great length between myself, the Deputy Commandant, and the Superintendent. As we saw it, continued existence of the silence was unwarranted."[47]

A later Military Academy publication postulated a direct connection between ending use of the silence and the next major crisis of honor at West Point. When the Corps decided to end the practice of the silence, stated this assessment, "the number of cases going to officer boards rose. The System then unravelled because there were two different review boards applying what cadets interpreted as two different standards to almost every case. Without the 'silence,' the Cadet Honor Boards were relatively meaningless. Within three years, the EE304 honor scandal occurred."[48]

We will turn now to consideration of that traumatic event, the most serious honor scandal in the Military Academy's existence, and one which fundamentally changed elements of the Honor System which had been in place for a century or more.

Notes

1   Papers of William C. Westmoreland, Box 31, Interview, Charles B. MacDonald with Gen. Westmoreland, 17 June 1973, Lyndon Baines Johnson Presidential Library.
2   "MacArthur's Speech," *2000 Register of Graduates*, p. 1-50. The date was 12 May 1962.
3   Ibid.

4 Gen. Edward C. Meyer (USMA 1951), who later (1979–1983) himself served as Chief of Staff. Interview, 9 January 1995.

5 General Harold K. Johnson, "Think on These Things," *Assembly* (Summer 1968), p. 31.

6 Ibid., pp. 31-32.

7 Lt. Gen. Sidney B. Berry, *The United States Military Academy: A Fundamental National Institution*, p. 23.

8 Remarks, Lt. Gen. Sidney B. Berry, at Royal Military College Centennial Symposium on Military Education, 15 June 1975.

9 Remarks, Lt. Gen. Sidney B. Berry, at Royal Military College Centennial Symposium on Military Education, 15 June 1975. The USMA Historian, Dr. Stephen Grove, reports that on a similar questionnaire administered to the Class of 1970 the same percentage, only 47 percent, indicated that they would, if they had it to do over again, choose to attend West Point.

10 Col. Manley E. Rogers, Director of Admissions, Memorandum for Record, Subject: Comparison of Admissions Data, 14 June 1976. The contrast over the period 1960–1978 is even more dramatic, from 802 admissions to 1435, an increase of nearly 79 percent.

11 Remarks, Lt. Gen. Sidney B. Berry, at Royal Military College Centennial Symposium on Military Education, 15 June 1975.

12 Col. Lance Betros, comments on draft manuscript.

13 Col. Robert G. Gard Jr., "The Military and American Society," *Foreign Affairs* (July 1971), p. 699.

14 Ibid., p. 698.

15 Ibid., p. 705.

16 The last draft calls were in the closing months of 1972. From 1973 forward, then, the Army depended entirely on volunteers to fill its ranks.

17 Memorandum, Maj. Gen. Sidney B. Berry (Superintendent USMA) to Commandant of Cadets and others, Subject: Superintendent's Special Study Group on Honor at West Point, 9 October 1974, USMA Archives.

18 Eulogy for General Creighton W. Abrams, Delivered by Maj. Gen. Sidney B. Berry, Superintendent USMA, 6 September 1974.

19 Memorandum, Patrick Finnegan, Cadet Honor Committee Chairman, to All Cadets, Subject: Cadet Honor Committee Procedures, 8 September 1970, File: Honor Code—Historical (JUL 70–JUN 72), USMA Archives.

20 Ibid.

21 Report of Honor Review Committee—1969, 22 April 1969, USMA Archives.

22 Finnegan Memorandum.

23 Memorandum, Honor Review Committee to Superintendent, Subject: Report, 4 May 1964, USMA Archives. The committee included in its report a tabulation of honor separations in recent academic years: AY 1961–1962: 21. AY 1962–1963: 20. AY 1963–1964: 21. These numbers differ substantially, however, from those recapitulated in the 1966 Honor Review Committee report, where they were given as: AY 1961–1962: 29. AY 1962–1963: 41. AY 1963–1964: 24.

24 USCC Regulations 600-1, 21 August 1976.

25 Note, SBB [Lt. Gen. Sidney B. Berry, Superintendent USMA] to General Bard (Commandant of Cadets), 3 March 1977, Adjutant General Files, 1011-01 Curriculum Approval Files: Honor Code (1977), USMA Archives.

26 Memorandum for the Record, Maj. Gen. Philip R. Feir, Commandant of Cadets, Subject: After Action Report, 12 April 1975, p. 34, USMA Archives. Hereafter Feir MFR.

27 Ibid.

28 Memorandum, Committee Appointed to Review Cadet Honor Code, to Superintendent USMA, Subject: Report of Committee Appointed to Review Cadet Honor Code, 13 May 1957, Adjutant General Files, 351.1 Honor System, USMA Archives.

Committee members were Col. Vincent J. Esposito (Chairman), Col. Charles R. Broshous, and Col. Julian J. Ewell.

29 Memorandum, Brig. Gen. T. D. Stamps (Dean of the Academic Board) for Superintendent, Subject: Recommendation of Committee Appointed to Review Cadet Honor Code (Esposito Committee), 18 June 1957, Adjutant General Files, 351.1 Honor System, USMA Archives.

30 Ibid.

31 Maj. John S. Brown, Maj. Dueltgen Interview, 7 June 1984, USMA Historian's Files.

32 *News of the Highlands* (4 October 1975), Honor Code Suit 1973 File, USMA Archives.

33 Opinion in White v. Knowlton, 361 F. Supp 445, 449 (S.D. N. Y. 1973), as cited by the government in Supplemental Memorandum in Support of Motion to Dismiss or in the Alternative for Summary Judgment, Cadet Paul Williamson, Plaintiff, vs. United States of America et al., Defendants, Civil Action No. 76-0300.

34 Opinion and Order, United States District Court, Southern District of New York, Cadet Timothy D. Ringgold et al., against the United States of America, Martin R. Hoffman [sic] . . . et al., Defendants, 76 Civ. 2442. District Judge Owen.

35 Ibid.

36 *USCC Pamphlet 632-1*, June 1977, pp. 2-3.

37 Feir MFR, p. 35.

38 Memorandum, Brig. Gen. Philip R. Feir, Commandant of Cadets, to Superintendent, USMA, Subject: Voluntary Chapel, 4 January 1973, USMA Archives. Emphasis in the original.

39 In a 16 April 1951 memorandum to the Corps, Honor Committee Chairman Stanley M. Umstead Jr. listed eight elements of the "Silence," including the provision that it lasted for a silenced person's entire Army career and that such person would not be permitted to wear a class ring. Adjutant General Files 351.1 Honor, USMA Archives.

40 *USCC Pamphlet 632-1*, August 1992, p. 2.

41 Compilation, Lt. Col. Roger H. Nye, Department of Social Sciences, 1 February [1968?], File: Honor Code—Historical (JUL 67–JUN 70), USMA Archives.

42 Feir MFR, p. 41.

43 Memorandum, Honor Review Committee to Superintendent, Subject: Report, 2 April 1962, USMA Archives.

44 Ibid., p. 42.

45 The record is less than definitive on this matter. Some commentaries maintain that the cadet in this instance was the only one who ever persisted through the silence and remained to graduate. A contemporaneous journalistic account, however, made this claim: "Although many cadets who are silenced leave at the end of a semester, 15 have finished their West Point stay in silence within the last 50 years, a spokesman said." Rod Allee, "Cadets Scrap Silencing," *Middletown Times Herald Record* (12 September 1973).

46 "Honor Committee Ends Silence," *Pointer View* (14 September 1973), p. 1. The article described the Silence as "the 102-year-old tradition of formally silencing cadets found in violation of the Honor Code who did not resign and who were not recommended for dismissal by a Board of Officers." It further stated: "As a practice in recent years, the Silence meant that a cadet affected by it was to eat at a separate table; he was not permitted to wear a class ring; he had to room alone; he was to be shunned by fellow cadets at snack bars, movies, and cadet hops; he was barred from participating in the Fourth Class System; and he was to be addressed only on official business and then as 'Mister.' "

47 Feir MFR, p. 42.

48 *USCC Pamphlet 632-1*, August 1992, p. 3.

6 | Crisis and Response

New Crisis

In March 1976 the Class of 1977, then in their third year as cadets, were assigned a take-home computer problem in a course designated Electrical Engineering 304 (or EE 304 for short). The instructions for completing the work, for which two weeks were allowed, specified there was to be no collaboration. Each cadet was to do his own work.

When, two weeks later, the completed problems were submitted, one cadet had written on his paper: "This computer project does not represent all my own work."[1] That alerted departmental instructors to a possible problem, which further investigation soon revealed was a very serious problem indeed. "As graduation approached," explained the Military Academy's Public Affairs Office, "it became clear that the Honor Committee would be unable to process honor cases being referred to them. It was deemed necessary to appoint an Internal Review Panel consisting of faculty members, legal advisors, and cadet representatives." The cadet chairmen of both the 1976 and 1977 honor committees agreed with this course of action.[2]

Officer board hearings were completed in September 1976. "Eventually," reported a West Point fact sheet, "152 cadets, through self-admitted involvement or honor and officers board guilty verdicts, were separated from the Military Academy."[3]

Particularly saddening was the fact that the Honor Committee itself was tainted by this scandal. "Of the 44 members elected during 1975–1976," reported Honor Chairman Michael Ivy in his 1977 Honor Book entry, "five members were found to be guilty of cheating in EE304. Five more resigned from the Committee for various reasons. Those figures represent a turnover of almost one-fourth of the Honor Committee in less than two years."

"If the majority of the [C]orps was innocent and honorable, as the [A]cademy stoutly maintained," wrote the distinguished author Rick Atkinson, "a sizable minority was guilty of at least tolerating the cheats."[4] Atkinson cited as pertinent context "the colossal changes that had swept through the nation in the past ten years. Church, family, school—all of the temples of authority and moral instruction—had been weakened." Thus: "Unconsciously, West Point had presumed that the sons it received every July were precisely like those it had always received, imbued with a basic reverence for truth, honor, and authority. That presumption, regrettably, had been wrong."[5]

Brigadier General Jack Capps, during these years Head of the Department of English, provided some insights into how the crisis had developed and some of the influences leading to such a breakdown. "The Class of 1977," he observed, "had been introduced to the Corps by the Class of 1974, who themselves had grown up under the pressures of the Vietnam War. In the Vietnam era upperclass cadets quite reasonably suggested that they be given increased responsibility and authority for better preparation for the heavier responsibilities obviously in the offing. That was a reasonable request endorsed by returning Vietnam veterans and sanctioned by the faculty. As has been true for generations, successive cadet classes sought more of whatever had been granted to their predecessors. In time, cadet authority began to exceed cadet judgment because the experience and wisdom acquired by one cadet class did not accrue to the next, and the initially sound proposition gradually went wrong." What went most wrong, and the later Borman Commission (about which more will be said shortly) pointed this out, was a breakdown in self-discipline. "It was that pervasive deficiency," said General Capps, "that required the extensive revisions in honor proceedings and institutional practices that followed."[6]

This fall from grace had serious practical consequences. As observed by Cadet Ivy, "the traditional issues concerning intervention into the Honor System from individuals outside the Corps drew great attention."[7] In fact, "interference into Honor proceedings came from multiple sources, from lawyers to cadets to chaplains." This was the result, at least in part, of internal deficiencies. "Discrepancies within the Honor Committee raised doubts concerning the validity of the entire System," acknowledged Ivy, "and justifiably so."

A West Point graduate who became a military attorney, John Beasley (USMA 1970), later wrote a useful paper giving his view that, "over the years, attitudes among cadets and the level of acceptance of the Code has continually fluctuated." Thus, he concluded, "it is difficult to fully appreciate the procedural and due process modifications without some idea of the human dynamics occurring behind the scenes."[8]

In testimony before a Senate subcommittee, Colonel Harry Buckley, who had chaired the Superintendent's Special Study Group on Honor at West Point, addressed the matter of contextual change and its influence by quoting the Study Group's general conclusion, a statement of epic ambiguity: "The Honor Code will never be anachronistic, but the specific applications of ideal principles are invariably linked to the conditions in which they operate."[9] That didn't seem to make matters any clearer—far from it.

There had been very disturbing precursors of this major honor crisis, identified and described by the very department in which the problem erupted. Wrote Colonel Elliott Cutler Jr., Professor and Head of the Department of Electrical Engineering, in a 1970 memorandum to the Dean, Brigadier General John Jannarone, "The annual EE Department effort to have cadets in the core curriculum write a computer program has again produced frightening results." The problem, in retrospect a major one, related to lost, and possibly stolen, computer decks and printouts. "The bulk of the cadets questioned," wrote Colonel Cutler, "felt that definite dishonesty was involved in the computer work and expressed the opinion that a surprising number of classmates (10–15%) were so upset with having to execute a computer problem, and felt so 'dumped-on' by the EE Department, that they felt somewhat justified in ignoring any honor implications and felt that they were 'getting even' by cheating."[10]

Looking back at this crisis from the perspective of a decade or so later, the Posvar Commission noted that "by 1974–1975 the Honor Code and its operation were described as being in a very troubled state by the Chairman of the Honor Committee and a Superintendent's Special Study Group. This was so for two principal reasons: enforcement of the Code was increasingly hampered by a procedural emphasis

---

Service

A republic, however free, requires the services of a certain number of men whose ambition is higher than mere private gains, whose lives are inseparable from the life of the nation, and whose labors and emoluments depend absolutely upon the honor and prosperity of the Government, and who can advance themselves only by serving their country.

President James A. Garfield
North American Review (1878)

---

and there was marked weakening of support from the cadets themselves for the spirit and letter of the Code." This is an important observation, underscoring the reality that over time cadet observance of and adherence to the spirit of the Honor Code has fluctuated, however much we might wish that were not the case. Thus "the next mass cheating scandal, in 1976, was the culmination of a process of erosion of confidence and trust in the Honor Code," concluded the Posvar Commission.[11]

An insightful summary of the situation in the years leading up to this crisis was later prepared by an officer serving at West Point. During the "preceding two or three decades," wrote Colonel Larry Donnithorne, "the Vietnam War and its broad, anti-military sentiments had created a hostile environment for the Academy—and for its current and prospective students as well as its graduates. The nation's rising sense of litigiousness contributed to pressures on the Honor System to protect due process rights of accused cadets, and it led to a successful court challenge of the Academy's requirement that cadets attend chapel services." Then: "Internally, the size of the Corps of Cadets had nearly doubled." Also, "women cadets were assimilated into the Corps of Cadets for the first time. Finally, "a major honor scandal [the 1976 crisis] erupted in the midst of a pervasive breakdown in morale in the Corps of Cadets."[12]

Honor instruction in more recent years has been gratifyingly candid in discussing these problems, their origins, and their effects. By the end of the 1974–1975 academic year, noted a later version of *The Four-Year Honor Education Program*, "the Honor Code and Honor System appeared to be having serious problems." Evidence of this was provided by a Special Study Group on Honor convened by the Superintendent during that year. Based on "extensive cadet surveys and interviews," the group "reached some disturbing conclusions regarding the level of cadet support of the Honor Code and System." Looking back on that time, the honor education handbook tellingly observes: "Less than a year later, one of the most serious cheating incidents in Academy history occurred, commonly known as the EE 304 cheating incident."[13]

Every cadet of the modern era is familiar with the "Blue Book," the *Regulations USCC* (United States Corps of Cadets), a volume that over the years has gone up and down in size according to various reform movements and personalities in the Department of Tactics.[14] In 1877, to cite one fairly early example, the document was 43 pages long and included the prescription that "cadets are required to take at least one bath a week." While they were in summer camp, cadets were authorized to "bathe in the river, at or near Gee's Point." Subdivision inspectors were instructed to "inspect immediately after taps, with lanterns."[15] By 1886 the document had grown to 95 pages, more than doubling in size in just nine years, while the 1899 version formally adopted the nickname: "This book shall be officially known as the Blue Book."

For our purposes, given the recurring honor problems of the mid-1970s, the 1976 version of the Blue Book is of particular interest. In a cover letter transmitting the document, Commandant of Cadets Brigadier General Walter Ulmer Jr. wrote that this version of the regulations had been written to be "long on spirit and short on letter" and expressed the hope that cadets living under, and up to, these rules would develop a recognition that " 'mission' and 'our soldiers' forever take precedence over 'self.' " Two excerpts of these regulations warrant being quoted in their entirety. Taken together, they constitute a clear, succinct, and inspiring statement of a way of life and its ethical dimensions:

> Paragraph 102. Professional Ethics. Cadets are expected to adhere to the professional ethics of commissioned officers in the United States Army. In this regard, cadets must conduct themselves with propriety and decorum. Cadets are expected to exercise moderation in all things and must not engage in any activities which violate the provisions of the Uniform Code of Military Justice, state, or federal laws. Cadets will abstain from vicious, immoral, or imprudent conduct of any type prejudicial to good order and discipline within the organization. A cadet's word is binding; his or her signature or initials attests to the truth and accuracy of its contents. A cadet's behavior must at all times, at West Point or away, reflect credit upon the individual, the Military Academy, and the Army.
>
> Paragraph 103. Integrity. Commissioned officers are entrusted responsibility for life and property. Consequently, they are expected to reflect the highest standards of integrity in fulfilling their awesome responsibility. Historically, the Cadet Honor Code has been the primary means by which this excellence of character and integrity is developed in the Corps of Cadets: to instill and promote a life-long adherence to the attainment of this standard. All cadets at the Military Academy are obligated to live by and support the Cadet Honor Code and the Cadet Honor System.

Awesome responsibility indeed. Thus far, every class ever graduated from West Point has eventually been tested in battle. Now, well into the Military

Academy's third century, that pattern seems likely to continue to be the destiny and defining mission of all those who take their place in the Long Gray Line.

Borman Commission

Secretary of the Army Martin Hoffmann appointed an external review panel to look into the causes of the EE 304 honor violations and make recommendations for remedial measures. Chaired by Frank Borman (USMA 1950)—retired Air Force colonel, former astronaut, and president of Eastern Airlines—the panel thus became known as the Borman Commission.[16] This group was asked to seek underlying causes for the recent honor problems and to take a "broad-based sensitive, non-intrusive look" into the future of honor at West Point.[17]

Near the end of the year Chairman Borman sent the Commission's report to the Secretary of the Army. In his letter of transmittal Borman wrote that "West Point remains a unique institution where young men and women, in a spartan military environment, learn the academic and military skills to be a professional soldier."[18] It seemed strange that in forwarding this key document, one engendered by grave challenges to the traditional Honor Code, Borman made no mention at the outset of requisite ethical or moral skills, only those in the academic and military realms.

The report did, however, strongly endorse the central importance of honor at the Military Academy. "West Point must retain its unique nature," said Chairman Borman. "The failure of some cadets to adhere fully to the Honor Code cannot detract from the fact that the overwhelming number of cadets are honorable men and women who will, we are certain, become fine officers in the United States Army." Also, stressed Borman, "the Commission unanimously endorses the Honor Code as it now exists."[19]

The Commission, Borman told Secretary Hoffmann, "concurs unanimously with the actions that you have taken to provide a 'second chance' for certain cadets involved in the Electrical Engineering cheating incident last spring." Borman added this rationale: "The cadets did cheat, but were not solely at fault. Their culpability must be viewed against the unrestrained growth of the 'cool-on-honor' subculture at the Academy, the widespread violations of the Honor Code, the gross inadequacies of the Honor System, the failures of the Academy to act decisively with respect to known honor problems, and the other Academy shortcomings."[20] That thoroughgoing indictment offered no explanation of why, if the conditions described were so dysfunctional, by far the majority of cadets nevertheless continued in word and deed to be committed to honorable behavior.

The body of the report likewise reflected some questionable judgments and conclusions. "We see nothing to be gained by further action against these cadets and much to be lost by continuing with the divisive and unrealistic attempt to purge all who have violated an Honor Code that is perceived in widely differing ways," Colonel Borman told Secretary Hoffmann. The Commission professed itself unable to understand cases in which, it said, "cadets have been found guilty for isolated conduct which cannot fairly be characterized as having made them dishonorable." To illustrate, it cited a case in which a third classman (whose class was not eligible to attend movies, although second classmen were) "was found guilty . . . of 'intentionally deceiving' in that he 'wore a second class dress coat'" to pose as a second classman and thereby gain admission to the movie which, as a third classman, he was not authorized to attend. It is difficult to understand what the Commission could have been thinking, or how that cadet's actions could have been viewed as other than intentional deception.[21] For many years cadets were taught that, in cases of doubt as to whether a contemplated action would violate the Honor Code, they could clarify the situation by asking themselves two questions: Am I attempting to deceive? Am I taking unfair advantage? To both those questions the cadet in question would have had to answer "yes."

> ### Integrity
>
> Nobody can take your integrity away from you. If you're going to lose it, you have to give it up yourself.
>
> General Creighton W. Abrams
> USMA Class of 1936

The 1976 Honor Committee Chairman, reflecting on these matters while on graduation leave, wrote to the 1977 Honor Committee to express his views. "The Honor Code is correct and it is right," he told them. "In its beautiful simplicity it acts as a timeless guide to graduates as well as non-graduates of the Academy. It has not in the past, nor should it now be changed, so as to fit in more easily with the social norms of the American society." But, he added, "in light of recent events, we could conclude that the Honor Code is not doing as well as it might in instilling these values."[22]

The Borman Commission placed much of the blame for the 1976 honor incident on deficiencies in honor education. "We believe that education concerning the Honor Code," wrote Chairman Borman, "has been inadequate and the administration of the Honor Code [System?] has been inconsistent and, at times, corrupt."[23] In its recommendations the Commission stated its conviction that "there must be instruction in ethics introduced into the core curriculum, to provide a base for continuing instruction in honor matters."[24]

Secretary of the Army Hoffmann took the matter under advisement, including findings of the Borman Commission and a number of internal review panels, and decided that there had been sufficient institutional responsibility for the honor problems to justify giving the cadets found guilty another chance, provided they first complied with certain stringent conditions. Thus he directed that those cadets could apply for readmission in the spring of 1977 (approximately a year after the date of their offenses) and, if cleared by a special readmissions committee at West Point, be readmitted. Mr. Hoffmann also waived what would otherwise have been a two-year service obligation in these cases.[25]

It should be noted that, in expelling the offenders from the Academy, albeit for only a year, the tradition of non-toleration was technically upheld. From another point of view, however, allowing cadets to eventually return to the Academy after an honor violation conviction bespoke abandonment of the single sanction, at least in this one series of cases.

Readmissions

In early 1977 it was announced that cadets who had been dismissed in connection with the EE 304 incident, but who applied and were accepted for readmission after screening by a special readmissions committee at West Point, would be readmitted in 1977, joining the Class of 1978, one year behind their original class.[26] Being turned back to the class behind one's own was not an inconsequential punishment. Moreover those so punished would, to some indeterminate degree, become marked men.

Secretary Hoffmann told a congressional subcommittee that "those who violated the Honor Code represent a wide range of apparent motivation, aptitude for commissioned service in the Army, self-discipline, and integrity." He said "criteria similar to those required for admission and commissioning will be used to identify those cadets potentially suited for eventual graduation from the United States Military Academy."[27]

The principal readmission criteria decided upon were "suitability for commissioning in the United States Army and an expressed commitment to the standards and principles of the Military Academy, including the Honor Code." Each case was to be considered and decided upon individually.[28]

Cadets who were dismissed and subsequently sought readmission were to include with their applications assessments and recommendations from people who had supervised them in the interim. Some had gone to college elsewhere and had academic advisors and instructors who could evaluate their performance. Others had taken jobs in the civilian sector and could seek endorsements from their supervisors. A smaller number had gone into the Army as enlisted men, yielding an interesting result. "By far the strongest recommendations," read a draft readmissions committee tabulation, "appeared in the references of those individuals who undertook the option of enlisted service. Some 10% of the applicants made this choice, and without exception they were commended by their commanders and, significantly, their first sergeants."[29]

Readmission was eventually offered to 105 of 152 dismissed cadets. Some declined the offer but, in late June 1977, 98 dismissed cadets returned for a second chance.[30] Of the total, 92 were former members of the Class of 1977; 85 of those continued on to graduate with the Class of 1978 the following June.[31]

In looking back on this extremely traumatic period in the Military Academy's history, General Berry said this: "I think our chief institutional failing was not being sensitive enough to those great society changes—Vietnam, different values of young people. . . . We thought the same words would have the same meaning to a young fellow who came in in 1973 as to one who came in in 1955."[32]

In fact, several cross-reinforcing trends and events had combined to put the Military Academy's standards and socialization of incoming classes under unprecedented strain. Societal changes as identified by General Berry were occurring throughout a long and controversial war, while at West Point from about 1975 on the leadership was largely preoccupied with planning and preparations for admitting women to the Academy for the first time, beginning in 1976. Any one of these factors would have produced significant strains. In combination they more or less overwhelmed the adaptive capacity of the institution and its leaders, cadets as well as officers.

Revised Procedures

In September 1976 company meetings were held throughout the Corps at which honor representatives presented a concept for restructuring Honor Committee and Officer Board hearings. "The concept of the change," wrote Commandant of Cadets Brigadier General Ulmer in a memorandum to the Superintendent, "is to return the balance of decision making to cadet level by providing due process at Honor Boards." Cadet boards would be supported by three officers—a recorder, a defense counsel, and a legal advisor to the board. Such boards would have twelve members, four of them Honor Committee representatives and the remainder cadets drawn from the Corps at large. Henceforth a 10-2 vote would be required for a guilty finding. After staffing, the revised procedures were to be presented to the Corps for a vote. More basically: "As soon as is reasonable following the vote on procedures, the Honor Committee plans to submit to the Corps the proposal that for certain categories of cases there be a sanction less than mandatory separation."[33]

In February 1977 the Superintendent, General Berry, wrote West Point's graduates a six-page letter in which he described procedural changes being adopted for operation of the Honor System. "Working closely with military legal advisors," he said, the Honor Committee had "developed and presented to the Corps of Cadets a broad range of revised Honor Committee procedures designed to provide increased due process to cadets accused of violating the Honor Code. On November 9th [1976] the Corps voted overwhelmingly to adopt the revised procedures." These included legal counsel for the accused in proceedings, a legal advisor to the cadet chairman of an honor board, a military lawyer to assist the Honor Committee in presenting its case, revised investigative procedures, and provision for regular cadets of all classes (not just honor committee members) to sit on honor boards. "These revised procedures," observed General Berry, "eliminate the requirement for a subsequent board of officers."[34]

The 1976 Honor Committee Chairman later described these modifications in a memorandum for the 1977 Honor Committee. "In the past eighteen months, the Honor System has undergone some very definite changes," wrote then-Lieutenant William E. Andersen. "These changes resulted in removing much of the mystique which has previously cloaked the Honor System. The Committee received a badly needed injection of due process in the form of codified and carefully considered procedures to guide our conduct. The newly existing procedures took those methods of operation handed down by tradition (in a rather haphazard manner) [and] solidified them, locking in safeguards to individual rights and more obvious and structured assurances of justice."

Also, noted Lieutenant Andersen, "A long held cadet belief has been that the Honor System is to be run solely by cadets. This is and should be a fallacy. It has not been true for at least half a century. The Superintendent and Commandant have, and will continue to have, tremendous input into the operation and functioning of the Cadet Honor System. Any other mode of operation would be improper and unacceptable."[35]

Later honor education materials noted that, even before publication of the Borman Commission's report, cadets had voted to "revamp the Honor System. With 85 percent of the Corps of Cadets voting in favor of the proposed revisions, the cadets completely eliminated the two-tier system in favor of a single 'due process' hearing at the Cadet Full Honor Board level. . . ." Three days later the Superintendent approved the cadet recommendations for implementation. The need for such reforms had become widely apparent to both cadets and the authorities. "With more and more cadets requesting officer boards," observed an honor education handbook, "the cadet hearing was having less impact and was becoming less and less a critical stage in the process." The two-tiered system had also become "a tremendous source of antagonism between the cadets and the Academy administration. Although there was one Honor Code, the two-tier system now seemed to create different standards of enforcement, something that neither the Academy nor the Corps of Cadets could tolerate."[36]

The new procedures soon proved to be cumbersome and excessively time-consuming, involving cadets in detailed legalistic procedures that resulted in the honor hearings process being dominated by attorneys, almost to the exclusion of the cadets who were in theory responsible. The revised procedures, the later Posvar Commission observed, "created even more complexities, having sacrificed the simplicity and timeliness of the earlier system, whatever its faults in creating antagonism between the cadets and the USMA administration."[37] It would be no surprise when, only two years after these new procedures were implemented, they were essentially scrapped and simplified new procedures adopted.

Some changes in regulations also reflected changing times. For generations cadets had felt secure in leaving their wallets, watches, and other valuables on their desks or otherwise unsecured. The 1976 *Regulations USCC*, however, established a different standard. A section on security read as follows: "Cadets are responsible for ensuring that their valuables are safeguarded. Articles of value such as rings, watches, or cash will not be left exposed in cadet rooms, basements, in the gymnasium, or in any other conspicuous place."[38]

It is hard not to conclude that something important had been lost with the publication of that requirement. Lieutenant General William Lennox Jr. (USMA 1971) commented when he was Superintendent on how things had been during his cadet days: "I thought it was a great way to live, you know, leaving your doors open, not having to worry about anybody taking anything, trusting every-body's word. And I don't think I had a problem with that at all; in fact, I valued that quite a bit."[39]

Later studies, however, seemed to substantiate the need for the new security procedures. The Superintendent's Honor Review Committee of Academic Year 1990–1991 noted as a "troublesome area" problems with cadet '"borrowing" and barracks theft. "Loss of personal items appears common in the barracks and classroom areas," the committee found, expressing its concern that this situation might "foster disillusionment and cynicism among cadets." They were almost certainly correct in that conclusion.

Indeed, the whole concept of cadet "borrowing" seems to have been invented in a futile attempt to mask what had become a troubling and widespread reality, and not a new one. Wrote the Superintendent's Honor Review Committee in 1973: "Indiscriminate 'borrowing' has become a cadet euphemism for suspicion of outright theft. It is a widespread phenomenon and seriously undermines cadet confidence in the honor code." Not just cadets themselves were the victims, moreover, as equipment and uniforms belonging to the Army Athletic Association frequently came up missing and, noted a 1983 report, the Library "permanently loses between 500 and 800 volumes per year."[40]

The Superintendent's Honor Review Committee of 1966 noted its finding that "over a period of years an undesirable situation has developed wherein borrowing has become widespread and abusive in the Corps of Cadets." Explaining: "The more serious instances result when one cadet takes the property of another without his permission and without leaving a note to explain that the item was borrowed. Too often the borrower fails to return the item and, in some instances, breaks or damages the item and then returns it without identifying himself to the owner." Surprisingly, the report then adopted this position: "The Committee feels that this problem should be solved by the Chain of Command and not be considered as a problem for the Cadet Honor Committee."[41]

The 1984 Honor Review Committee stated its conviction that cadet borrowing "is a cancer that eats away at the fiber of the Honor Code, and cadets seem unwilling to tackle this problem." Just how widespread the problem had become was indicated by a cadet survey in which 58 percent of respondents stated that "they had been deprived of their property by theft, cadet borrowing, or wrongful appropriation in the previous twelve months."[42]

Academic testing procedures, long valued as affirmations of trust in the integrity and reliability of cadets, also underwent significant change. Prior to the 1976 cheating scandal, identical tests were administered to all sections over a two-day period, relying on cadets who had already taken the tests to refrain from discussing them with those who had not yet been tested. All that changed in 1976. "The Academic Board has reviewed procedures," Secretary of the Army Martin Hoffmann stated in an August 1976 congressional hearing, "and has decided that take-home projects of the type administered in the EE 304 course will no longer be given. Further, Academic Departments will prepare separate examinations for each attendance period."[43]

The "Real" Army

Living by the precepts of the Honor Code is of course not something only for cadet days, just as being a cadet is not an end in itself. Both are preparation for going out into the Army and society as principled leaders, a high privilege and even higher obligation.

The question has often arisen over the years as to whether the Honor Code is applicable to cadets while they are away from West Point. The matter was eventually resolved in the proper way, for it would clearly have been untenable for cadets to live by one standard at West Point and another when they were elsewhere. The Buckley Study Group said that "the issue concerning the physical domain of where the Honor Code applies was not formally addressed until the 1950's, and the question was finally resolved in 1960 with the policy that the Code and System are binding on a cadet wherever he is."[44] That was a logical conclusion with respect to the Honor Code, although not all elements of the Honor System have consistently been applied away from West Point. Absence cards, for example, when still in use at West Point, were not used on cadet class trips. *The Honor Code and Honor System* pamphlet defined the Honor Code's reach unequivocally: "This standard's applicability is not defined by any geographical boundaries. Cadets are expected to live by this standard both at West Point and away from West Point. The Honor Code is applicable anywhere that a cadet may go."[45]

In the larger context of what some would call the "real" Army, not all those whom young graduates encounter choose to live up to the high standards taught at West Point. In the modern era cadets have learned this while serving as aspirant leaders in Army units on many posts and stations. Not only will they have encountered challenges to their own integrity, but they will have witnessed lapses of integrity (some unpunished) on the part of others. This dichotomy constitutes, especially for the young officer fresh from West Point, both a challenge and an opportunity. Former Superintendent General William Lennox discussed his aspirations for young officers just out of the Military Academy: "We want them carrying that standard [of the Honor Code] into the Army . . . and we want them not exploding when they don't find it, but actually bending down [and] pulling up what they find to the standard that they are accustomed to."[46]

This matter was addressed in some detail, and quite sensibly, in the West Point pamphlet *Honor Guide for Officers*. Cadets are going to ask you for advice on honor matters, officers assigned to West Point's staff and faculty were told. Especially is it likely that junior officers will be asked about "honor situations that sometimes obtain in the active service." Examples are provided, including cheating by student officers at branch schools, false scoring of targets on rifle ranges, and inaccurate reporting of readiness statistics. "There is no need for an officer to be defensive in discussing this problem," states the guide. "Any cadet can understand that the Army is a little more complicated than the Corps of Cadets . . . ." But: "The cadet must realize that he has been trained for the purpose of setting high standards. When he graduates he must approach each problem in the honor area with fairness and understanding and do what he thinks is right. . . . In the long run complete honesty is the best policy and the Army policy."[47] Such weighty considerations illustrate why it continued to be essential, as a former Commandant put it, to convince cadets that "they are in a very serious profession, and that they need to be prepared for the expectations."[48]

Meanwhile, at West Point very significant new departures in the Honor System lay ahead. Most importantly, they would institutionalize one of the elements that had been, as we have seen, informally applied from time to time by both cadets and the administration. The term that would come into use to characterize the new procedures was "discretion," meaning the exercise of discretionary judgment in meting out punishment for honor violations. We turn to that topic next.

Notes

1 I am indebted to the USMA Historian, Dr. Stephen Grove, for the language of the cadet's statement as quoted from the *1977 Superintendent's Annual Report*.
2 Fact Sheet, Public Affairs Office, USMA, 6/77.
3 Fact Sheet, "The 1976 Honor Incident," Public Affairs Office, USMA, 6/78, USMA Archives. This was the largest number of cadets ever separated in the wake of a single honor incident. A contemporary commentary cited a particularly relevant historical antecedent: "At Eton during the 19th century, the then headmaster Thomas Arnold expelled a score of students for misbehavior. He then assembled the rest of the student body in the chapel and said: 'It is not necessary that there be 350 students at Eton. It is not necessary that there be 50 students at Eton. But it is necessary that they be Christian gentlemen.' " Jeffrey Hart, "West Point in Trouble," Manchester (NH) *Union Leader* (5 June 1976).
4 Rick Atkinson, *The Long Gray Line*, p. 399.
5 Ibid., p. 400. The USMA Historian, Dr. Stephen Grove, later wrote of the Class of 1977 that "this class was identified relatively early as having an unusually low level of support for the honor system. One-half of the class did not believe the system to be fair and just; two-thirds did not believe the code and system were realistically enforced. This lower level of support for the Honor System was frequently attributed to cadets entering the Academy at a particularly difficult period of recent history. This was a time when the American participation in Viet Nam was winding down, questions concerning the integrity of military personnel were well publicized, and the Watergate scandal was unfolding. In addition, the 1974 Honor Committee Chairman, who presented much of the honor instruction to this class, was himself graduated but not commissioned because of honor-related difficulties." USMA Historian, Disposition Form to Superintendent, Subject: Environmental Factors Which Led to the Honor.
6 Letter, Brig. Gen. Jack L. Capps to Sorley, 5 May 2007.
7 In August 1976 Secretary of the Army Martin R. Hoffmann had received a letter on matters at West Point signed by the Speaker of the House, the House Majority Leader, the Chairman of the House Armed Services Committee, and 170 members of the House of Representatives.
8 Maj. John H. Beasley, JAGC, *The USMA Honor System: A Due Process Hybrid*, p. 7.
9 Statement, Hearing before the Subcommittee on Manpower and Personnel, Committee on Armed Services, U.S. Senate, 2nd Session, 94th Congress.
10 Memorandum, Col. Elliott C. Cutler Jr., Professor and Head of the Department of Electrical Engineering, for Dean of the Academic Board, Subject: Lost

Computer Decks and Printouts, 12 March 1970, File: Honor Code—Historical (JUL 67–JUN 70), USMA Archives. A 1974 Superintendent's Honor Review Committee report portrayed the experience of honor enforcement during a year not long before the 1976 episode as follows: "For the year ending in April 1974, 82 cases were heard by honor boards and 43 cadets were found guilty. Another six resigned in lieu of having their cases heard. Fourteen of those convicted chose to appeal to a board of officers. Of these, nine were separated and five were reinstated, notwithstanding the honor board's unanimous determination of guilt." Information Paper, Subject: Honor Code, DCSCOMPT, 18 June 1976, File: Honor Committee (1 Jun 76–31 Aug 1976), USMA Archives.

11 *Final Report of the Special Commission of the Chief of Staff on the Honor Code and Honor System at the United States Military Academy,* 30 May 1989, p. 11.

12 Col. Larry R. Donnithorne, *Preparing for West Point's Third Century,* p. 1.

13 *The Four-Year Honor Education Program* (USMA, West Point, NY, August 1992), p. 19.

14 The term "Blue Book" may now be obsolete, however, as such documents are distributed electronically and the familiar blue cover would no longer be in evidence. At least some cadets of today do seem to be familiar, however, with the Red Book (Academic Program) and Green Book (Military Program), whereas what once was known as the Blue Book I am told now just goes as "The Regs."

15 *General Orders U.S. Corps of Cadets,* 29 March 1877, passim. For many years cadet barracks consisted of "divisions," four-story structures arranged about a single staircase, with four rooms on each floor. A "sub-division" constituted part of a division, usually either the top two or bottom two floors, assigned to a given barracks inspector.

16 Other members of the Commission included Gen. Harold K. Johnson, a former Army Chief of Staff; A. Kenneth Pye, Chancellor and Dean of the Duke University School of Law; Dr. Willis M. Tate, President Emeritus of Southern Methodist University; Bishop John T. Walker, Bishop Coadjutor of the Episcopal Diocese of Washington; and Maj. Gen. Howard S. Wilcox, Chairman of the USMA Board of Visitors and an Indianapolis businessman. An anecdote concerning General Johnson is instructive in terms of the crucial importance of one's professional reputation. The Army Chief of Chaplains, Major General Charles E. Brown Jr., was an amateur clockmaker. One afternoon he visited the home of Secretary of the Army Stephen Ailes to fix a clock for him. Afterward they were sitting on the back stoop, having a beer, when Mr. Ailes asked General Brown what he thought of General Johnson. "Stephen," replied Brown, "he's the strongest spiritual strength in the Army today." Two or three weeks later the selection of General Harold K. Johnson as the next Army Chief of Staff was announced. Brown Telephone Interview, 23 October 1994.

17 Fact Sheet, Public Affairs Office, USMA, 6/78, USMA Archives.

18 As reprinted in *Assembly* (March 1977), p. 4.

19 Borman Commission Report, 15 December 1976, Letter of Transmittal.

20 Ibid., Chairman's Cover Letter, pp. [1]-[2].

21 Ibid., p. 5.

22 Memorandum, 2nd Lt. William E. Andersen to 1977 Honor Committee, Subject: Cadet Honor Code and Honor System, 30 June 1976, File: Honor Committee (1 Jun 76–31 Aug 1976), USMA Archives.

23 Borman Commission Report, Letter of Transmittal.

24 Ibid., p. 16.

25 Fact Sheet, Public Affairs Office, USMA, 6/77, USMA Archives. Brig. Gen. Jack L. Capps, who served as Chairman of the Special Readmissions Committee in the aftermath of the EE 304 scandal, later calculated how those cadets readmitted and subsequently commissioned had done in comparison to the rest of their class. He found that "of those readmitted, 19.5% reached the grade of colonel; the average for their class was 20.7%." Letter, Capps to Sorley, 5 May 2007. The Secretary of the Army's decision to waive the two-year call to active duty for cadets separated in this

case may have been influenced by the views of Col. Frederick C. Lough, Head of West Point's Department of Law, who had suggested in a 29 June 1976 memorandum to the Superintendent that "at this particular time, there is no absolute requirement that an Army so proudly made up of volunteer soldiers should be encumbered by some 150 disenchanted, disgruntled ex-cadets who most probably will contribute little if anything to the morale of the Army and for that matter to the defense of the Country."

26 Special Supplement, *Pointer View* (7 January 1977).

27 Fact Sheet, Key Features of Secretary Hoffmann's Remarks before Armed Services Subcommittee on Manpower and Personnel, 23 August 1976, Brig. Gen. Jack L. Capps Papers.

28 Letter, Lt. Gen. Sidney B. Berry, Superintendent, to West Point Graduates, 18 February 1977, USMA Archives.

29 Draft article, Special Readmissions Committee cadet members, 15 July 1977, Brig. Gen. Jack L. Capps Papers.

30 Newburgh Evening News (30 June 1977).

31 Fact Sheet, Public Affairs Office, USMA, 6/78, USMA Archives.

32 Quoted in Phil McCombs, "The Painful Death of a West Point Myth," Part 3 of a Series, *The Washington Post* (21 December 1976).

33 Memorandum, Brig. Gen. W. F. Ulmer Jr., Commandant of Cadets, for the Superintendent, Subject: Honor Committee Procedures, 23 September 1976, USMA Archives.

34 Letter, Lt. Gen. Sidney B. Berry, Superintendent, to West Point Graduates, 18 February 1977, USMA Archives.

35 Memorandum, 2nd Lt. William E. Andersen to 1977 Honor Committee, Subject: Cadet Honor Code and Honor System, 30 June 1976, File: Honor Committee (1 Jun 76–31 Aug 1976), USMA Archives.

36 *The Four-Year Honor Education Program*, p. 19.

37 *Final Report of the Special Commission of the Chief of Staff on the Honor Code and Honor System at the United States Military Academy*, 30 May 1989, p. 11.

38 *USCC Regulations 600-1, Regulations for the United States Corps of Cadets*, 21 August 1976, p. 35.

39 Lt. Gen. William J. Lennox Jr., Dr. Stephen Grove Interview, 22 September 2005, USMA Historian's Files.

40 *Report of the Honor Review Committee—1973*, 10 May 1973, and *Report of the Superintendent's Honor Review Committee AY 82-83*, March 1983, USMA Archives.

41 Memorandum, Honor Review Committee to Superintendent, Subject: Report, 17 May 1966, USMA Archives. The committee was chaired by Col. Elvin R. Heiberg and also included Col. Frederick C. Lough and Col. George K. Maertens. All three were very experienced and highly regarded officers, and all were West Point graduates. Colonel Lough was then Professor and Head of the USMA Department of Law.

42 *Report of the Superintendent's Honor Review Committee AY 83-84*, March 1984, USMA Archives.

43 Statement by the Honorable Martin R. Hoffmann, Secretary of the Army, Before the Subcommittee on Military Personnel, Committee on Armed Services, U.S. House of Representatives, Second Session, 94th Congress, Hearings on USMA Honor Code, 25 August 1976.

44 *Report of Superintendent's Special Study Group*, p. 11

45 *The Honor Code and Honor System*, 1984, p. 4.

46 Lt. Gen. William J. Lennox Jr., Dr. Stephen Grove Interview, 22 September 2005, USMA Historian's Files. Emphasis in the original.

47 *Honor Guide for Officers*, p. 14.

48 Maj. Gen. David A. Bramlett, Dr. Stephen Grove Interview, June 1992, USMA Historian's Files.

7 | Adaptation

Discretion

For many years the Honor System had generally provided only one punishment for violations of the Honor Code—dismissal, commonly known as the single sanction. This rigidity (or, as viewed by others, faithful adherence to principle) caused a number of problems. In the wake of the EE 304 scandal, those problems came under intense scrutiny and, after long and agonized consideration, it was decided that under certain circumstances lesser penalties than expulsion might be levied against convicted honor violators. General Berry, the Superintendent at that time, later observed that in a previous assignment as a division commander he "had far more latitude in dealing with honor issues according to circumstances" than he did as Superintendent, a limitation he viewed as unfortunate. Thus in his view "the System supporting the Honor Code needed great improvement, correction, and strengthening."[1] Those measures, unfortunately precipitated by the major honor crisis of 1976, lay ahead.

Over the years the issue of having a range of penalties for convicted honor violators, not just the "single sanction" of dismissal, had frequently been debated. As was noted earlier, in isolated cases some lesser penalty was formally determined, while at times Honor Committee members were thought to have voted against conviction, despite believing the accused to be guilty, because they viewed dismissal as too harsh a measure. The Honor Book entry for 1936 in fact implies that discretion was sometimes applied. "Unless the personal equation is considered, great injustices may be done. A man whose record and whose reputation for truth and veracity show that he has at all times abided by the principles of our system should not be dismissed for a minor slip," wrote the Honor Committee Chairman. "The unforgivable offense," he added, "is the premeditated crime or a series of crimes showing a dishonest frame of mind."

In his 1960 Honor Book entry Cadet Roy O'Connor reported that for the first time the Honor Committee had been given "the right to grant leniency during New Cadet Barracks in cases in which the accused demonstrated a lack of understanding of the honor code and honor system when he in fact committed an honor violation. This meant," said O'Connor, "we were able to keep a potentially honorable man here at the academy."

Such leniency was subsequently extended to three members of the Class of 1963 (two of whom later resigned). Apparently this innovation was viewed as successful. The report of an officer review committee in 1965, for example, told the Superintendent that the committee "notes with satisfaction that the present Honor Committee has shown considerable maturity in its use of the Option to prevent the dismissal of a fourth classman before he could fully comprehend the Honor Code and Honor System."[2]

Likewise in the following year a similar officer committee expressed its confidence that "the Cadet Honor Committee, during NCB [New Cadet Barracks] 1965, exercised extremely mature judgment in evaluating Honor violations involving New Cadets." The committee added a description of the Option "which permits the Honor Committee to base its decision on careful evaluation of the New Cadet's understanding of the Honor Code and System, his degree of indoctrination, and the circumstances of NCB pressure during which he committed the offense."[3]

A trend toward favoring something less than strict adherence to a single sanction was becoming apparent in both cadet and faculty outlooks. In 1962, for example, an officer committee tasked to review honor matters reported to the Superintendent its finding that "there is some sentiment toward the mitigation of the traditional punishment of separation from the Academy for a self-reported offense." After deliberation, these officers reflected a somewhat similar feeling, recommending that "the Commandant of Cadets and the Honor Committee consider the feasibility of substituting a severe penalty less than separation (such as special punishment for six months or a year's suspension) for a cadet who voluntarily reports himself for an intentional violation of honor, providing it can be established that the offense would not otherwise have been detected." Not all were yet ready for such a step, however; the Superintendent, then Major General William Westmoreland, disapproved the recommendation.[4]

Writing in mid-1975, the Commandant of Cadets recorded his view that "the Cadet Honor Committee, but not the institution, has in the past applied a 'second chance' rule when in its opinion the offense was self-reported and consisted of a minor infraction. The vote for reinstatement had to be unanimous." This practice, he continued, was eliminated by the Honor Committee during the Academic Year 1973–1974 "because, as a practical matter, it had become too difficult to justify to the Corps different findings in cases perceived by the Corps to involve the same circumstances." Also, noted this officer, "some 'discretion' is applied during New Cadet Barracks wherein the Cadet Honor Committee warns [only] new cadets alleged to have violated the Honor Code until in its opinion the new cadet class has received sufficient honor instruction to be held responsible."[5]

Major General Philip Feir pondered this matter over some two and a half years as Commandant of Cadets, finally arriving at an impasse. "With respect to results," he wrote, "I have concluded on the one hand that for a violation of the Code separation or nothing is too rigid; on the other, that the seriousness of separation as a consequence results in inconsistency and unfairness."[6] After discussing differing viewpoints on the "second chance" issue, this officer stated presciently that "times change, and with them views change also."[7] The precipitating factor this time would of course be the EE 304 crisis, lying just over the horizon.

The Buckley Study Group, meeting over a period of more than eight months in 1974–1975, incorporated surveys of officer and cadet outlooks and attitudes in its report. On the matter of discretion and sanctions, it said, "Generally, both cadets and officers support the use of discretion in the application of sanctions for honor violations. Both groups identify a gradation in guilt, and they generally endorse some alternative to the absolute sanction of separation."[8] In keeping with that outlook, the Buckley Study Group recommended that "the Cadet Honor Committee be authorized to recommend that a cadet found guilty of an honor violation be considered for retention when it has been determined that some combination of the following circumstances existed at the time of the violation: unusual pressure involved in the incident; self-reported violation; limited experience under the Honor Code."[9]

Earlier attempts by the Cadet Honor Committee to introduce discretion into their deliberations had fallen short. Honor Chairman William Reid recorded his disappointment in a 1975 Honor Book entry. "In the past year I attempted to guide the Committee into adopting reforms I felt were essential," he wrote to his successor, "to include a system of explicit discretionary powers, or 'second chance,' to be employed in certain cases. As you know, I was unable to muster sufficient support from the committee in this and other instances."

In February 1976, recalled the Honor Committee Chairman, 54 percent of the Corps of Cadets "voted in favor of what was considered a very new idea, but in fact a very old and basic idea—that of having more than one punishment, separation, for cadets found guilty of violating the Honor Code." That fell short of the level of support specified for adoption of such a change. Cadet Andersen recalled that "a majority of the Corps of Cadets were in favor of some form of punishment less than expulsion in certain unusual and different cases," but "the proposal presented in February 1976 was not solid enough and many considered it too vague to be voted in favor of." Andersen suggested a determinative factor in that outcome: "There are very good indicators that the Class of 1976 voted in [a] very solid block against the proposal."[10] Andersen, by this time a new lieutenant, wrote to his successors his view that "on its own merits, some form of discretionary judgment should be and must be implemented—not because the Honor Code and System are now under great scrutiny but because it is the correct and proper thing to do."[11]

This matter was resolved by external intervention when in January 1977 Secretary of the Army Hoffmann directed a landmark change in USMA regulations. Language specifying that a cadet violating the Honor Code "shall be" separated would, ordered Secretary Hoffman, now be changed to read "shall normally be" separated. The effect of this change, wrote General Berry, was "to permit the Superintendent to exercise his judgment (or to use

---

Honesty

I have only one simple requirement—
I felt that I walked in here as an
honest man. I am going to endeavor
to go out the same way.

General Harold K. Johnson
USMA Class of 1933
Army Chief of Staff 1964–1968

---

his 'discretion') in matters concerning cadet honor violators in the same way in which he previously has been free to use his judgment in the other sensitive and important personnel actions." The Secretary directed the Superintendent "to exercise his discretion conservatively in accordance with the guidelines proposed by the Honor Committee and supported by 66% of the cadets in the December 1976 vote." He also specified that, in exercising discretion, "in those few cases where that decision is made, the Superintendent will insure that his reasoning is clearly understood by the Corps, its leadership, and the community at West Point."[12] General Berry, for his part, pledged to graduates that he would "exercise this authority prudently and infrequently."[13]

There is some reason to believe that senior Army officials, both the top civilian leaders and uniformed officers, were influenced in establishing some kind of discretion by an effort to keep the Congress from intruding itself and perhaps, in the most extreme case, doing away with the Honor System altogether. Even after a readmission plan had been promulgated, for example, a congressman wrote the *New York Times* to express his view that West Point persisted with "an archaic plan and unrealistic expectations." The readmission plan, he claimed, was "totally unacceptable and inadequate" and "the honor code must be revised."[14] That kind of rhetoric from a member of the national legislature could only have sent tremors through those who viewed West Point's high standards as not just worthy of perpetuation but essential to development of the nation's military leaders. In response the Superintendent invited his senior associates at the Academy to "consider life at USMA without the Honor Code."[15]

Significant insight regarding the temper of the times, and the West Point leadership's reaction to it, was provided in a speech by the Superintendent to a West Point Society at Fort Myer, Virginia, in October 1976. "Berry laid most of the responsibility for the decision to allow reapplication by code violators [in the EE 304 exam] at the doorstep of Congress," reported the *Pentagram News*, "saying that 'political realities forced the decision.' He said that if the Army had not acted forcefully and quickly, Congress would have stepped in and taken action of its own. Both he and Secretary Hoffmann, in discussing the impact of the decision on the Point, felt that the threat of Congressional intervention was sufficient justification for the decision to allow reapplication."[16]

Two months earlier General Berry had said, in a letter to West Point graduates explaining the Secretary of the Army's involvement, that his action had been necessary in view of the way in which "the Congress, the Courts, higher authorities in the Defense Department, and other outside agencies have become directly and actively involved" in the cheating incident and its aftermath. "As these new dimensions in the dispute emerged," he said, "the potential for the most serious consequences for the Military Academy and the Army became clear to the Secretary from his vantage point in Washington, and to those of us involved here at West Point. It was in this context that the Secretary made his decisions."[17] The key elements to which he referred were of course Superintendent's discretion and readmission of honor violators.

"The Secretary did not take his personal intervention lightly," General Berry added. "In fact, the decision to intervene at all, given his deep commitment to the prerogatives of the Corps in these matters, was in itself a momentous decision. He believed that he could most effectively equalize the pressures from all sides which were becoming involved in the situation by intervening directly on a one-time basis. His intervention was intended, among other things, to allow the Military Academy to complete the mechanics of the solution unfettered by continued outside involvement from a multitude of sources."[18]

There were views on the other side, however, often expressed with considerable passion. Editorialized the *San Diego Union* in September 1976, for example, there are those, "particularly those on the campuses of public and private colleges today," to whom the honor code seems to be "an anachronism in a changing era." Said the *Union*: "We think not." Should West Point be easier? "We say no. West Point calls for a peculiar breed of men and women. Tampering with the honor code can do nothing but erode an honorable and proven legacy."[19]

Others, of course, including some significant number of cadets, were in favor of a range of sanctions proportional to the perceived seriousness of the offenses committed by honor violators. Their number, as reflected by successive polls of the Corps of Cadets, gradually increased over time, in due course reaching the two-thirds majority that had been established as the threshold for making such a change. They were joined in such a view by some graduates, perhaps represented in the extreme case by an officer tasked to coordinate the defense of cadets charged with EE 304 honor violations. "The System here is unfair," he was quoted in the press as saying. "It's arbitrary and capricious and it's biased."[20]

An even more significant viewpoint on the matter was subsequently expressed by General Berry, Superintendent not only during the crisis but through much of its resolution. "I do believe," he said in a question-and-answer session at West Point in January 1977, "that one of the flaws of the current situation, the single penalty for all honor violations—that is, separation from the Corps—I think that is too rigid and inflexible."[21] The Secretary of the Army, General Berry told the cadets with whom he was meeting, "is really pondering how to deal with the discretion, because he believes that it's right, that it is necessary that discretion be fully incorporated into this Honor System. So do I. So does the Chief of Staff. So does the First Captain. So does the Chairman of the Honor Committee and so do 66 percent of the cadets."[22]

In the wake of the EE 304 cheating episode a number of remedial steps had been taken. Perhaps most important was the assignment of General Andrew Goodpaster (USMA 1939) as Superintendent. In his person he represented the absolute best of the military profession, and of West Point's graduates over the years. His brilliant career had involved a long series of very challenging assignments carried out with distinction, but perhaps his extended stint as Staff Secretary to President Dwight Eisenhower, when Goodpaster was still a colonel, was most representative. He held the post through nearly the entirety of Eisenhower's two terms, a tenure derived from the universal conviction that he was an honest broker, a man to be trusted, one who was invariably fair and discreet and who had the total confidence of the President. Those qualities resulted in a progression of subsequent responsible assignments, culminating with service as Supreme Allied Commander, Europe, the top NATO post, during the period 1969–1974.

Before agreeing to come out of retirement to take the post of Superintendent, General Goodpaster had discussed his outlook and prospective policies with the Secretary of the Army. "I would want to go beyond the minimum legal requirements in terms of the moral/ethical character of the environment that we maintained here," he told the Secretary, meaning that he intended to restore an exemplary standard, not just meet some legalistic and more easily attainable minimum. And, he told the Secretary, "I would expect support in that regard." General Goodpaster also stated that, if he were to undertake the task, he "would do so with the intention of maintaining the Honor Code . . . and restoring it to as much health as [he] could."[23]

General Goodpaster later gave his rendition of the subsequent sequence of events. Describing the two votes of the Corps of Cadets on the matter of discretion during 1976, the latter of which fell just short of achieving two-thirds approval, he noted that, "with the evidence before him that a majority of the Corps supported 'discretion,' and with a similar recommendation from the Borman Commission, the Secretary of the Army decided to delegate 'discretionary' authority to the Superintendent, to be applied according to the Superintendent's judgment, but in a conservative manner. This action," reported General Goodpaster, "was well received by the Corps of Cadets."[24]

Another aspect had to do with the possibility that cadets themselves, through the operation of the Honor Committee, might recommend the exercise of discretion by the Superintendent in selected cases. In February 1977 General Berry reported to graduates on that situation. "On 9 December 1976," he wrote, "the Honor Committee again proposed to the Corps of Cadets that the Honor Committee be given the authority to recommend to the Superintendent an exception to the sanction of mandatory separation." He articulated some factors which the Honor Committee might consider in deciding whether to make such a recommendation. These included, but were not limited to, "the education and experience of the cadet under the Honor Code; whether the offense was self-reported; attitude, or an indication that the cadet has truly learned from the experience and demonstrates an understanding of the value of personal honor now and in the future; any previous violations of the Honor Code."[25]

When, in February 1976, the Honor Committee had first decided to put the matter to a vote of the Corps of Cadets, specifying that a two-thirds approval would be required for the new procedure to be implemented, the proposal failed to carry. A second vote was held in December 1976, and again the measure failed to carry, but this time by the narrowest of margins, less than one percent. As a result, reported General Berry, as of that time "mandatory separation remain[ed] as the only penalty the Honor Committee can recommend to the Superintendent until such time as the Corps of Cadets indicates adequate support for an alternative."[26] A few months later a committee of officers and cadets appointed by the

Superintendent submitted this recommendation: "That the single sanction be modified in favor of a dual sanction which allows, under certain circumstances, a cadet found guilty of an honor violation to return to the Corps."[27]

It should be noted that this dialogue pertained to what the Cadet Honor Committee could or could not recommend in this realm, the Secretary of the Army having already decided that the Superintendent would henceforth have authority to exercise discretion when cases reached his level. Thus, from early 1977 on, there were in place provisions for the Superintendent to exercise his discretion in determining the appropriate penalty for convicted honor violators, and for the Honor Committee to offer its recommendations as to the Superintendent's use of that authority.

Not everyone was happy with this new approach. Especially among older graduates, who had lived under the more stringent regimen and found it both workable and admirable, the weakened standards were viewed with disdain. Many who had served on the Academy staff and faculty, and were thus closer to the current environment, had a different view, one conditioned by their estimate of prevailing realities and their impact on what was possible. "It seemed to me then a reasonable move," said a former Commandant of the introduction of discretion, "and I still support it." In advancing his rationale for that position, this officer added: "I don't believe today's American society produces cadets who can manage an Honor System without alternatives to dismissal."[28]

As the new Superintendent, General Goodpaster faced multiple challenges, not least determining the true state of honor in his new command. "I felt that the Academy was in serious difficulty," he later said while looking back during an oral history interview near the end of his tenure. "The rot had spread very extensively."[29] At West Point, though, General Goodpaster also found a strong reservoir of support for the historic ideal. In the autumn after his appointment he noted in congressional testimony his belief that there was a "strong consensus at West Point that the honor system is presently one of the most healthy systems at the Military Academy." But, he cautioned, "By its very nature it is also one of the most fragile."[30]

Only six weeks later Colonel Dana Mead, Professor of Social Sciences at West Point, reported the results of a Superintendent's honor review: "Unfortunately it appears that at this point there is rather widespread dissatisfaction with, and/or indifference to, the Honor Code/System among cadets. The perception that the Code and System no longer belong to the Corps, but rather are now officer-run, is almost universal." Thus: "Understandably the current attitude is not strongly supportive. We are thus confronted with the problem of rebuilding strong Corps support for the Code as soon as possible."[31]

Cadets leading the Honor Committee had a much different perception. The Honor Committee Chairman, the Vice Chairman for Investigation, and the Secretary were interviewed as part of the same Superintendent's Honor Review in which Colonel Mead was taking part. "None felt that toleration within the Corps is a problem. The number of cases being reported was cited in support of this belief."[32] In other words, the fact that a significant number of honor cases were reported by other cadets acting in accordance with the dictates of the non-toleration clause demonstrated the viability of that provision.

Some sanctions short of dismissal were decided at West Point, but others took place in Washington. In 1988 a cadet found to have been untruthful about preparation of a Rhodes Scholarship application was dismissed, then reinstated and allowed to graduate (late) by authorities in Washington who deemed expulsion too harsh a punishment. (Late graduation, it should be noted, was itself a punishment of some moment, since it relegated the offending cadet to a position at or near the end of his class.) At West Point, the Superintendent accepted the inevitable. "It happened the way it was supposed to happen," he was quoted as saying, meaning that higher authorities reviewed the case and, as they were entitled to do, had overridden the Academy's decision. "Obviously," added the Superintendent, "I didn't agree with it."[33]

Since its inception, the use of discretion in honor cases by the Superintendent has varied according to the incumbent in that position. The original guidance, issued by the Secretary of the Army in 1977, was that dismissal would "normally" be the penalty for convicted honor violators, implying that the use of discretion and imposition of a lesser penalty would be abnormal or unusual. At least as perceived by cadets, however, that has not necessarily been the case. The 1998 Honor Committee Chairman noted in the Honor Book several meetings with the Honor Committee Executive Staff during which "the staff expressed a concern that the Superintendent was using discretion too much." As a result, "the Superintendent decided to consult with cadets and receive their recommendations for the future of the cadet in question."

Such consultation as may have taken place apparently did not ameliorate the problem, however, since in 2000, with the same Superintendent in office, the Honor Committee Chairman wrote in the Honor Book that, "despite an overall effective system, we have seen some disturbing trends." He identified as one such trend "discretion as the standard sanction despite what our literature states." Reinforcing the point, he stated that "wide and liberal use of discretion has now made it the standard sanction for an honor violation."

The viability of the exercise of discretion had been strengthened, concluded an evaluation a number of years after initial implementation, "by an expansion of the developmental alternatives available to [the Superintendent]. Among these is reprimand, turnback, and separation with right to apply for readmission. Cadets separated may elect to spend the time in enlisted status on active duty with the Army. All developmental alternatives require, in addition, that the cadet prepare an oral or written presentation on honor under the tutelage of an officer mentor."[34]

Contemporarily, however, such a conclusion is not universally endorsed, at least insofar as the mentorship program is concerned. In a thoughtful and substantive memorandum submitted at the close of his tenure, the 2007 Honor Committee Chairman stated his view that "effectiveness of the Honor Mentorship Program, as currently applied, is questionable." For one thing, in his view "the program has a very weak means of enforcement, so there are many cadets that are able to pass the program without learning from their experiences." With the standard response to a poor packet (the journal and collateral materials each mentored cadet is required to maintain and present as evidence of his rehabilitation) being to extend the program until the packet is up to par, wrote the Chairman, this "puts the onus on the Honor Executive Staff to prove that the cadet did *not* learn from his or her violation." In addition, during the year just concluded, "for the first time in the history of the Honor Code, a firstie found [meaning convicted] on three allegations was shown discretion." The Chairman's recommendation was for a more stringent standard, such that if, at the conclusion of a six-month mentorship, "the packet is still not up to par, the cadet should be immediately separated from the United States Military Academy."[35]

"I firmly believe," wrote the 2007 Honor Committee Chairman, "that too many cadets are retained after committing an honor violation. The standard sanction is technically separation, though this is no longer the reality." What is more, while many observers periodically express concern as to the extent to which cadets of today wholeheartedly support and exemplify the Honor Code, what is evident here is a strong desire on the part of cadets for a more stringent standard to be applied in dealing with honor violators, with the administration (at least in this cadet view) being the party taking the more permissive approach.[36]

Honor and Regulations

An issue that simply won't go away has been whether the authorities or, more specifically, the Tactical Department, have unfairly or illegitimately used honor to enforce regulations. "The first known official expression of cadet concern on this matter," found the Posvar Commission, "was in 1899."[37] Cadets typically have argued the affirmative and, over a number of years, have made impressive inroads in rolling back any practices that could be so defined.[38]

For many years, for example, cadets maintained in their rooms a card (known as an absence card, discussed briefly earlier) which was to be marked to show their status when they left the premises. Each card had slots for individual cadets living in the room to post their nametags, then use a marker (similar to a button on a string) to indicate their whereabouts. The card had one slot designated "Unmarked,"

Integrity

Uncompromising integrity is not an idealistic goal. It is an operational necessity every bit as critical as any other phase of our combat readiness. Without this trait of character in our officer corps, this Army will cease to function. An atmosphere created of distrust, half-truths, and hypocrisy can only destroy the mutual confidence and respect which are necessary for peacetime training and wartime operations.

Lieutenant General Garrison
H. Davidson
USMA Class of 1927

serving as a home base for the marker, and others showing such destinations as Guard, Hospital, Trip and Leave.[39]

In marking his card, the cadet was giving his word of honor that he was where the card said he was and nowhere else. In addition, in exchange for the privilege of moving about unsupervised, he promised to obey the regulations concerning what were known as the "five points": no gambling, no hazing, adherence to limits, no liquor, and no narcotics. Cadets of an earlier time, going back as far as the middle of the last century, found this a fair quid pro quo, and many old-timers of today have trouble understanding why later generations of cadets found it objectionable.

A 1930 entry in the Honor Book defended the absence card with this rationale: "To obtain certain privileges, a man gives an all right, promising not to do certain things. It is up to him to keep his promise." But a 1957 faculty committee appointed to review the Honor Code struck a more dubious note: "It is often said that the Honor System is not used to enforce regulations," their report began. "However, when one considers the use of the absence card, the All Rights, and the various sign-outs and signatures, a cadet is placed on his honor by regulations much of the time. This procedure is well established and understood by all and has a definite character-building value. On the other hand, it runs counter to the idealist concept of an Honor System. We feel that we should mention this basic conflict in philosophy, but any further consideration of it is for higher authority."[40]

The record seems to show that successive generations of cadets, viewing the absence card and its use in a gradually changing light, simply began to disregard it in such numbers that its use was no longer viable. Writing in the spring of 1975, Commandant of Cadets Feir described this as "a continuing problem. Cadets simply do not relate the absence card to integrity in the way they should. They see it primarily as a limits affair. Anything beyond that is viewed as a use of honor by the institution to enforce regulations. Absence card violations rarely even get to the Cadet Honor Committee."[41]

General Goodpaster reflected on the absence card late in his tenure as Superintendent in context of a discussion of "honor proofing" certain cadet activities, a term which meant formulating policies and procedures in such a way that the temptation to do something dishonorable was reduced or eliminated. Said General Goodpaster in May 1981, "I'm engaged in 'honor proofing' one more major area at the present time, the Absence Card. That's a great disappointment to me." In his view, the necessity to "honor proof" the absence card reflected "very badly on the state of honor, the sense of honor within the Corps." Still, he considered it less costly to "honor proof" the card than it would be "to have a spreading sense [among cadets] that we are making false statements, and we don't mind doing that because we disagree with the necessity for making that statement. I think that [such a cadet outlook] would be even worse, and it's on that judgment that we're moving in that direction."[42]

There was a connection, thought General Goodpaster, between proliferating cadet privileges and cadets' increasingly skeptical outlook on such mechanisms as the absence card. "The privileges that have been given to cadets were so extensive and had been given so unconditionally," he said in speaking of his time as Superintendent, "that you would almost have to change a culture to go back to where they saw the granting of the privilege as related to the fact that they had this honor commitment." In his own cadet days (Class of 1939), recalled Goodpaster, "when you signed out [in the company departure book], that was a privilege. You didn't have to sign out, you didn't have to go to a hop, you could sit in the barracks if you wanted to. But when you did sign out, you were making a commitment that could be depended on, [that] you were going to an authorized place and nowhere else and that no advantage would be taken."[43] While it took another fifteen years for this sea change to play out, use of the absence card was finally abolished during Academic Year 1989–1990.[44]

In 1946, as previously noted, while he was serving as Army Chief of Staff General Dwight Eisenhower had written to the Superintendent stating his view that it was "important that individuals now at the Academy, both officers and Cadets, clearly and definitely understand . . . that under no circumstances should [the Honor System] ever be used at the expense of the Cadets in the detection of violations of regulations."[45] Despite the immense weight that Eisenhower's opinions carried, that was not necessarily the last word on the matter. An *Honor Guide for Officers* published at West Point a dozen years later had this to say to members of the staff and faculty: "It is often said that the Honor System is not used to enforce regulations. This statement is not particularly true as many aspects of the system revolve around the idea that a cadet gains a privilege in return for his word that he will obey regulations."[46]

As with many aspects of cadet life, the approach to enforcing regulations has undergone periodic change. The 1947 Honor Committee Chairman advised his successor: "Don't hesitate to call upon your advisor for help or to see the Commandant on any question relative to honor. You will find them very helpful and not the least dominating or bullying to get you to work their way. Remember that although the Honor System belongs to the Corps and the committee runs it, the officers are very interested in seeing that the Honor System remains with the cadets. They will not use it to enforce regulations." Clearly there had been, over a period of years, some fairly dramatic fluctuations in the realm of honor and enforcement of regulations, or at least in the principals' understanding of those matters.

When he was Commandant of Cadets in the early 1970's, Brigadier General Feir became very dissatisfied with the regulations, finding them excessively legalistic and characterized mostly by a cataloging of prohibitions. He thus formed a working group charged with revising the Blue Book to achieve a more appropriate version, one that would stress the spirit of discipline and obedience that cadets should achieve. He specifically related the desired changes to honor, stating that "the concept and use of honor as a means of enforcing regulations should be in terms of integrity. This can be related to life in the Army where integrity, as a function of regulations, is on the line every day."[47]

There have thus proven to be limits to how far the authorities are willing to go to exempt cadets from being called to account. After all, in the Army an officer is expected to be reliable in both word and deed, and to report honestly as well as reply honestly to official inquiries. "When a man leaves the academy," wrote the Honor Committee Chairman in 1932, "his code of honor goes with him, influencing and guiding him throughout his life, and what he receives here [at West Point] will be his code." A Commandant of Cadets, completing a three-year tour in that office in 1975, summed up his aspirations and expectations for cadets like this: "We want to teach young men at West Point to be open and honest, to answer questions promptly and correctly, and having answered in this fashion, to accept the consequences, good or bad, for those answers."[48] Noted one officer member of an honor review committee in the late 1980s, "A lot of cadets are saying 'you're using honor to enforce regulations.' Yes, we are," he affirmed. "Their word is their bond."[49]

Honor Committee Chairman William Doyle probably achieved the definitive judgment on this matter in his 1987 Honor Book entry, observing regarding the continuing tension between honor and the enforcement of regulations: "This has been an issue since dinosaurs roamed the Plain."

Social Tact

In modern times those responsible for interpreting and applying the Honor Code have come to concede that there are certain situations, arising in the course of normal unofficial activities, in which allowances should be made for statements which, while not strictly accurate, are intended to spare the feelings of others while at the same time not gaining any advantage for the person making such statements. Thus there developed the concept of what is now called "social tact."

In honor education that concept is often illustrated by describing a situation in which a cadet who has dined at an officer's quarters is asked by his hostess how he enjoyed the meal. The potatoes may have been a bit lumpy, the roast a little dry, and the rhubarb pie not his favorite, but in responding the cadet takes into account both the lady's feelings and his own gratitude for being invited into her home. "It was a wonderful dinner!" would, under the circumstances, probably be considered acceptable as an exercise in social tact. Perhaps even better, though, would be, "It's been wonderful being with you and your family! Thanks for inviting me!"

Official publications have stated flatly that "Cadets are expected to exercise tact in social situations." Then a guideline is provided for determining whether, in a given situation, social tact had been properly understood and applied: "As a general rule, if a cadet makes an untrue statement intending to protect the feelings of others <u>and</u> the cadet <u>does not</u> gain any benefit from this statement, then the cadet has correctly applied the principle of social tact."[50]

In most situations requiring tact there are three options: tell the truth, lie, or remain silent. In a famous comment on dealing with the press, an observation that may have some relevance when considering social tact, Winston Churchill returned from the United States and wrote to President Harry Truman about an approach he had discovered during his visit. "I think 'no comment' is a splendid expression," he observed. "I am using it more and more." The equivalent in social tact might be an oblique response that avoids giving unnecessary offense. Another version of remaining silent is tactfully changing the subject.

Social tact and its application were explained to officers assigned to West Point in a 1958 pamphlet entitled *Honor Guide for Officers*, which had this to say about the matter: "Some cadets become so rigidly honor conscious that they lose their sense of perspective. The most frequent example of this is the cadet who shows a complete lack of tact in a social situation by blurting out the awful truth instead of bypassing the situation with some harmless (but true) comment. These cadets need assistance in recognizing that tact and honesty are compatible. Cadets sometimes overlook the fact that honor is a living concept and that common sense is one of its necessary ingredients."[51]

In her classic treatise on lying, Sissela Bok has this to say about what are often called white lies: "Silence and discretion, respect for the privacy and for the feelings of others must naturally govern what is spoken." She also introduces a due regard for compassion into the calculation of what one might or ought to say in given situations: "The self-appointed removers of false beliefs from those for whom these beliefs may be all that sustains them can be as harmful as the most callous liars."[52]

Variable Interpretations

The vital role of the Honor Committee, both as a body and in the persons of individual cadet company honor representatives, is especially apparent in the matter of certain variable interpretations of given acts over the years. The classic example involves what is known as "bed stuffing," defined in one official publication as "the act of placing articles in one's bed in an attempt to give the impression to an individual, the barracks inspector, that there is a cadet present in the bed."[53] At certain times bed stuffing has been interpreted as an Honor Code violation, while at other times it has been condoned as no more than a "prank." An early (1928) entry in the Honor Book maintained by Honor Committee Chairmen records "several important interpretations of regulations (given by the Commandant) which are changes from the past." First among them: "1. Putting dummy in bed (intent to deceive) is a violation of honor."

Only a few years later, in 1939, the Honor Chairman recorded in the Honor Book a "major change in the interpretation of the honor system" which had arisen during the year. "I refer," he said, "to the ruling on the practice of cadets putting dummies in their beds and then going out after taps. It has been decided that such action involves an honor violation in that it is deceitful."[54] Apparently, therefore, sometime between the 1928 Honor Book entry concerning a change from bed stuffing's not being an honor violation to its being considered one, it had once again been declared not to be such a violation, since here in 1939 we read that it is henceforth again going to be so considered. This kind of inconsistency in understanding and interpretation of the honor code, with an apparent four changes on this one issue alone in a matter of just over a decade, is of course asking for trouble.

Cadet Robert Little understood this hazard very clearly. "A major change such as this," he wrote in the Honor Book, "causes trouble for this reason: ever since the men in the first, second, and third classes have been at the academy, the practice of using dummies has been frowned upon, but was not considered an honor violation. A sudden 'about face' such as involved in the new ruling invites criticism because it makes the honor system appear to be an arbitrary code subject to frequent change. The more firm and stable the code can be made, the more respect it will hold." We can be grateful to Cadet Little for reminding us that true honorable behavior does not change according to the whims of those in authority.

Obviously, however, Mr. Little's observation was ignored. In almost comic opera fashion, the issue of bed stuffing continued to flop back and forth. Honor Committee Chairman Jeffry Schmidt reported in his 1984 Honor Book entry that since 1921 bed stuffing "has changed from a regulatory matter to an honor matter no less than 11 times."

Many of these perennial issues, including variable interpretations, social tact, and the honor-regulations nexus, represent challenges each new generation of cadets must address and resolve in the context of their times.

Notes

1 Telecon, Lt. Gen. Sidney B. Berry, 3 December 2007.
2 Memorandum, Honor Review Committee to Superintendent, Subject: Report, 30 April 1965, USMA Archives.
3 Memorandum, Honor Review Committee to Superintendent, Subject: Report, 17 May 1966, USMA Archives.
4 Memorandum, Honor Review Committee to Superintendent, Subject: Report, 2 April 1962, USMA Archives.
5 Memorandum for the Record, Maj. Gen. Philip R. Feir, Commandant of Cadets, Subject: After Action Report, 12 April 1975, p. 36. The Commandant was promoted from brigadier to major general during his tenure and is shown in various citations with the rank held at the time of the document cited.
6 Ibid., p. 46.
7 Ibid., p. 37.
8 *Report of Superintendent's Special Study Group*, p. 17.
9 Ibid., p. 20.
10 Memorandum, 2nd Lieutenant William E. Andersen to 1977 Honor Committee, Subject: Cadet Honor Code and Honor System, 30 June 1976, File: Honor Committee (1 Jun 76–31 Aug 1976), USMA Archives.
11 Ibid.
12 Letter, Secretary of the Army Martin R. Hoffmann to Lt. Gen. Sidney B. Berry, Superintendent USMA, 20 January 1977, USMA Archives.
13 Letter, Lt. Gen. Sidney B. Berry, Superintendent, to West Point Graduates, 18 February 1977, USMA Archives. Emphasis in original.

14   Letter to the Editor, Cong. James H. Scheuer (11th District of New York), *New York Times* (6 September 1976).

15   Note, Superintendent General Berry to General Ulmer, Colonel Rhyne, and Cadet Ivey, 3 October 1976, USMA Archives.

16   Steve Abbott, "West Point Society Speaker," *Pentagram News* (7 October 1976).

17   Letter, Lt. Gen. Sidney B. Berry, Superintendent, USMA, to "Dear West Point Graduate," 26 August 1976, USMA Archives.

18   Ibid.

19   *San Diego Union* (5 September 1976).

20   Capt. Arthur Lincoln (USMA 1966), as quoted in Charles T. Powers, "The Juice Test," *Miami Herald* (15 September 1976).

21   Transcript, Lt. Gen. Sidney B. Berry, Question and Answer Session, West Point, 5 January 1977, USMA Archives.

22   Ibid.

23   Lt. Gen. Andrew J. Goodpaster, Interview by Dr. Stephen Grove, 12 May 1981, USMA Historian's Files.

24   Statement, Lt. Gen. Andrew J. Goodpaster, Superintendent USMA, before the Subcommittee on Military Personnel of the Committee on Armed Services, House of Representatives, West Point Honor Code, 5 October 1977.

25   Ibid.

26   Ibid.

27   Memorandum, Superintendent's Special Committee on Nontoleration, to Superintendent, Subject: Report of Superintendent's Special Committee on Nontoleration, 27 May 1977, Adjutant General Files, 1011-01 Curriculum Approval Files: Honor Code (1977), USMA Archives.

28   Brig. Gen. Walter F. Ulmer Jr. (USMA 1952 and Commandant of Cadets 1975–1977), Message to Sorley, 10 October 2007.

29   Lt. Gen. Andrew J. Goodpaster, Interview by Dr. Stephen Grove, 12 May 1981, USMA Historian's Files.

30   Statement, Lt. Gen. Andrew J. Goodpaster, Superintendent USMA, before the Subcommittee on Military Personnel of the Committee on Armed Services, House of Representatives, West Point Honor Code, 5 October 1977.

31   Memorandum, Col. Dana G. Mead (Acting Head, Department of Social Sciences) to Col. [Jack M.] Pollin, Subject: Superintendent's Honor Review, 15 November 1977, USMA Archives.

32   Memorandum for Record, Minutes of the Superintendent's Honor Review Committee, 8 November 1977, dated 10 November 1977, USMA Archives.

33   Lt. Gen. Dave R. Palmer as quoted in Soraya Sarhaddi, "West Point Honor System on the Line," *Middletown Sunday Record* (3 July 1988).

34   Col. Larry R. Donnithorne, *Preparing for West Point's Third Century*, p. 73. The term "turnback" means being reassigned to a later class than the one with which the cadet entered the Military Academy, thus being "turned back."

35   Memorandum, Cadet Christopher J. Hostler to Multiple Addressees, Subject: Chairman's Final Thoughts and Recommendations, 26 May 2007.

36   Ibid.

37   *Final Report of the Special Commission of the Chief of Staff on the Honor Code and Honor System at the United States Military Academy*, 30 May 1989, p. 12.

38   As every tactical officer knows to a certainty, cadets are remarkably adept at dealing with regulations, even though their record may be less than perfect. At one point a revision in uniform regulations specified that cadets would wear ties with their class shirts, a requirement that had been relaxed in previous years. One cadet, finding himself about to enter the classroom, but without the requisite tie, knew that he would be "quilled" for the offense. Thinking fast, he ducked into the nearest latrine and removed a sock, which he then wrapped around his neck and tucked into his

shirt in his best imitation of a necktie. All in vain, however; he hadn't gone more than a few steps down the hall toward the classroom when a sharp-eyed math instructor stopped him and wrote him up—for not wearing a sock.

39 In an earlier day a similar reporting mechanism, known as the Hours-of-Instruction Card, was in use. An example is on display in one of the replicas of early cadet rooms located in Nininger Hall (formerly the 1st Division of Central Barracks). Surprisingly, no sample of the later Absence Card seems to have survived.

40 Memorandum, Subject: Report of Committee Appointed to Review Cadet Honor Code, 13 May 1957, USMA Archives.

41 Memorandum for the Record, Maj. Gen. Philip R. Feir, Commandant of Cadets, Subject: After Action Report, 12 April 1975, p. 39.

42 Lt. Gen. Andrew J. Goodpaster, Interview by Dr. Stephen Grove, 12 May 1981, USMA Historian's Files.

43 Gen. Andrew J. Goodpaster, Interview by Lt. Col. James M. Johnson, 7 March 1988, USMA Historian's Files.

44 As noted in Cadet Thomas Clancy's entry in the 1990 Honor Book.

45 As quoted in "Honor Violations at West Point, 1951: A Case Study," USMA Archives. Eisenhower's son John had graduated only two years earlier in the Class of 1944, so his father presumably had a convenient pipeline for information on such matters in the recent past.

46 *Honor Guide for Officers*, August 1958, p. 12.

47 Memorandum for the Record, Maj. Gen. Philip R. Feir, Commandant of Cadets, Subject: After Action Report, 12 April 1975, USMA Archives. General Feir cites "times when large numbers of cadets are involved as a group in violations such as occurred during spring 1973 (physics) and spring 1974 (engineering)," p. 40.

48 Feir MFR, p. 36.

49 Soraya Sarhaddi, "Pentagon Panel," *Middletown Sunday Record* (8 January 1989).

50 *USCC Pamphlet 632-1*, June 1984, p. 9.

51 *Honor Guide for Officers*, p. 13.

52 Sissela Bok, *Lying*, p. 76.

53 *USCC Pamphlet 632-1*, June 1984, p. 9.

54 The Buckley Study Group of 1975 determined that the domain (either honor or regulations) under which bed stuffing was classified changed in 1928, 1932, 1948, 1956, and 1963. *Report of Superintendent's Special Study Group on Honor*, p. 11.

8 | Modern Times

The years since the mid-1980s at West Point have featured a large and diverse Corps of Cadets, adaptation to the use of discretion with respect to honor violations, the usual preoccupation with who owns the Honor Code and System, and a combination of residual and newly emerging problems to be addressed by the Honor Committee and the Corps. Recent graduating classes have almost immediately marched off to war, taking with them the values learned and practiced as cadets. In combination, these factors have made honor education even more crucially important than it has ever been.

Posvar Commission

We have had reference to the work of the Posvar Commission a number of times in the course of this book, but it deserves another brief look in today's context. In 1989 the Army Chief of Staff, General Carl Vuono (USMA 1957), appointed a Special Commission of thirteen members, chaired by Dr. Wesley Posvar (USMA 1946), President of the University of Pittsburgh, to conduct an inquiry into the current state of the Honor Code at West Point. "This was," noted Dr. Posvar, "an unprecedented assignment because, for the first time, the Code would be systematically examined in a period of relative calm."[1]

The Posvar Commission reached refreshingly different conclusions than those of the earlier Borman Commission, which had labeled the Honor Code "a goal toward which every honorable person aspires." Dr. Posvar and his colleagues instead found the West Point Honor Code "a practical mode of behavior that benefits its practitioners in the Military Academy and the Army."[2] In a 30 May 1989 report to the Army Chief of Staff, Posvar and his colleagues also said that they strongly endorsed the Honor Code, supported it "in substance and intent," and viewed it as "a commanding ethical force in the Academy's military and academic environment." Far from finding it a perhaps unattainable goal, they stated their specific conviction that the Honor Code represented "a standard of ethical behavior that functions effectively for cadets, to which all American professionals can aspire, and which all citizens should appreciate as a national asset."[3]

Borman and his colleagues had at some points seemed confused about the distinction between the Honor Code and the Honor System. Here again the Posvar Commission demonstrated greater clarity and understanding, reflected in succinct definitions of the two elements. The Honor Code, they stated, is "the mandate for honest and truthful behavior by cadets," the Honor System "the means, rules, and procedures for application and enforcement of the Code."[4]

The Cadet Honor Committee also confronted the Borman conclusions head-on. "It [the Honor Code] does not encompass all ethical behavior," it stated on the opening page of a 1984 version of *The Honor Code and System*, "rather it is the minimum <u>standard</u> of behavior required of cadets." Moreover, said the Honor Committee flatly, "The Code is not an unduly difficult standard to live by."[5]

Ownership of the Honor Code

"Through the decades," acknowledged an official publication, "there has been continued great debate over the concept of ownership of the Honor Code. Many believed that the Code should belong solely to the cadets, and that the Honor System should be shielded from external influence, to include that of Military Academy officials." There was a time when such a belief seemed largely correct, particularly in the days when Vigilance Committees flourished with at most unofficial sanction by the authorities. But many changes over the years, both societal and procedural, acted to modify such a one-dimensional arrangement. One reality posited in the document cited was that "cadets are indeed 'active duty soldiers,' [and hence] statutory requirements necessitate the active involvement of the Academy and Department of the Army staff."[6]

As late as 1958, however, an *Honor Guide for Officers* published at West Point noted that "the firm policy of the Military Academy is that the Honor Code and System 'belongs' to the Corps of Cadets and is operated by the Corps. This policy, which is rather unusual in a military organization, is based on tradition and custom as well as on the principle that the maintenance of such a high ethical standard requires the common assent and enthusiastic support of the entire Corps. Thus, even though the Honor System is based on the Uniform Code of Military Justice and Army Regulations, the authorities here meticulously avoid arbitrary interference with it."[7]

Only three months into his tenure as Superintendent, Major General Sidney Berry established a Special Study Group on Honor. In the appointing memorandum sent to officers and cadets he made this statement: "I acknowledge that the West Point Cadet Honor Code and System will be meaningful and workable only if fully understood, supported, and administered by the United States Corps of Cadets. The Honor Code and System must belong to the Corps of Cadets; it cannot be imposed nor manipulated by external authority."[8] In contrast, it should be recalled, the Borman Commission had taken an exclusionary rather than inclusive view of the matter: "No one 'owns' the Honor Code," read its report. "Everyone must work to insure the effectiveness of the Honor System."[9]

"The strength of the system," wrote a former Commandant of Cadets in a restatement of the traditional view, "is that it belongs to the Corps of Cadets; it is theirs to manage; it is as good as they collectively and individually wish to make it. Officers play a role in it, certainly, and I believe that role is clear and accepted by all. But I say again, for emphasis, the real strength of the system flows from the fact that it is a cadet system."[10]

General Goodpaster told an Honor Review Committee convened early in his tenure as Superintendent that "no one will take the Honor Code away from the cadets and this should be known to them. The Honor Code and its wellbeing is a shared responsibility. One of my prime responsibilities is to look after the well-being of the Honor Code. But this responsibility cannot be accomplished without the wholehearted support of the code by the cadets."[11]

By the time the June 1977 version of the USCC pamphlet on the Honor Code and System was published, the Honor Committee Chairman would advise cadets that "through its history, the Honor Code has belonged to the cadets, the officers, and all those associated with the United States Military Academy. History shows," he continued, "that though the cadets have been the executors of the Honor Code and System, the Honor Code has never been the exclusive property of any segment of the West Point community. This shared interest and ownership are the strengths that have resulted in the success of the Honor Code and System in providing an ethical and moral bedrock for the cadets throughout the Academy's history."[12]

Most of those with a stake in the Military Academy would today acknowledge that, while cadets have the primary responsibility for administering and perpetuating the Honor Code and System, there are other important constituencies who care deeply about honor at West Point and who view themselves as sharing "ownership" of the Code. These include of course West Point's graduates of earlier days, most of whom remain passionate in their commitment to honor and their belief in its essentiality to perpetuation of the Military Academy in its historic role and stature. Also included, and of necessity, are the current authorities at West Point and at Department of the Army. This has in fact always been the case, since cadets have always had responsibility for determining honor violations, but never (at least since days of the Vigilance Committee) authority for deciding or ordering punishments, and even the Vigilance Committees did so outside of legal bounds.

> ### Soldier's Legacy
>
> A soldier . . . can never leave his children much in the way of wealth. But what he can leave them is a rich heritage of courage, of loyalty, of service to his country.
>
> General Lewis B. "Chesty" Puller
> United States Marine Corps
> VMI Class of 1921

There are others in what might be called the West Point "family" who also care deeply about honor matters, and thus have a stake in how effectively cadets of the current day carry out their responsibilities of ownership. These "family" members include the Military Academy's staff and faculty, the parents and other relatives of cadets past and present, and the larger Army whose ranks graduated West Pointers are joining. Some would argue, and with justification, that the entire nation has an interest approximating "ownership" of West Point's Honor Code and System.

Near the end of his tenure General Goodpaster observed that in the realm of honor "there is an <u>absolutely</u> fundamental role, indispensable role for the cadets, but it's not an exclusive role. I <u>think</u> they've come to understand that in their minds, but in their hearts they'd like to have it otherwise."[13]

When he was Superintendent, Lieutenant General Dave Palmer addressed the ownership issue eloquently. "Cadets today," he said, "know that while they are clearly custodians of the Code, they are joined by graduates and friends in veneration of it and share with the institution's leadership a responsibility for administering the system, which includes educating each incoming class." Thus he concluded that "in this sense . . . each of us who cherishes the ideals of West Point 'owns' the Code."[14]

The Current Honor System

In contrast to the relatively stable but evolving Honor Code, the Honor System has been in nearly constant flux, especially over the past several decades. After the 1976 scandal was sorted out, a number of changes were made in how the Honor System functioned. It was later concluded that, initially, they had gone a little too far in "due processing" proceedings and otherwise providing safeguards for the rights of individuals accused of honor violations. Three attorneys had been introduced into the process, for example, one representing the accused, one assisting the prosecution, and one functioning as a legal advisor at large. An Academy officer of that day who was responsible for honor matters described the disadvantages, with lawyers dominating the action, cadets bogged down in time-consuming and complicated legal wranglings, and an unduly adversarial flavor introduced into the proceedings.[15]

In 1979, only two years after institution of the new procedures, some significant changes were found necessary. "The Corps of Cadets last week," it was reported in May 1979, "ratified the Cadet Honor Committee's decision to change the procedures used by the Honor Committee to investigate and resolve alleged cadet violations of the Honor Code. The [existing] procedures, instituted during Academic Year 1976–1977, proved to be extremely complex, cumbersome, overly legalistic, and unfairly time consuming."[16]

By the mid-1980s procedures had evolved to the point of better balancing protection of individual rights and the need for an efficiently functioning system. The hearing panels included some members from the Corps of Cadets at large, along with members of the Honor Committee, and convictions required ten affirmative votes out of the twelve panel members, a safeguard against any one or two holdouts being less than objective. A few further adjustments were later made, such as reducing the panels hearing honor cases to nine members, with six votes required for conviction.

Further evidence of how society at large, and therefore inevitably to some degree the unique interior life of cadets, had become more legalistic was provided by the demise of the term "quibbling." Variously defined over the years as "omitting pertinent information" or "stretching the truth," the essential element had always been an intent to deceive. A survey of upperclassmen in 1964 asked them to define quibbling. "All of them replied that they knew what quibbling was and all of them were able to offer a suitable definition," read a subsequent report to the Honor Committee Chairman. Among the definitions were these: a half-truth, short of a lie; an attempt to deceive through evasive statements; avoiding the truth for purposes of personal gain; intentionally conveying a false impression with a statement not necessarily false; attempting to deceive without committing oneself to a positive oral statement; and allowing someone to believe something which is not true.[17]

The 1964 Honor Committee Chairman in turn issued an instruction to honor representatives on the topic: "Quibbling is not a direct lie; however, it is not the whole unequivocal truth either." And: "A necessary part of quibbling is the intent to deceive, either by telling the truth in such a way as to have it interpreted another way or by omitting part of the truth to gain a misinterpretation."[18]

The term quibbling was dropped from official use some years ago, but a subsequent official definition of lying seems clearly—and appropriately—to subsume what had previously been known as quibbling. "Cadets violate the Honor Code by lying if they deliberately deceive another by stating an untruth, or by any direct form of communication, to include the telling of a partial truth or the vague or ambiguous use of information or language, with the intent to deceive or mislead."[19]

For many years cadets trying to decide whether a contemplated action might constitute an honor violation were counselled to ask themselves two questions: Am I attempting to deceive? Am I trying to take unfair advantage? More recently there have been three such questions taught, now characterized as rules of thumb. The reformulation of the two deriving from an earlier day serves to illustrate the increasing complexity and legalism of modern times. Hence the first question as now constituted: "Does this action attempt to deceive anyone or allow anyone to be deceived?" And the second: "Does this action gain or allow gain of a privilege or advantage to which I or someone else would not otherwise be entitled?" With some effort it is still possible to identify the original bedrock values evoked by those two questions. The third current question, one added more recently, seems oriented more to consideration for the rights and feelings of others than to honor: "Would I be unsatisfied by the outcome if I were on the receiving end of this action?"[20]

Fortunately common sense has helped counterbalance the modern tendency toward excessive legalism. A case was reported in which an official received a call from a man who accused a cadet of lying to his daughter by telling her he loved her. Thankfully, the Commandant set that matter aside.[21]

From very early days, interference in governance of the Military Academy by officials in Washington has been a problem. Indeed, such meddling with what he viewed as his legitimate authority was the key factor in Sylvanus Thayer's decision to leave West Point after sixteen years as Superintendent. Thus it was encouraging when, in October 1988, the Honor Committee Chairman informed the Corps that "the Secretary of the Army has only overturned four honor cases in the last ten years. Cases of this nature," he observed, "are certainly the exception, not the rule."[22]

The current Honor Code and System are defined and articulated in two publications designated USCC (United States Corps of Cadets) Pamphlets. Pamphlet

632-1 deals with "The Honor Code and System," while Pamphlet 15-1 covers "Honor Committee Procedures." Thus every cadet has at hand a definitive exposition of these most important matters, a long, long way from the days when no authoritative guidance existed in writing and, before that, when even the basic tenets and procedures were in a state of flux and evolution.

As noted by Honor Committee Chairman Cadet Christopher Hostler when the 2007 version of Pamphlet 632-1 was published, its purpose is "to serve as the authoritative document on matters relating to the Honor Code and the Honor System." Thus it "explains and codifies an ethical values system for the purpose of practical application and enforcement of the Cadet Honor Code."[23]

The pamphlet opens with a short essay entitled "On Honor" by Robert Wood, reprinted from the 12 April 1929 issue of *The Pointer*, the cadet magazine of an earlier day. An Honor Code or System, he wrote, "must spring from the brains, and yes, the hearts of those who live by it. It must be lived up to in order to endure." Following this essay is an articulation of the Honor Code in its current formulation: "A cadet will not lie, cheat, steal, or tolerate those who do." More than that is expected, however. "West Point expects that all cadets will strive to live far above the minimum standard of behavior and develop a commitment to ethical principles as a guide to moral actions. West Point's core mission is to develop leaders of character for our Army."

Next is an explication of the spirit of the Honor Code, "an affirmation of the way of life that marks leaders of character." That spirit goes beyond mere external adherence to rules. "Cadets who embrace the Spirit of the Code think of the Honor Code as a set of broad and fundamental principles, not as a list of prohibitions." From such a spirit there derive truthfulness, fairness, respect for others, and professional responsibility. This extensive document tabulates and discusses the essential elements of lying, cheating, and stealing, as well as toleration of such acts on the part of others, so that there can be no confusion or uncertainty about what adherence to the Honor Code requires. Elsewhere the spirit of the Honor Code has been officially described as "reverence for the truth, a commitment to fair and just behavior, and an enduring respect for the dignity of others and their property."[24]

From the historical fragments available to us, we perceive an early period in which cadets not only episodically felt the need to uphold a nascent Honor Code, then formed ad hoc groups that determined guilt or innocence, but also established, then carried out, what they viewed as appropriate punishment. Banishment, perhaps occasionally accompanied by an additional distinction such as being tarred and feathered en route, was the usual—in some periods probably the invariable—sanction applied.

The "system" of those days, if we may call it that, had certain virtues. It was entirely cadet-administered and therefore enjoyed, it appears, nearly universal and enthusiastic cadet support and commitment. It was swift. It may have had very significant deterrent power. In most cases it was final, although we have some knowledge of interference by political figures—both in the administration of the day and in Congress—to reinstate individuals found guilty by their fellow cadets. This phenomenon appears to have given rise to the silence, which in the small Cadet Corps of an earlier day seems to have been an effective means of reestablishing the primacy of cadet judgments in matters of honor.[25] All this evolved and flourished with, it must be assumed, the knowledge of the authorities, and for the most part their tacit approval.

The flaws of such an approach are obvious. Accused cadets had little or no time or opportunity to prepare or offer an explanation or defense, no legal or other counsel, no route or means of appeal, no due process of any kind. Those rendering judgment did so in the heat of the moment, with little or no time for reflection or weighing of evidence. No record was created or maintained of deliberations, if indeed there were any. The equities resided entirely with the accusers rather than with the individual being judged.

As in any system or proceeding in which values in conflict are mediated, some desirable attributes are given up or attenuated in order to attain others. In the Honor System as we know it today, compared with the vestigial arrangements of much earlier days, two aspects stand out: swiftness has given way to what many might view as ponderousness, or at least burdensome and time-consuming process; and helplessness of the accused has been replaced by a robust set of rights, rules, procedures, representation, and appellate judgment (Superintendent's discretion).

Equally dramatic is the contrast between the unwritten, semi-secret, and ad hoc procedures of the early days and the extensively documented and transparent system of today. USCC Pamphlet 15-1 sets forth—at nearly a hundred pages' length—the procedures now in use, which include most notably an open process observable by the Corps of Cadets at large and an extensive written record of cases and their outcomes.

The Cadet Honor Committee is of course the central mechanism prescribing and implementing the Honor System. Along with its adjudicative function is its all-important responsibility for honor education. Each cadet company has an elected Honor Representative (chosen by his or her classmates in the company) from the First and Second Classes and, during the year, similarly elects a representative from the Third Class who will move up to membership on the committee upon becoming a Second Classman. To be eligible for election as Honor Representatives, cadets must meet certain specified standards in conduct, academic proficiency, and other realms.

The newly constituted Honor Committee then elects its Chairman and members of the Executive Staff. Those positions are now fairly numerous, reflecting both how extensive (and significant) are the duties of Honor Representatives and the wide range of the Committee's contemporary concerns. Among the staff roles to be filled are an Executive Officer, six Vice Chairs (for investigations, education, mentorship, special projects, information systems, and liaisons respectively), and a Secretary.

Suspected honor violations are resolved in a specified sequence of events, beginning with an approach by the potential accuser to the person suspected with a request for clarification. If the explanation provided is not considered satisfactory, the suspected person is encouraged to personally report the matter to an honor representative. If that is not done, the accuser then takes the matter to an Honor Committee member. After investigation, those cases considered to warrant it are referred to an appropriate panel (depending on whether the suspected violation is admitted or contested).

The investigative phase begins at cadet company level, with results and recommendations then forwarded to the regimental honor representative for review and formulation of a recommendation to the Vice Chairman for Investigations to either forward or drop the case. In those cases where it is decided to proceed with the case, it is referred to an Honor Investigative Hearing (contested cases) or a Cadet Advisory Board (admitted cases). A three-member panel then evaluates and renders a judgment on the adequacy of the evidence in the case. Members swear an oath of privacy to ensure that no information regarding the case becomes public knowledge. That panel is authorized to forward the case to an Honor Investigative Hearing, return it for further investigation, or cause it to be dropped.

In those cases where a hearing is indicated, the Commandant of Cadets now becomes involved, with the matter proceeding to him via his Special Assistant for Honor (an officer) and the Staff Judge Advocate (for legal review). The Commandant then decides whether to refer the case for a hearing or take other action (order it dropped or return it for further investigation).

Cadets under investigation for a possible honor violation are notified of that fact in writing and, also in writing, advised of their right to remain silent and of their right to consult with legal counsel. They acknowledge in writing having received such advice, and their signature so acknowledging is witnessed by another cadet, who also signs a statement that he has done so. Under current arrangements, in fact, cadets under investigation for honor violations are required to visit the legal assistance office to discuss their rights and responsibilities and to receive advice concerning their case. All steps are conspicuously orderly and proper. Very little slips through the cracks in the modern process.

Cases forwarded to an Honor Investigative Hearing are brought before a board of six voting members, three members of the Honor Committee and three members of the Corps at large. The accused now has a wide range of legal and procedural protections under due process, including the rights to remain silent, to consult legal advisors, to call witnesses, to present evidence, to appear personally, to be present during all open sessions, to question witnesses, to challenge board members for cause, to obtain copies of all official documents relating to the investigation, and to have a cadet advisor present during the hearings. A military lawyer is also present to act as hearing advisor. After hearing all the evidence, board members vote on whether a violation of the Honor Code has been committed. Four votes are required to convict.

Every case in which a cadet is found guilty of an honor violation eventually reaches the Superintendent, who has final responsibility for its disposition. He makes two determinations: first, whether to approve or set aside the findings of the board which heard the case, a decision he will base on his consideration of due process and the facts of the case; and second, whether or not discretion should be granted, this to be based on such factors as how long the cadet found guilty has served under the Honor Code, the manner in which the violation was reported, the degree to which the convicted cadet has demonstrated resolve to live honorably in the future, the likelihood that the honor violation reflects the true character of the cadet found guilty, and whether or not there was any evidence of duress in the case.

In making these determinations, the Superintendent gives due weight to input from members of the cadet hearing board, who provide in writing their assessment of the convicted cadet's character, his or her resolve to live honorably in the future, any duress in the case deriving from unusual external personal circumstances, and the convicted cadet's potential for service as an officer. Finally the cadet hearing board members give the Superintendent their recommendations as to sanctions, including whether or not they view discretion as appropriate in the case and, in the event they do, which of several options they recommend. The range of possible sanctions when discretion is granted includes being turned back one class year, being turned back half a year so as to graduate in December, and being allowed to graduate with their current class.

The newest major innovation in the Honor System, one stemming from the possibility of discretion which allows a cadet found guilty of an honor violation to continue under certain circumstances as a member of the Corps of Cadets, is the honor mentorship program. The premise is that some violators can, through an intensive program of guided self-examination and self-evaluation, be able to overcome the ethical lapses in decision making that resulted in their violation of the Honor Code. The mentorship program is defined by cadets as "a reflective practicum." As such it involves working with a faculty officer on intensive counselling sessions, development of a portfolio of written work on honor-related topics and a character development plan, completion of a case study, maintenance of a journal, presentation of honor instruction, and other developmental tasks. At the conclusion of the six-month mentorship program, the officer mentor makes a recommendation to the Superintendent as to whether the cadet should be continued in service and commissioned upon graduation.

No doubt in future years further modifications of the Honor System will be implemented, as has been the case almost continuously over the past several decades. The System as currently constituted and operated, however, represents what can certainly be viewed as a model of fairness, conscientiousness, and due process.

Contemporary Problems

The very first written articulation of the Honor Committee's responsibilities, as approved by the Superintendent in 1928 and copied into the Honor Book by that year's Honor Committee Chairman, included "To guard against the springing up of practices inconsistent with our honor code." That has, over the years, been a challenging task as such issues as unauthorized copying of software, use of fictitious identification cards, misappropriation of library materials, mass use of hotel rooms by unregistered guests, claiming unauthorized tax deductions, driving improperly licensed vehicles, and other questionable practices have arisen. As always, the key to maintenance of ethical practices has been education, a responsibility every Honor Committee seems to have taken very seriously. Ultimately, though, as pointed out to the Corps by the First Captain in a 1969 message, it comes down to individual responsibility. "We cannot set down clearly defined guidelines for every possible situation which may arise," he stressed. Thus: "We must . . . be able to rely on the integrity of each individual."[26]

Contemporary debates in the nation have centered around highly publicized lapses of honor, especially in corporate settings. Many analyses and not a few surveys have suggested a declining commitment to honorable behavior in our society in settings ranging from academia to the workplace and even to the family. James Bowman, a resident scholar at the Ethics and Public Policy Center in Washington, has recently written a book entitled *Honor: A History* which analyzes both negative and positive aspects of concepts of honor through history. In an essay on honor codes he has suggested that "honor is passé in the Western world today. Some see it as too 'judgmental,' too much at odds with the spirit of equality that has introduced us to honor's ersatz and forever-unsatisfying substitute: self-esteem. This fact cannot but have a powerful effect on the coherence and the usefulness of honor codes."[27] It should be added that the author's purpose in rendering this judgment is to then consider how such an unfavorable situation might be reversed.

In a companion essay, Lad Sessions, Professor of Philosophy at Washington and Lee University, takes a more optimistic position. "Personal honor," he writes, "is neither dead nor decadent. . . . It depends entirely on the honor group and its code. Honor for us—honor that can inspire and guide admirable modern lives—is not easy, but it is achievable." To that Professor Sessions adds, speaking of honor systems: "They may rise above the rules [the letter of the law] to inculcate a sense of honor, a settled disposition to value honorable conduct in all areas of life. Such honor systems are fundamentally not penal but educational and inspirational."[28]

What seems clear, despite the pressures of contemporary societal outlooks on traditional conceptions of honor, is that people—individually and in groups, especially smaller groups—can *decide* to be honorable, to behave honorably, to support honorable behavior within their chosen group, and to enforce group standards of honor by imposing sanctions on those who fail to abide by them.

The late Stephen Ambrose once made an observation that has applicability in many contexts, not least in the realm of value-laden courses of action. "Nothing in life is inevitable," he said. "That is my most basic conclusion as an historian. People make choices, and choices have consequences."[29]

Honor Education

There is widespread agreement that honor education is the most important teaching done at West Point. It is noteworthy that this most important teaching is done primarily by the least experienced teachers, cadets themselves. The Honor Book and many other documents make clear that cadets understand their heavy responsibilities for imparting an understanding of the Honor Code and System to incoming plebes, and for inspiring them to embrace the code wholeheartedly, and that they work hard at meeting those responsibilities.

Over the years the importance of honor education has grown significantly as changing societal values, ethnic and cultural diversity of the entering classes, and thus a less reliable (or at least less predictable) shared value base has characterized each cohort of new plebes. Similarly, with regard to the larger society, Morris Janowitz has emphasized the "need to reconstruct a sense of patriotism," particularly in the years since World War II, due to an "immense proliferation of civic rights and welfare-state benefits" and the sense of entitlement (as distinct from responsibilities) they have engendered.[30]

The 1948 Honor Chairman, Cadet Lee Doyle, stressed to his successor that it was not enough to simply lecture new plebes on honor during Beast Barracks. "They are too bewildered to know what is important and too tired to absorb the honor system in its entirety in just a few hours of lecturing," he pointed out. Also "it must be realized that a very large percentage of the men entering the Academy have ideas on the importance of lying, cheating, and stealing which differ greatly from the concepts of our code of honor." If that was true then, many would agree it is even more so six decades later. Cadet Doyle recommended informal talks to the Fourth Classmen by company honor representatives throughout the academic year as the most effective means of educating them on matters of honor.

> ### Service
>
> What is important is how you look back on your service. Your view will depend more on what you gave than on what you received.
>
> General John A. Wickham Jr.
> USMA Class of 1950

A typical introduction to the Honor Code and Honor System, as presented by the Honor Committee Chairman to new cadets in their very first period of honor education, begins with a statement of the Honor Code and its significance. "It is ours to guard, protect, and uphold," he stated. "It is a great responsibility, but you will find it makes you a better man for having lived with it, a prouder man for having accepted it in spirit as well as in the letter, and a richer man for the mark it will leave on your character."[31]

A significant increase in emphasis on honor education was implemented during Academic Year 1975–1976. Acknowledging that for the past few years "too much emphasis has been placed upon the reprimanding of violators and too little upon education of the Code's membership," Cadet Jose Cueller advised the Corps that the Honor Committee had recently designated a vice chairman for education (along with one for investigations). Cueller, who held the education post, also noted that "in the past, Cadet honor instruction has been limited to two summer sessions—one prior to Plebe year and one prior to third class year. This amount of instruction was discovered to be totally inadequate."[32]

In 1976 a widely admired Tactical Officer, Major Boyd "Mac" Harris, wrote a landmark paper critiquing honor education as it had been practiced. "Honor is one of the most crucial, complex, and difficult things we teach here," he noted. "True professional integrity is a concept that requires maturity, age, and experience to understand. We should leave the 'running' of the honor system to cadets, but, concurrently, instructors and officers should be deeply involved in teaching professional integrity to cadets."[33]

In that same season a respected Chaplain, Colonel Kermit D. Johnson (later the Army's Chief of Chaplains), published an incisive essay on ethical issues in military leadership. His analysis concentrated on the leadership climate and its relationship to ethical behavior. "All decisions, practices, goals, and values of the entire institutional structure should be examined," he stressed, "beginning with the following: First, blatant or subtle forms of ethical relativism which blur the issue of what is right or wrong, or which bury it as a subject of little or no importance. Second, the exaggerated loyalty syndrome, where people are afraid to tell the truth and are discouraged from it. Third, the obsession with image, where people are not even interested in the truth. And last, the drive for success, in which ethical sensitivity is bought off or sold because of the personal need to achieve."[34]

The importance of more extensive (and perhaps more effective) honor education was indirectly stressed by General Goodpaster in remarks to the 1979 Board of Visitors to the Military Academy. The board's report subsequently quoted the Superintendent's remarks on reinforcing high standards of morals, ethics, and conduct. Such reinforcement was, said General Goodpaster, in his view a matter "of very great importance at a time when elsewhere in our country the same cannot be said. There has been a deterioration in morals and ethics and conduct, and in the sense of service and sacrifice across the country. There have been pressures, as all of us well know, to conform to that trend here. It has not been easy in the past, it is not easy now, and it will not be easy in the future for us to try to maintain a higher standard of morality and ethics and conduct here than is seen across the country."[35] Not easy—just essential.

When the Class of 1981 arrived as new plebes in the summer of 1977, with the Military Academy working hard to rebuild after the trauma of EE 304, it was decided that a ceremony would be conducted at the conclusion of Cadet Basic Training to emphasize responsibilities under the Honor Code and to dramatize acceptance of those responsibilities. An oral oath was devised for those purposes: "I, [name], about to become an accepted member of the Corps of Cadets, do solemnly swear that I will accept my responsibility to live by the Honor Code, that I accept this Code freely without any mental reservations or fraudulence possible, that I am prepared to take full responsibility for my actions and that I will not lie, cheat, or steal nor tolerate those who do[,] so help me God."[36]

In March 1982 a Superintendent's Honor Review Committee stated its view that "the new Four Year [Honor] Education Program is, without doubt, the most dramatic step taken in recent years to provide cadets the means to develop within the Corps a positive, healthy attitude toward the Honor Code and System; many improvements are needed but the program is well underway."[37]

The 1983 Superintendent's Honor Review Committee also praised the four-year program of honor education, at the same time urging that it focus more on the spirit of the Honor Code: "Honor education must convince cadets to seek to do the right thing, avoid the ethically gray areas, and abandon efforts to discover the fine line between behavior that will or will not be punished by the Honor System." Stating its view of what cadets should reasonably be expected to achieve, the 1983 Committee added that the four-year honor education program "cannot hope to make every cadet a candidate for sainthood. It can, however, explain that the Military Academy has a right to expect of all cadets candid and forthright behavior in all things and a desire to avoid any conduct that might threaten their reputation for honesty, aspects of the professional reputation that cadets begin to build even while at West Point and will carry with them into commissioned service."[38]

In many annual editions of *Bugle Notes* there appeared a toast rendered by one of the most revered figures at West Point, Colonel Herman Koehler. Not himself a graduate of the Military Academy, Colonel Koehler was appointed Master of the Sword—West Point's antique term for the director of physical education—in 1885, serving in that role for the next thirty-eight years. It was estimated that, between his tenure at West Point and detached service in Officer Training Camps around the country, he had personally instructed at least 200,000 officers and men, and that upon his retirement at the end of 1923 there were in the Army fewer than 200 graduates who had not been trained by him while they were cadets. In his toast Colonel Koehler expressed the hope that he too had been influenced by the spirit of West Point during his long years of service there. That spirit, he said, "leaves its indelible impress upon all who come in contact with it, be they graduates or not, by bringing out all the best that is in them. It is a spirit, gentlemen, that once it holds you in its grip is ever binding, ever immutable; the Academy's chiefest asset, the army's greatest reliance, and the country's best safeguard."[39]

Colonel Koehler made it clear that honor was the base plate of the spirit of West Point. "To me it is like a religion," he said, "for in it I find the unification of those principles of practical ethics and such physical and mental attributes as go toward the production of a manly man, in all which that term implies: vigorous of body; quick of intellect; clean of morals; sensitive of honor and honoring; of justice and duty keen; and to authority subservient. A combination, gentlemen, that gives the courage to dare because of the consciousness to do."[40]

In 1995, Honor Committee Chairman Mark Kappelmann noted in the Honor Book that the time allocated for honor education had increased from about twenty hours to fifty hours of instruction over the previous four years. An important feature of contemporary honor education is that, contrary to the practice in earlier days, all classes now receive such education, not just the plebes. As cadets progress through their years at West Point, the focus of honor education also evolves from the basic tenets of the Honor Code and System to the responsibilities of leadership and ethical aspects of officership. Not all honor education derives from briefings and lectures by members of the Honor Committee, of course. In fact, insistence on the value of a curriculum-wide concern for honor education or, even more broadly construed, an environment-wide concern for imparting high standards of honorable behavior, and for maintaining a climate supportive of honorable behavior, has repeatedly been stressed by honor study groups at West Point.

A 1977 study group comprising both officers and cadets included in its report the interesting and useful observation that "the Honor Code is a secular code of behavior."[41] That is a centrally important point, one made even more so by the increasing diversity of backgrounds in the modern Corps of Cadets. It is also worth noting that the majestic, venerable, and inspiring Cadet Prayer may be read as a secular document of great instructive and inspirational value. "Strengthen and increase our admiration for honest dealing and clean thinking" and "make us to choose the harder right instead of the easier wrong, and never to be content with a half truth when the whole can be won," are fundamentally worthy aspirations, whatever one's theological or metaphysical outlook, as is the aspiration "to maintain the honor of the Corps untarnished and unsullied and to show forth in our lives the ideals of West Point."

Chaplain Clayton Wheat composed the Cadet Prayer in 1919, just a year after taking up his post. His comments on the origins of his creation are noteworthy. "Corps honor, corps justice, corps integrity, corps loyalty, corps trustworthiness are instinctive group values which have long dominated the action of the Corps," he was quoted as saying in the *1939 Bugle Notes*, "even though the individual member may at times have failed in his effort to live up to those ideals." "In the Cadet Prayer, I attempted to compose a petition which would set forth in their own lives the ideals and principles which have long been fostered in the Corps." Again, therefore, we have an example of the central values that guide and inspire the Corps having their origins in the Corps itself.

In the modern era, with chapel attendance no longer mandatory, the Cadet Prayer is reportedly not as universally known among cadets as in an earlier day. That is a significant loss, for it deserves to be among the fundamental source documents for those preparing for careers of principled leadership.

Many cadets, at least among those in what turned out to be the latter days of mandatory chapel attendance, professed a certain cynicism about the experience, but there is anecdotal evidence of residual influence of great inspirational power upon at least some of those of an earlier day. Frederick Mayer, longtime organist at the Cadet Chapel and a gentleman known to generations of cadets, edited and published a collection of West Point songs that went through many editions. In a moving foreword he expressed his conviction that the Cadet

Alma Mater

Hail, Alma Mater dear!
To us be ever near,
Help us thy motto bear
Through all the years.
Let Duty be well performed,
Honor be e'er untarn'd,
Country be ever armed,

West Point, by thee.
Guide us, thy sons, aright,
Teach us by day, by night,
To keep thine honor bright,
For thee to fight.
When we depart from thee,
Serving on land or sea,
May we still loyal be,
West Point, to thee.

And when our work is done,
Our course on earth is run,
May it be said, "Well done.
Be thou at peace."
E'er may that line of gray
Increase from day to day,
Live, serve, and die, we pray,
West Point, for thee.

Paul S. Reinecke
USMA Class of 1911

Chapel, "with its beautiful Gothic architecture, reverential atmosphere, and inspiring Services, is undoubtedly a powerful influence in developing the more serious, idealistic nature of that splendid body of young manhood composing the Corps of Cadets."[42]

The tasks of honor education and exemplification today have never been more important, and perhaps never more challenging. "They come with values; we reinforce them," Captain Robert Lamb observed while serving as a tactical officer at West Point.[43] In an era when the larger society is perceived as less homogeneous, particularly in terms of the values espoused, helping cadets discover their best values and live by them is more critical than ever. The fact that many young men and women self-select for West Point precisely because they admire and want to live by the values taught there provides very positive reinforcement.

Formal and informal training and education on honor and the Honor Code and System are, in the contemporary West Point environment, complemented and buttressed in many ways. While religious influences are clearly more limited for many cadets than in an earlier day, a comprehensive program of education in aspects of the professional military ethic (referred to in shorthand terms as PME2) explores a wide range of value-related topics. These include team building, ethical reasoning and decision making, aspects of a profession, respect and consideration for others, and of course duty. The future of West Point depends on the success of such comprehensive approaches to inculcating the values and inspiring the devotion to duty required to lead American soldiers.

Notes

1 *Final Report of the Special Commission of the Chief of Staff on the Honor Code and Honor System at the United States Military Academy*, 30 May 1989, p. 5.
2 Ibid., p. [1]. Dr. Posvar and his colleagues were not entirely prescient, however, writing in May 1989: "If sensible national security policy prevails, there shall be no more grand wars and famous commanders of theater forces," p. 6. Less than two years later Gen. H. Norman Schwarzkopf (USMA 1956) gained fame by leading a massive armored force to victory in Operation Desert Storm. Of course Posvar and his colleagues had made their prediction conditional, so perhaps they would have maintained that it was still accurate.
3 Ibid., p. [1].
4 *Final Report of the Special Commission of the Chief of Staff on the Honor Code and Honor System at the United States Military Academy*, 30 May 1989, p. 9.
5 *USCC Pamphlet No. 632-1, The Honor Code and Honor System*, 1 June 1984, p. 1. Emphasis in the original.
6 *USCC Pamphlet 632-1*, August 1992, p. 3.
7 *Honor Guide for Officers*, p. 6.
8 Memorandum, Maj. Gen. Sidney B. Berry (Superintendent USMA) to Commandant of Cadets and others, Subject: Superintendent's Special Study Group on Honor at West Point, 9 October 1974, Adjutant General Files, 1011-01 Curriculum Approval Files: Honor Code, USMA Archives.
9 *Report to the Secretary of the Army by the Special Commission on the United States Military Academy*, 15 December 1976, p. 20. Hereafter *Borman Commission Report*.

10 Memorandum for the Record, Maj. Gen. Philip R. Feir, Commandant of Cadets, Subject: After Action Report, 12 April 1975, p. 44.

11 Goodpaster comments as reported in Memorandum for Record, Col. Jack M. Pollin, Subject: In Process Review, Superintendent's Honor Review Committee, 7 December 1977, dated 15 December 1977, USMA Archives.

12 *USCC Pamphlet 632-1*, June 1977, p. 4. This version of the periodically revised and reissued basic publication on the Honor Code and System is much more detailed and informative than, for example, even such a recent predecessor as the 1973 version, perhaps reflecting greater attention paid to the document in the wake of the 1976 honor crisis.

13 Lt. Gen. Andrew J. Goodpaster, Interview by Dr. Stephen Grove, 12 May 1981, USMA Historian's Files. Emphasis in original.

14 Ibid., p. 4, quoting from the Superintendent's letter to graduates in *Assembly* (July 1988).

15 John MacCormack, *Middletown Times Herald* (18 May 1979), quoting Major M. C. MacLaren.

16 *Pointer View* (25 May 1979), p. 7.

17 Disposition Form, Subject: Quibbling, Cadet Hatfield to D. K. Culp, 3 March 1964, File: Honor Code (JUL 63–JUN 64), USMA Archives.

18 Memorandum, Dennis K. Culp, Chairman, Honor Committee, to Honor Representatives, Subject: Instruction to Honor Representatives, 17 February 1964, File: Honor Code—Historical (JUL 63–JUN 64), USMA Archives.

19 *USCC Pamphlet 632-1*, August 1992, p. 10.

20 2007 *Bugle Notes*, p. 35.

21 Ibid.

22 *The Honor Newsletter* (Vol. 3, No. 1, October 1988), p. 2.

23 Cadet Captain Christopher Hostler, Memorandum, Subject: The Honor Code and System, 1 February 2007, Cover Memorandum to *USCC Pamphlet 632-1*, same date. Cadet Hostler notes in this memorandum that the Cadet Honor Committee is publishing the document "with the approval of the Commandant of Cadets and the Superintendent, United States Military Academy."

24 *Years of Continuity and Progress: 1991–1996*, p. 13.

25 Col. Matthew Moten, Professor and Deputy Head of the USMA Department of History, has commented in reviewing this manuscript with respect to the silence: "Another problem with ostracism was that it had also been used for purposes other than honor enforcement. Most egregiously, in the late 19th and first half of the 20th centuries the Corps shunned black cadets who had done nothing dishonorable. This practice surely tended to confuse, perhaps to conflate, honor with racism."

26 Memorandum, Cadet Captain Robert H. Baldwin Jr., Brigade Commander, to Members of the Corps of Cadets, Subject: Clarification of Honor Implications in Automobile Licensing and Registration, 10 March 1969, File: Honor Code—Historical (JUL 67–JUN 70), USMA Archives.

27 James Bowman, "Honor," *Richmond Times-Dispatch* (5 August 2007).

28 Lad Sessions, "Teaching Such a Concept," *Richmond Times-Dispatch*, 5 August 2007.

29 The History Channel, 25 September 1998.

30 Morris Janowitz, *The Reconstruction of Patriotism*, pp. x-xi.

31 Lesson 1, Honor Instruction, New Cadet Barracks, 1969, p. 1-5.

32 Memorandum, Cadet Jose A. Cuellar, Vice Chairman for Education, Honor Committee, to United States Corps of Cadets, Subject: Honor Education, 21 January 1976, File: Honor Code—Historical (1 AUG 73–JUN 73), USMA Archives.

33 Memorandum, Maj. Boyd M. Harris to Superintendent USMA, Subject: Recommendations for Constructive Change at West Point, 4 November 1976, USMA Archives.

34 Chaplain Kermit D. Johnson, "Ethical Issues of Military Leadership," *Parameters* (Vol. IV, No. 2, 1974), as quoted in Charles W. Hudlin, "Morality and the Military Profession: Problems and Solutions," *Military Ethics*, p. 85.

35 Report of the Board of Visitors to the United States Military Academy, 28 December 1979, USMA Archives.

36 As described in Letter, Lt. Gen. Sidney B. Berry to Gen. Bernard W. Rogers (Chief of Staff), 10 June 1977, USMA Archives.

37 Report of the Superintendent's Honor Review Committee AY 81-82, March 1982, USMA Archives.

38 Report of the Superintendent's Honor Review Committee AY 82-83, March 1983, USMA Archives.

39 "A Toast by Col. H. J. Koehler," *1924 Bugle Notes*, pp. 21, 23-24.

40 Ibid., p. 24.

41 Letter, Lt. Gen. Sidney B. Berry to Gen. Bernard W. Rogers (Chief of Staff), 10 June 1977, USMA Archives. Emphasis in original.

42 Frederick C. Mayer, *Songs of the United States Military Academy*, p. vi.

43 As quoted by Ward Poche, "Cadets' Honor," *Newburgh Evening News* (2 June 1986). Capt. Lamb (USMA 1978) had as a cadet been chairman of the Honor Committee.

Epilogue

Continuity

Most graduates of the Military Academy undoubtedly share the view of Major General Philip Feir, who stressed when he was Commandant of Cadets that the honor system is the "cornerstone" of West Point. "It is something we must have. If we lost it or if it fails—not much difference there—then I believe that the need for the Military Academy would be diluted significantly."[1]

In earlier times most officers assigned to the Military Academy's staff and faculty were graduates of the institution, but more recently highly qualified officers from other fine colleges and universities have also been given such assignments, as have a significant number of civilian educators, and eventually certain carefully selected non-commissioned officers as well. These instructors have played a key role in honor education, and have done remarkably well in that role. But this diversity of instructor background has also meant that some formal articulation of key elements of the Honor Code and System was in order. As Commandant of Cadets Brigadier General David Bramlett (USMA 1964) did that clearly and succinctly in a memorandum for his tactical officers. "The Cadet Honor Code and System," he began, "continue to be the bedrock upon which this institution pursues its singular purpose: developing leaders of character."[2]

Some years later, in the early 1990s, it was decided to designate two realms of behavior as those in which "bedrock" values of the Corps of Cadets were involved. Not surprisingly, the first chosen was honor, since bedrock values were defined as "the irreducible, inviolate, and unchanging standards for men and women of character who lead American soldiers."[3] Among the obligations of those serving honorably, it was specified, were "establishing a proper command climate within a unit, demonstrating proper behavior, and influencing others to do what is right." That was in 1992. The following year a second bedrock value was designated, this one defined as "consideration for others," an obligation intended to foster "professional trust and respect for the sanctity of life and property."[4]

A document summarizing the years 1991–1996 at West Point, the period during which the bedrock values had been highlighted, included this key observation: The United States Military Academy "recognizes that America and the Army need good leaders, and we are increasingly aware that the difference between good and bad leaders is often more a question of character than of technical proficiency." Following that insight to its logical implication: "Every activity at the Military Academy must contribute to developing leaders of character, and character development is the fundamental goal of the West Point experience."[5]

General Bramlett had also stressed, in his earlier remarks, the broader application of these values, and their historical origins. "The principles of the Honor

Code and System," he wrote, "are the foundation for the professional officer ethical code; these principles are not unique to West Point, but the Academy has codified them into a way of life that prepares its graduates to assume the awesome responsibilities of a commissioned officer." And: "Honor is integral to everything we do here at West Point."[6]

Colonel Thomas Griess, longtime Head of the USMA Department of History, set forth an admirable standard in describing the officers he wanted coming back to his department: "I want, as teachers of cadets, only bright, mature, and dedicated officers whose personal fidelity to service remains unwavering; I want only those men who feel a keen sense of moral obligation to repay, with service of the highest quality, the society which has seen fit to educate them to leadership, trust, and responsibility."[7]

Increasing faculty diversity has been paralleled, as we have noted, by greater diversity of background and prior outlook among incoming cadets, both realities that further underscore the importance of honor education. Changes in the day-to-day experience of cadets, also in important ways constituting a centrifugal force, make effective honor education even more imperative. Every successful leader knows that cohesion is crucially important in building a high-performing unit. A former Commandant of Cadets also identified cohesion as "one of the things that makes the honor code work," calling it "absolutely essential to the proper function of the honor code and the sense of duty and everything else we're trying to inculcate in people around here." But the task of building cohesion in the Corps of Cadets, he noted, was more challenging (as he viewed it in 1985) than ever before. Among the factors he enumerated were the admission of women, elimination of mandatory chapel attendance, introduction of academic majors, proliferation of extracurricular activities, and an expanded number of corps squads. Thus "people are going in all different directions doing all sorts of things."[8]

The key factors in achieving cohesion in such an environment would seem to be strong leadership—from both officers and the cadet chain of command, and effective acculturation imparting West Point's historical traditions and values—and inspiring their emulation. The USMA Department of History has an engaging slogan that relates to this handing down of values: "At West Point, much of the history we teach was made by the people we taught."

Today and Tomorrow

The Honor Code clearly does not attempt to catalogue and proscribe all forms of dishonorable behavior. Murder, rape, failure to live up to marital vows—all are eschewed by honorable persons, yet none of these is included in the Code. As many have observed, then, the Honor Code is a desirable standard of honorable behavior, necessary but not sufficient in and of itself as a complete guide to an honorable life. A Posvar Commission observation is pertinent: "As an ethical rule, [the Honor Code] happens to be stated in proscriptive terms, specifically

against lying, cheating, stealing, or tolerating those who do. This list has
changed, and can change again."[9]

General Goodpaster commented
perceptively on this matter, stressing
that "the simple negatives are just the
price of admission, that you don't lie,
cheat, steal, or tolerate those who
do. . . . There's a lot more to ethics and
to honorable behavior than that. It's
being honest in word and deed, stand-

Service

I don't know what your destiny will
be, but one thing I know; the only
ones among you who will be really
happy are those who have sought
and found how to serve.

Albert Schweitzer

---

ing up to your responsibilities. . . . You don't just stay within regulations or just
within the law, you try to carry out the purpose of the institution as reflected in
the regulations and in the law."[10]

Lieutenant General Dave Palmer, another former USMA Superintendent,
has recently written a book about George Washington and Benedict Arnold.[11] In
an intriguing sub-title, he describes them both as patriots, then in the text justi-
fies that assertion before demonstrating that what brought the two patriots to
such disparate ends was character, or in Arnold's case the lack of it. "Know
what is right, and have the moral courage to do what is right—that is character,"
General Palmer has said, reducing the matter to its essence. That brief formulation covers a lot of ground.

As we have seen, the Honor Code has evolved over time, at first applying simply to the sanctity of one's word. Even then, however, other forms of dishonorable behavior now proscribed by the Code were not tolerated, but were
dealt with separately, usually being punished under the laws of war. Stealing
is the prime example from those earlier days. This suggests that, even though
they are literally carved in granite at the Military Academy, the terms of the
Honor Code could conceivably be supplemented at some future time by
inclusion of other forms of prohibited behavior. The Posvar Commission stated
flatly that "the Honor Code will succeed or fail based upon the degree of
commitment of the Corps of Cadets to honor as a virtue, not merely to the literal
Code itself."[12] Such a comprehensive view could also, at some future point, lead
to expanded coverage of the Honor Code itself, just as in earlier times.

Honor and Duty

There is another realm in which honor, above and beyond the basic requirements of the Honor Code, comes into play. For those in military service, under-
taking thereby the solemn obligations that leadership of soldiers entails, the
demands of duty also come very close to obligations of honor. Some indeed have
argued that, for military professionals, the individual responsibility to be competent amounts to an ethical imperative.[13]

When a Military Academy pamphlet on the Honor Code and System was
issued in August 1976, the transmittal memorandum was signed jointly by the

Commandant and the Honor Committee Chairman. "Concepts of Honor and Duty are inseparable," they said right at the outset. "Both represent obligations of loyalty to the highest ideals of public service and military professionalism."[14]

A former Commandant commented perceptively on the full range of expectations for cadets. "The first goal is to develop as a good human being," said Brigadier General John Moellering. Along with that he stressed development of character and individual leadership.[15] Any unit in the Army would be proud to have a leader who was striving to, as the great recruiting slogan of the past put it, "be all you can be" in those three realms.

Speaking at West Point's Centennial celebration in 1902, Lieutenant General John Schofield, President of the Association of Graduates, reminded all those assembled that "the honor as officers and gentlemen, of which Cadets have justly been most proud, is very largely in their own keeping."[16] It is of fundamental importance to understand that living by honorable standards as cadets is not an end in itself, but rather preparation for living an honorable life as an officer. "Looking ahead to their service life," wrote the Posvar Commission, "cadets should be made aware that their subordinates, especially enlisted soldiers, will rely on them as officers to be honorable, consistent, and fair, that indeed a unit draws its strength from the character of its officers, both in respect to their real qualities and the impressions imparted by their behavior."[17]

An important part of such expectations is that officers' conduct be consistent, that they adhere to the same high standards in private life as they do on duty. When he was Chief of Staff, General Abrams made that point in the strongest possible terms (and with his usual crusty candor) in addressing the issue of racial prejudice. He told a conference of his senior subordinates that it would not do to act one way on duty and another way "off duty." We have only one life, he said, and that's our military life. No dual standards can be tolerated. "Is there anyone left who thinks his soldiers don't know all that—and realize what a damned fraud he is? If you're a leader you can't do it. If you can't live with that, you're just in the wrong outfit."[18]

General Abrams spoke often of service, and of the privilege of service. "There must be, within our Army," he said, "a sense of purpose and a dedication to that purpose. There must be a willingness to march a little farther, to carry a heavier load, to step out into the darkness and the unknown for the safety and well-being of others."[19] Many, many graduates have lived lives and careers inspired by that outlook. Remembering one departed husband and father in a memorial article, his family and classmates recalled how he had written that he went to West Point because "it was an opportunity for a good education." Then, they said with affection and admiration: "He got that good education, and in return he gave back a lifetime of dedicated service: service to his country, to his family, to the Army, to his church, to his community, to his alma mater, and to his classmates and friends."[20] Thus are concepts of honor and duty ever intertwined.

Cadet Joseph Dougherty, Chairman of the 1956 Honor Committee, stated the fundamental point that inculcation of honor was a matter not just for one's years at West Point but was rather for a lifelong commitment. The main purpose of the Honor System, he wrote in the Honor Book, "is to develop a high sense of

Honor in <u>each individual</u> so that he may be a better person and better officer to serve his country. This is not a Code of Honor that will be left behind at West Point upon graduation, but one that will follow the cadet until the day he dies." A later Honor Chairman, Cadet James Coe, put it this way in his 1980 Honor Book entry: "The spirit of the Code is what is sought here, a spirit that transcends the West Point experience and is carried on through life."

In an act of both symbolic importance and practical import, entering cadets sign and swear to an oath of allegiance and agreement to serve. Those who measure up, who persevere to graduation and commissioning, qualify for the inestimable privilege of leading American soldiers.

On the distant battlefields of Afghanistan and Iraq young West Pointers of today are showing valor and devotion to duty worthy of the best of the Long Gray Line. Lieutenant General Benjamin Freakley, the senior officer now responsible for Army accessions from all sources, is one of many attesting to that. "I want to assure you that the United States Military Academy is producing phenomenal leaders in a time of war," he said recently to an audience of "old grads."[21] Gratifyingly, there are many indications that today's soldiers share that view.

Other young graduates have shown equally inspiring courage and serenity not in combat, but in the midst of dire personal crises. William Stallworth graduated in the Class of 1988 and was commissioned in field artillery. Athletic, handsome, full of energy and optimism, he was a natural leader with a great career ahead of him. Then, only two years out of the Academy, he was stricken with a rare and ultimately fatal form of muscle cancer. An hour before his death this brave young man dictated a message that spoke volumes about who and what he was, and about the values that had guided his short life: "To fellow classmates, friends, and the rest of my family: Thank you for the love, peace, dignity, strength, and honor which you have shown to me. Your gift is priceless. Goodbye, everyone."[22]

The mission statement of the Military Academy has in recent times been the subject of a number of revisions.[23] In its classic formulation, taken in this instance from the *1941 Bugle Notes*, that statement reads like this: "To instruct and train the Corps of Cadets so that each graduate shall have the qualities and attributes essential to his progressive and continued development throughout a lifetime career as an officer of the Regular Army." That issue of *Bugle Notes* also includes an interesting statement linking the Cadet Honor Code to what many have viewed as its ancient source: "The Code of the Soldier demands courageous and fearless honesty in setting forth the truth, regardless of consequences."

Today the mission statement, after many excursions, again reads much like the classic version: "To educate, train, and inspire the Corps of Cadets so that each graduate is a commissioned leader of character committed to the values of Duty, Honor, Country and prepared for a career of professional excellence and service to the Nation as an officer in the United States Army."[24] An essential element in accomplishment of that mission is, and has always been, wholehearted acceptance of the powerful dictates of the Honor Code. Wrote an Honor Committee Chairman to a civilian collegian who inquired about the matter: "Our System is a set of rules; our Code is a way of life."[25]

Strong affirmation of the overall success of the Military Academy in promulgating and perpetuating an admirable set of values has been provided by a fairly recent study conducted by civilian academicians. "All service academies," they wrote, "while by no means perfect, had honor code compliance far superior to civilian colleges and universities." Cadets past and present could take heart, strength, and encouragement from their final conclusion: "The USMA honor code seems to stand head and shoulders above all others."[26]

Pride in that finding must, however, be tempered by the knowledge that such a reputation must be earned anew by each cohort, indeed by each class and each cadet, as they take their places in the Long Gray Line. The privilege of being a West Pointer carries with it the sacred duty to teach and to inspire, by precept and example, those who follow to themselves adopt and exemplify the Military Academy's highest ideals, and to pass them along in their turn.

At the time of West Point's bicentennial celebration a longtime former Cadet Chaplain, the Rev. Richard Camp, was invited back as guest preacher in the Cadet Chapel. He took as his theme continuity amidst change, for over the years many, many things had changed at the Military Academy. But Chaplain Camp stressed the timelessness of West Point's essential character and spoke movingly of its enduring values. "Everything is different," he observed, "but nothing has changed."

A quarter century after his graduation, an officer then serving as Commandant of Cadets spoke about what West Point had meant in his life: "In a lot of ways West Point was the place I was born," said Brigadier General Peter Boylan in an oral history interview. "It was a place where I learned what it was that I wanted to be, what it was that I wanted to become. It was a place that provided me the wherewithal, the resources to become that sort of person. It nurtured me."[27] James Salter, who entered West Point with the Class of 1945, later recalled his first impressions of the place as a plebe: "It was the hard school, the forge." On that forge "West Point did not make character, it extolled it. It taught you to believe in difficulty, the hard way, and to sleep, as it were, on bare ground. Duty, Honor, Country. The great virtues were cut into stone above the archways and inscribed in the gold of class rings, not the classic virtues—not virtues at all, in fact, but commands. In life you might know defeat and see things you revered fall into darkness and disgrace, but never these."[28] Many thousands of graduates, reflecting on their lives and careers as shaped and guided by West Point, could relate to those inspiring recollections. And many could also subscribe to a famous sentiment expressed by General of the Armies John Pershing (USMA 1886) soon after the close of the First World War: "The longer I live, and the further I have gone in the Service, the more I reverence the things that inspire the heart and soul of young men at West Point."[29]

As the Military Academy moves through the 21st century, the Honor Code remains as it has always been, a precious thing, fragile, entirely dependent on each new cohort of cadets to adopt it, make it their own, fiercely protect it, and march forward in its service. That this process shall continue in perpetuity is the heart-felt hope and dream of all those—proud and grateful members of the Long Gray Line—who have shared the privilege of living by its inspiring standard.

The Corps

The Corps! The Corps! The Corps!
The Corps! Bareheaded salute it,
With eyes up, thanking our God
That we of the Corps are treading
Where they of the Corps have trod.
They are here in ghostly assemblage,
The men of the Corps long dead,
And our hearts are standing attention
While we wait for their passing tread.
We sons of today, we salute you,
You sons of an earlier day;
We follow, close order, behind you,
Where you have pointed the way.
The long gray line of us stretches
Through the years of a century told,
And the last man feels to his marrow
The grip of your far-off hold.
Grip hands with us now, though we see not,
Grip hands with us, strengthen our hearts,
As the long line stiffens and straightens
With the thrill that your presence imparts.
Grip hands, though it be from the shadows,
While we swear, as you did of yore,
Or living, or dying, to honor
The Corps, and the Corps, and the Corps.

Bishop Herbert S. Shipman
Chaplain, USMA

Notes

1 Memorandum for the Record, Maj. Gen. Philip R. Feir, Commandant of Cadets, Subject: After Action Report, 12 April 1975, USMA Archives.

2 Memorandum for Tactical Officers, Subject: Command Guidance: The Honor Code and System, Brig. Gen. David A. Bramlett, Commandant of Cadets, 4 April 1990, USMA Archives.

3 *Years of Continuity and Progress: 1991–1996*, p. 11.

4 Ibid., pp. 1-2.

5 Ibid., pp. 7-8.

6 Ibid.

7 Letter, Col. Thomas E. Griess to Officers Going to Graduate School, 13 December 1971, Box Labelled "Knowlton Correspondence with Lt. Gen. Kerwin, DCSPER," USMA Archives.

8 Brig. Gen. John H. Moellering, Commandant of Cadets, Dr. Stephen Grove Interview, 5 June 1985, USMA Historian's Files. At the time of this interview General Moellering observed that there were 27 different corps squads and 92 extracurricular activities in which cadets could take part.

9 *Final Report of the Special Commission of the Chief of Staff on the Honor Code and Honor System*, 30 May 1989, p. [1]. When he was Superintendent General Goodpaster stated a formulation in positive rather than negative terms: "Commitment to the concept of honorable behavior—of being honest in word and deed, as I like to put it, to put it in a positive context rather than in not lying, stealing, cheating, or tolerating." Interview by Dr. Stephen Grove, 12 May 1981, USMA Historian's Files. In 1998 the Cadet Honor Committee, apparently stimulated by a thirst for what they (perhaps mistakenly) considered grammatical correctness such that it overcame any regard for historical continuity, conspired with the Department of English to recast the Honor Code as follows: "A cadet will not lie, cheat, steal, or tolerate those who do." *USCC Pamphlet 632-1*, p. 2-2. The Honor Committee Executive Officer announced the change in a 5 October 1998 memorandum.

10 Gen. Andrew J. Goodpaster, Interview by Lt. Col. James M. Johnson, 7 March 1988, USMA Historian's Files.

11 Dave R. Palmer, *George Washington and Benedict Arnold: A Tale of Two Patriots* (Washington: Regnery Publishing, 2006).

12 Ibid., p. 14.

13 See for example Lewis Sorley, "Competence as Ethical Imperative," *Army* (August 1982), pp. 42-48.

14 Pamphlet, *The Cadet Honor Code and System*, 30 August 1976. The transmittal memorandum was signed by Brig. Gen. W. F. Ulmer Jr., Commandant, and Cadet Michael E. Ivy, Honor Committee Chairman.

15 Brig. Gen. John H. Moellering, Interview by Dr. Stephen Grove, 5 June 1985, USMA Historian's Files.

16 *Centennial of the United States Military Academy*, I:62.

17 *Final Report of the Special Commission of the Chief of Staff on the Honor Code and Honor System*, 30 May 1989, p. 21.

18 As quoted in Lewis Sorley, *Thunderbolt*, p. 354.

19 As inscribed on a memorial to General Abrams at the U.S. Army War College, Carlisle Barracks, Pennsylvania.

20 "Memorial Article: John G. Driskill, USMA 1952," *Taps* (May/June 2007), p. 45.

21 Remarks, West Point Society of the District of Columbia Luncheon, Fort Myer, Virginia, 19 September 2007.

22 Memorial Article, *Assembly* (January 1992), p. 192.

23 These changes reflected at least in part an accommodation (and then, with later emendation, backing away from such accommodation) of graduates serving less than full careers as Army officers.

24 Briefing Slide, Simon Center for the Professional Military Ethic, Briefing for Chief of Staff General Casey, 20 April 2007.

25 Letter, Dennis K. Culp, Chairman, Cadet Honor Committee, to Paul T. Barnes, Fairfield University, 18 February 1964, File: Honor Code—Historical (JUL 63–JUN 64), USMA Archives.

26 Frederick V. Malmstrom and Solomon A. Fulero, "Do Service Academy Honor Codes Work?" p. 205.

27 Brig. Gen. Peter J. Boylan, Dr. Stephen Grove Interview, 22/24 July 1987, USMA Historian's Files.

28 James Salter, "You Must," *Esquire* (December 1992), pp. 146, 150. This was many years before Tom Hanks's memorable explanation to a flustered young female baseball player in the film *A League of Their Own*, but that also fit: "*Of course* it's hard. It's *supposed* to be hard. That's what makes it *great!*"

29 The *1919 Bugle Notes*, p. 34, identifies this as taken from an 11 January 1919 letter to the USMA Superintendent from Pershing as Commander in Chief, American Expeditionary Forces.

Acknowledgments

Researching and writing this essay has been a challenging but delightful task. First, it has brought me back to West Point, a place very dear to me and to my kinfolk. That is where I was born when my father was teaching Military Art & Engineering and my uncle was a tactical officer. It is where I was educated as a member of the great Class of 1956, proudly following my grandfather (Lewis Sorley, USMA 1891), my father (Merrow Sorley, USMA 1924), and my uncle (Lewis Sorley Jr., USMA 1919) as a member of the United States Corps of Cadets. It is where I made many of the friends who have sustained me personally and professionally over many years of shared service. It is where, as a captain of Armor, I was privileged to spend three years on the faculty as an instructor and then assistant professor in the Department of English. And it is where, at the end, I hope to return, to a final resting place somewhere near my father.

Over the years many scholars have found West Point a fascinating topic, and I am grateful to them for the cumulative work on which I have been able to draw. Those works are cited in the bibliography and many of the notes, but I would like to express special admiration for the late Colonel Russell P. "Red" Reeder, my father's Beast Barracks roommate and a friend to me for many, many years. After valorous though short-lived service as a regimental commander in the Normandy invasion of World War II, service that earned him the first Distinguished Service Cross awarded in the European Theater of Operations, Red served for many years at West Point as a mentor, role model, coach, and author whose influence over several generations of cadets was of inestimable value.

Another gratifying aspect of this task has been that almost without exception everyone who was approached for help responded willingly and enthusiastically. At West Point that begins with the Simon Center for the Professional Military Ethic, where I was welcomed, provided office space, encouraged, and assisted by the Director, Colonel Doug Boone (USMA 1979); two Deputy Directors in turn, Lieutenant Colonel (now Colonel) Pat Sullivan and his (unrelated) successor, Lieutenant Colonel Tim Sullivan (USMA 1989); the Professor of Officership, Dr. Rick Swain (USMA 1966), and his interim successor, Colonel Mat Moten (USMA 1982), who is also deputy head of the Department of History; the Commandant's Special Assistant for Honor, initially Lieutenant Colonel Leanne Meyer and then Lieutenant Colonel Todd Messitt (USMA 1987); Major Devon Blake (USMA 1995) the Education Officer for the Simon Center for the Professional Military Ethic; and the office manager, first Wolodymyr "Walt" Banach and then Ellen Peterson. I owe special thanks to Pat Sullivan, whose energy, imagination, ability, and good will made every aspect of this project go better. I am also grateful to General Frederick Franks (USMA 1959), the distinguished Visiting Scholar at the Simon Center, for encouragement and insights.

An editorial board for the project, chaired by Colonel Boone, has been most helpful. Its members have included Colonel Lance Betros (USMA 1977), head of the Department of History; Colonel Rick Kerin (USMA 1972), head of the Department of English; Colonel Maritza Ryan (USMA 1982), head of the Department of Law; and Gregory Louks (USMA 1988), and then later Nancy Calhelha, of the Association of Graduates.

During many weeks spent at West Point for research I developed great admiration and respect for the team of professionals with whom I worked. Dr. Steve Grove, USMA Historian, gave me access to the superb collection of oral histories of former Superintendents and other senior officials he has built up over the years, and in the process also became a valued friend. During many long days in the USMA Archives I received encouragement and valuable support from Suzanne Christoff, Archivist and Director of Special Collections, and her entire staff, to include Alicia Mauldin-Ware, Elaine McConnell, Susan Lintelmann, Pamela Kingsbury, Herbert LaGoy, Valerie Dutdut, and Deborah McKeon-Pogue. Another longtime member of the USMA Library staff and an old friend, Alan Aimone, was also most helpful. At the USMA Museum, Director David Reel and Art Curator Gary Hood took a friendly interest in the project. Diane Bernicker of the Office of Policy, Planning and Assessment assisted at a critical juncture. At the Military Academy's Five Star Inn, providing billeting for transient military people and my home away from home for many weeks, the late Laura Sheposh and Dale Notarte were particularly helpful.

I also had the pleasure of meeting a number of other impressive and dedicated members of the West Point community whose interest in this project provided encouragement. They included Lieutenant Colonel Tony Burgess (USMA 1990), who heads the innovative Center for Company-Level Leadership, and his colleagues Lieutenant Colonel Pete Kilner (USMA 1990) and Major Ray Kimball (USMA 1995). Also Lieutenant Colonel Joe Doty (USMA 1982), a broad-gauged scholar who teaches character-building aspects of sports in the Department of Physical Education with engaging energy and insight.

My involvement in this project derives directly from my friendship with and admiration for Lieutenant General Ted Stroup (USMA 1962), Chairman of the West Point Association of Graduates, who encouraged me to undertake the work "for the good of the team." Colonel Bob McClure (USMA 1976), the Association of Graduates' President, has been very supportive, as have been my much admired and longtime friend Colonel Morris Herbert (USMA 1950), Gregory Louks (USMA 1988), and Nancy Calhelha of the AOG staff.

Many others who care about West Point have come up on the net to offer assistance and, in a number of cases, valuable documents. These include my classmates Lieutenant General Dave Palmer (USMA Superintendent, 1986–1991), Lieutenant General Chuck Bagnal (Deputy Superintendent, 1977–1980), Lieutenant General Rick Brown, Major General Jim Ellis, Colonel Dick Curl, Colonel Fred Holmes and Colonel Jim McMahon (USAFR).

Also General Art Brown (USMA 1953 and Deputy Superintendent, 1980–1981), Lieutenant General Sid Berry (USMA 1948 and Superintendent, 1974–1977), Lieutenant General Walt Ulmer (USMA 1952 and Commandant of Cadets 1975–1977), General "Dutch" Kerwin Jr. (USMA 1939), Lieutenant

General Bob Pursley (USAF) (USMA 1949), Lieutenant General Dick Trefry (USMA 1950), Brigadier General Tom Carpenter (USMA 1958), Brigadier General Tony Hartle (USMA 1964), Colonel Tom Courant (USMA 1952), Major Jack Craigie (USAF) (USMA 1951), Colonel Rudy Ehrenberg (USMA 1963), Colonel Neal Ellis Jr. (USAR) (USMA 1970), Colonel Bill Epling (USMA 1954), Dr. John Feagin (USMA 1955), Colonel George Hall (USAR) (USMA 1958), Major Bruce Harding (USMA 1976), Colonel Max Kovel (USMA 1957), Colonel Len Marrella (USMA 1957), Lieutenant Colonel Tom McKenna (USMA 1953), Colonel Bill McWilliams (USAF) (USMA 1955), Colonel Tony Nadal (USMA 1958), Lieutenant Colonel George Psihas (USAR) (USMA 1951), Ann (Mrs. Paul S.) Reinecke, Lieutenant Colonel Jim Ryan (USMA 1955), Valerie Vesser, and Colonel Frank Wolak (USMA 1949). Brigadier General Jack Capps (USMA 1948) was especially helpful regarding events in 1976–1977, when he played a key role as Chairman of the Special Readmissions Committee.

I am particularly grateful to Colonel Lloyd Matthews (USMA 1954), my former colleague in the USMA Department of English and a valued friend for all the years since then, for meticulous review of the entire manuscript and many very helpful suggestions for its improvement.

Special thanks also to Colonel Jay Olejniczak (USMA 1961) and his publications staff at the West Point Association of Graduates. Their *Register of Graduates and Former Cadets* has been an indispensable resource for this and many other research tasks.

Financial support for this work was provided by the late Bernard Petrie (USMA 1946), whose original idea it was to underwrite such a volume in the interests of honor education. His dedication to West Point and his generosity in its behalf are inspiring. It is a source of great regret that he departed this life before his project reached completion. I hope the book he sponsored will nevertheless prove to have met his expectations.

Finally I record my loving thanks to my wife Virginia Mezey Sorley for her loyal support and encouragement in this as in all things.

This book is dedicated to the United States Corps of Cadets.

Lewis Sorley
Potomac, Maryland
16 March 2008

A Note on Sources

The literature on the United States Military Academy, and specifically on its Honor Code and System, is extensive, as are the document collections. The USMA Archives are in and of themselves an absolute treasure trove of primary source material, so engrossing that any researcher needs firm self-discipline to stick to his assigned topic and resist pursuing various side paths on all manner of unrelated but entertaining topics.

The coverage of successive periods in the Academy's history is not uniform, however. A major fire in 1838 destroyed much material pertaining to the very early years, a loss whose impact cannot be fully assessed in that even what was lost is not definitively known. Then there have been instances in which, long after the fact, extremely valuable and previously unknown materials have been discovered. In the 1920s, to cite one delicious example, a package of Colonel Sylvanus Thayer's personal correspondence was discovered under the flooring of the Superintendent's quarters.

Materials held by the Archives range from the official—Superintendents' Letter Books from the very early days, annual reports, records of periodic honor review committees and specific investigations, and much else—to individual and personal materials. A full collection of such cadet-produced publications as *The Howitzer* (the annual yearbook put out by the graduating class) and *Bugle Notes* (a handbook for study and use by new plebes) provides much material pertinent to honor issues.

Unpublished materials in the Archives that proved useful include a number of dissertations, many of them by West Point graduates, examining various eras of the Military Academy's history and development. Invariably issues relating to honor matters are given close attention in such studies.

The USMA Library's collection of secondary source material on the Military Academy is, as one might expect, voluminous, comprehensive, and unsurpassed. The Simon Center for the Professional Military Ethic at West Point also has a useful Honor Library of published materials.

Various interested graduates have, from their own files, provided on loan a wealth of valuable materials. Those assisting in this way included former Superintendents and Commandants, USMA faculty members, honor committee members of earlier days, a special readmission committee chairman, military lawyers involved at various stages, and individual graduates who had made their own studies of honor issues. Some of this material duplicated archival holdings, but much was unique and therefore particularly helpful.

Special mention must be made of the invaluable materials compiled over many years by the USMA Historian, Dr. Stephen Grove. In addition to the Superintendent's annual reports drafted by him, Dr. Grove has produced a fine collection of oral histories. Those interviewed include senior Academy officials such as Superintendents, Deans, and Commandants, many other members of the staff and faculty, cadets who served as First Captain or Honor Committee Chairman, and many people involved with the integration of women into the Corps. Taken in the aggregate, these materials constitute a rich contribution to the historical record.

Selected Bibliography

Books

Ambrose, Stephen E. *Duty, Honor, Country: A History of West Point*. Baltimore: Johns Hopkins Press, 1966.

Atkinson, Rick. *The Long Gray Line*. Boston: Houghton Mifflin, 1989.

Baumer, William H. Jr. *West Point: Moulder of Men*. New York: D. Appleton-Century, 1942.

Berman, Bennett H. and Michael E. Monbeck. *West Point: An Illustrated History of the United States Military Academy*. New York: Times Books, 1978.

Beukema, Colonel Herman. *The United States Military Academy and Its Foreign Contemporaries*. West Point: USMA Department of Economics, Government and History, 1943.

Bixby, William H. *Record of the Class of 1873 of the United States Military Academy*. New York: D. Van Nostrand, 1875.

Blackwell, James A. *On Brave Old Army Team: The Cheating Scandal That Rocked the Nation: West Point, 1951*. Novato: Presidio Press, 1996.

Blaik, Earl. *The Red Blaik Story*. New Rochelle: Arlington House, 1974.

Bok, Sissela. *Lying: Moral Choice in Public and Private Life*. New York: Vintage Books, 1979.

Bowman, James. *Honor: A History*. New York: Encounter Books, 2006.

Boynton, Captain Edward C. *History of West Point and Its Military Importance during the American Revolution and the Origin and Progress of the United States Military Academy*. New York: D. Van Nostrand, 1863.

Bradley, Omar N. and Clay Blair. *A General's Life: An Autobiography*. New York: Simon and Schuster, 1983.

Bugle Notes, Volume 44 (1952–1953). West Point: United States Corps of Cadets, 1952. Also other years.

Coffman, Edward M. *The Regulars: The American Army, 1898–1941*. Cambridge: Belknap Press, 2004.

Cowley, Robert and Thomas Guinzburg, ed. *West Point: Two Centuries of Honor and Tradition*. New York: Warner Books, 2002.

Crackel, Theodore J. *The Illustrated History of West Point*. New York: Harry N. Abrams, 1991.

_____. *West Point: A Bicentennial History*. Lawrence: University Press of Kansas, 2002.

Dupuy, R. Ernest. *Where They Have Trod: The West Point Tradition in American Life*. New York: Frederick A. Stokes Company, 1940.

Eliot, George Fielding. *Sylvanus Thayer of West Point*. New York: Julian Messner Inc., 1959.

French, Rev. J. W. *Practical Ethics*. New York: D. Van Nostrand, 1865.

Ganoe, William Addleman. *MacArthur Close-Up*. New York: Vantage Press, 1962.

Janowitz, Morris. *The Reconstruction of Patriotism: Education for Civic Consciousness*. Chicago: University of Chicago Press, 1983.

Lipsky, David. *Absolutely American: Four Years at West Point*. Boston and New York: Houghton Mifflin, 2003.

Marcus Aurelius. *Meditations*, trans. Maxwell Staniforth. London: Penguin Books, 1964.

Marrella, Len. *In Search of Ethics*, 2d ed. Sanford: DC Press, 2005.

Mayer, Frederick C., ed. *Songs of the United States Military Academy*, 7th ed. New York: G. Schirmer Inc., 1939.

McWilliams, Bill. *A Return to Glory*. Lynchburg: Warwick House, 2000.

Military Ethics: Reflections on Principles. Washington: National Defense University Press, 1987.

Palmer, Dave R. *George Washington and Benedict Arnold: A Tale of Two Patriots*. Washington: Regnery Publishing, 2006.

Schaff, Morris. *The Spirit of Old West Point, 1858–1862*. Boston: Houghton, Mifflin, 1908.

Sorley, Lewis. *Thunderbolt: General Creighton Abrams and the Army of His Times*. New York: Simon & Schuster, 1992.

Westmoreland, William C. *A Soldier Reports*. Garden City: Doubleday, 1976.

West Point Hand-Book, The. West Point: Young Men's Christian Association, 1907. First edition of what in subsequent years was published as *Bugle Notes*.

Articles and Pamphlets

Ahearn, David C. "The Recent Violations of the Honor Code at West Point: A Statement from the Corps of Cadets," *Assembly* (January 1952), p. 6.

Berry, Lieutenant General Sidney B. *The United States Military Academy: A Fundamental National Institution*. Address to the Newcomen Society, 17 November 1976. New York: The Newcomen Society, 1977.

Blaik, Earl. "A Cadet under MacArthur," *Assembly* (Spring 1964), pp. 8-11.

Blumenson, Martin. "America's World War II Leaders in Europe: Some Thoughts," *Parameters* (December 1989), pp. 2-13.

Center for the Professional Military Ethic. *White Paper on the Cadet Honor Code and Honor System*. West Point: CPME, 10 February 2000.

Devers, Jacob L. "The Mark of the Man on USMA," *Assembly* (Spring 1964), pp. 16-19.

Forman, Sidney. "Scandal Among Cadets: An Historical Verdict," *Teacher's College Record*, Volume 66, Nr. 6 (March 1965), pp. 485-491.

Gard, Colonel Robert G. Jr. "The Military and American Society," *Foreign Affairs* (July 1971), pp. 698-710.

Honor Code and System, The. USCC Pamphlet 632-1. West Point: United States Corps of Cadets, 1 February 2007. Also other dates.
Title sometimes rendered as *Cadet Honor Code and System.*

Honor Committee Procedures. USCC Pamphlet 15-1. West Point: United States Corps of Cadets, 1 February 2007.

Honor Guide for Officers. West Point: USMA, 13 August 1958.

Irving, Major General Frederick A. "The Recent Violations of the Honor Code at West Point," *Assembly* (October 1951), pp. 6-7, 12.

"MacArthur's Speech," *2000 Register of Graduates*, pp. 1-50–1-51.

Millett, Allan R. *Military Professionalism and Officership in America.* Columbus: Mershon Center of the Ohio State University, May 1977.

"Origin of the Motto: Duty, Honor, Country," *Assembly* (December 1978), pp. 32-33.

Salter, James. "You Must," *Esquire* (December 1992), pp. 145-156.

Sorley, Lewis. "Beyond Duty, Honor, Country," *Military Review* (April 1987), pp. 2-13.

_____. "Doing What's Right: Shaping the Army's Professional Environment," *Parameters* (March 1989), pp. 11-15.

_____. "Duty, Honor, Country: Practice and Precept," *American Behavioral Scientist* (May/June 1976), pp. 627-646.

Southworth, Stacy B. "The Life and Character of BG Sylvanus Thayer: An Address Delivered to the Officers of the United States Military Academy at West Point, NY, on 14 December 1922 by the Headmaster of the Thayer Academy, South Braintree, Massachusetts," *2002 Register of Graduates*, pp. 1-60–1-63.

Starz, Michael Henderson. "The Non-Toleration Clause: The Bedrock of the USMA Honor Code." On line at http://www.usafa.edu/isme/JSCOPE00/Starz00.html.

Taylor, Major General Maxwell D. *Leading the American Soldier.* West Point: USMA, 1953.

_____. *West Point Honor System: Its Objectives and Procedures.* West Point: USMA, 1947.

Studies and Reports

Annual Report of the Superintendent, United States Military Academy, 1921. West Point: United States Military Academy Press, 1921. Also other years.

Donnithorne, Colonel Larry R. *Preparing for West Point's Third Century: A Summary of the Years of Affirmation and Change, 1986–1991.* West Point: USMA, 1991.

Final Report of the Special Commission of the Chief of Staff on the Honor Code and Honor System at the United States Military Academy, 30 May 1989.

Honor Violations at West Point, 1951: A Case Study. West Point: USMA, 10 September 1990.

Malmstrom, Frederick V. and Solomon A. Fulero. "Do Service Academy Honor Codes Work? 38 Years of Graduates." Paper Presented at the Sixteenth Applied Behavioral Sciences Symposium, U.S. Air Force Academy, 22 April 1998.

Notes of a Board of Officers Appointed by Letter Orders, Headquarters, USMA, 13 August 1951. Bartlett Board Notes.

Platoon Leader Performance of USMA Graduates. West Point: Office of Institutional Research, June 1988.

Proceedings of a Board of Officers Appointed by Letter Orders, Headquarters, USMA, 13 August 1951. Bartlett Board.

Report to the Secretary of the Army by the Special Commission on the United States Military Academy, 15 December 1976. Borman Commission.

Report of Superintendent's Special Study Group on Honor at West Point. West Point: USMA, 23 May 1975. Also known as Buckley Study.

Documents

Association of Graduates, USMA. "Nomination of Sylvanus Thayer, Educator, to the Hall of Fame," n.d. USMA Archives.

The Centennial of the United States Military Academy at West Point, New York: 1802–1902. Volume I: Addresses and Histories. Washington: Government Printing Office, 1904.

The Four-Year Honor Education Program. West Point, NY: USMA, August 1992.

The Honor Code and Honor System, USCC Pamphlet No. 632-1. West Point: United States Military Academy, June 1984. Also version of August 1992.

Honor Guide for Officers. West Point: USMA, 1958.

Honor Instruction, New Cadet Barracks, 1969. West Point: Department of Tactics, USCC, 1969.

Official Register of the Officers and Cadets, United States Military Academy, West Point, New York, For the Academic Year Ending 5 June 1956.

Superintendent's Letter Book, 11 vol. USMA Archives.

USCC Regulation 600-1, *Regulations for the United States Corps of Cadets,* 21 August 1976.

West Point Association of Graduates. *2000 Register of Graduates and Former Cadets of the United States Military Academy.* West Point, NY: AOG, 2000. Also other years.

West Point Association of Graduates. *The West Point Thayer Papers, 1808–1872,* 11 vol. West Point, NY: AOG, 1965.

Unpublished Manuscripts

Beasley, Major John H. "The USMA Honor System: A Due Process Hybrid." Charlottesville: The Judge Advocate General's School, 1983.

Davidson, Lieutenant General Garrison H. "West Point at the Crossroads: A Return to Basic Principles," n.d.

Denton, Edgar III. "The Formative Years of the United States Military Academy, 1775–1833." Ph.D. dissertation, Syracuse University, 1964.

Dillard, Walter Scott. "The United States Military Academy, 1865–1900, The Uncertain Years." Ph.D. dissertation, University of Washington, 1972.

Griess, Thomas E. "Dennis Hart Mahan: West Point Professor and Advocate of Military Professionalism, 1830–1871." Ph.D. dissertation, Duke University, 1968.

Molloy, Peter Michael. "Technical Education and the Young Republic: West Point as America's Ècole Polytechnique, 1802–1833." Ph.D. dissertation, Brown University, 1975.

Morrison, James L. Jr. "The United States Military Academy, 1833–1866: Years of Progress and Turmoil." Ph.D. dissertation, Columbia University, 1970.

Index